THE PRESBYTERIAN CONTROVERSY

by

Patrick Baskwell

ISBN : 978-0-578-01196-7

Contents

Introduction

In the opening months of 1935 and continuing unabated into 1936, newspaper headlines told the story of a renegade Presbyterian professor and his 'unruly' band of misguided followers. On 9 March 1935, the front page of the prestigious *New York Times* screamed: 'Machen Charges Trial is "Unfair", Declares Presbytery Board in Limiting Scope, "Prejudiced Case Without a Hearing"' (quoted by Hart 1988:1). Neither were the smaller tabloids slack in their efforts to telegraph Machen's troubles abroad. One sentinel after another delivered sensational headlines such as: '5 Clerics Deposed by Presbyterian Church', 'Machen Loses Church Fight He May Secede', or the more provocative caption 'Presbyterian Vote Backs Modernists' (quoted by Atwell 1981:1). These headlines did not evoke the pathos, nor did they contain the mystique of a previous front page story chronicling a certain unsinkable ship's plunge into the ice waters of the North Atlantic. Neither did the Machen headlines contain the sheer drama and obvious far-reaching consequences of another earlier feature involving a political assassination of an archduke in Sarajevo, which plunged the whole world into war. Collectively, the Machen accounts could rival neither of these in immediately perceived importance. Their significance was, after all, confined to a religious denomination. Yet, these unobtrusive events would have an untold impact in years to come on how the Protestant world would ultimately view the Christian faith.

These were only some of the headlines that attended the last and most celebrated heresy trial in the Presbyterian Church. It culminated years of strife that tore at the very fabric of the Presbyterian Church in the USA. Yet, the bulk of this long, protracted ecclesiastical battle, which ended with Machen's disciplinary trial, actually lies in the preceding decades. These were the years when the church, both Protestant and Catholic, struggled as new questions were put to a once timeless faith. Definitions of the Christian Faith, held sacred for centuries, were subjected to a rigorous criticism. Many scholars and churchmen of the time came to conclusions that were quite at odds with the prevailing consensus. But then the consensus began to change. Ours is the story of this change in opinion regarding the very nature of the historic faith. Those opting for the newer views were labeled Modernists or Liberals. These, to a man, saw their researches and subsequent conclusions as building on the faith of their fathers. They were rescuing old doctrines and breathing new life into them; something they saw as consistent with the calling of the church in the world. But the opposition, embodied in J. Gresham Machen, said these pioneers were guilty of creating another religion; one, in fact, totally different in character from anything that could be classified as Christianity.

This struggle has come to be known in the annals of the Presbyterian Church by a variety of names, the most common of which are the Presbyterian Controversy or the Fundamentalist/Modernist Controversy. Those writing on this sad chapter in Presbyterian history have usually concentrated on the six year period from 1923 to 1929 as determinative. In a more recent offering, author William Weston prompts us to take notice of a much larger time frame for the events that climaxed in the headlines above (Weston 1997). One of the important features of his work is that it sees the Presbyterian Controversy of the 1920s and 1930s as the culmination of contention within the Presbyterian Church that began some forty years earlier with the addition of Charles Augustus Briggs to the faculty of Union Theological Seminary in New York in 1874. Additionally, Weston forces a reconsideration of the events of these fateful years; between the time of Charles Briggs and J. Gresham Machen, and their related significance.

In the main I heartily agree with the position taken by William Weston in recasting the Presbyterian Controversy between the 1890s and the 1930s. I would also like to show that these years were a watershed for change in the Presbyterian Church in the USA. It was during this time that a transformation took place in the self-understanding of the Presbyterian Church regarding its very nature. Weston's thesis is that this change was the result of the liberal, Charles Briggs, and conservative, J. Gresham Machen, vying for the allegiance of a more centrist group which he calls the 'institutional loyalists' (Weston 1997:49-81).

Weston's description of the Presbyterian Conflict is apt enough. However, the history of the conflict and the people involved do not necessarily fall into the clear-cut categories that he has established. While I would agree that at times there are three distinct camps, the liberals, the conservatives and the institutional loyalists, this cannot always be easily determined. Those individuals involved who may be classified as conservative at one point in the outworking of events may be classified more precisely with the loyalists at another point. Or, even a liberal may be found among the conservatives at another juncture in the story. So

10

while I greatly admire the contribution made by William Weston to the understanding of events in the Presbyterian Church in the early part of the twentieth-century, it seems appropriate to nuance more carefully the descriptions of people and the ecclesiastical camps to which they belonged. This is precisely what I will attempt to do.

In order to accomplish this objective it is necessary to inquire into the events that transpired between the time of Charles Briggs and J. Gresham Machen from the viewpoint of doctrinal development. This task is, of course, very complex indeed. The first question that emerges naturally is: what is development of doctrine? There was, and still is, much confusion and debate as to just what constitutes development. The second question follows naturally from the first: once it has been established what development is, can we then inquire as to its presence, or lack thereof, in the period before us?

In order to facilitate this study of the events and personalities of this period from a developmental standpoint, I wish to appropriate the categorical architecture developed by John Courtney Murray. Admittedly, the structure developed at length by Murray is applied by him only to events leading up to and surrounding the Council of Nicaea in 325AD. Still, the framework he developed is both helpful and adaptable. It has an uncanny workability that is appropriate for use in a variety of situations. Hence, with minor modifications, I will adopt Murray's frame of reference and employ it in interpreting the Fundamentalist/Modernist controversy in the Presbyterian Church

The controversy in the Presbyterian Church that spanned the forty-year period at the turn of the century was about: 1) the use of critical, literary approaches concerned with investigating what stands behind the sacred biblical texts, and 2) the perceived theological Liberalism, or, if you will, unbelief, that issued from such investigations. Charles Briggs and those who were associated with him at Union Seminary in New York believed that they were in the vanguard of scientific investigation as it applied to the Scriptures. Forging ahead with new, more objective, and more critical methods of inquiry, known as biblical criticism, they firmly believed that they were heralding a whole new world in theological investigation; opening up the riches of the Scriptures and the Christian Faith in ways previously unknown. In fact, the progress being made on this front made the theological foundations of yesteryear seem woefully inadequate. The word development is almost

11

insufficient to describe the optimism and expectation that attended these investigations. Others, however, were not so confident in this newly found scientific approach and many, like Professor Briggs, who followed the critical approach in dealing with the faith soon found their ideas branded as innovations, or worse.

In the ensuing years of the controversy, those who followed in the footsteps of Professor Briggs moved well beyond their mentor in the conclusions that they drew from their use of the critical method. In some instances, disillusioned with the current state of the church, they even sought a more politically motivated faith, one that brought the world of the hereafter to the here and now; where all of humanity's needs and desires were satisfied in the present. Forerunners of this political idealism were luminaries such as Harry Ward and Norman Thomas. Harry Ward, as a professor of ethics, was one of Briggs's contemporaries at Union Seminary in New York. Norman Thomas studied for the Presbyterian ministry there, later abandoning the ministry to devote more time to political ventures which he saw as the outworking of the Christian message.

Not everyone saw the critical ideas coming out of Union Seminary as a development of what had gone before. Briggs, and those championing these new ideas, met with staunch resistance. While much dissatisfaction with the new methods had filtered throughout the Presbyterian Church, the core of opposition was located at Princeton Theological Seminary in New Jersey. Charles Hodge, one of the fathers of Princeton Seminary, while also believing wholeheartedly in development of doctrine, dissented markedly from the offerings of the professor from Union. His ideas on this subject were woven into the very warp and woof of the Princeton school, continuing to influence all, both faculty and students, who came after him. But were the ideas of the elder Hodge on development really ones that allowed for development or were they just a bulwark against development of any kind? Herein lays a significant difference of opinion, one that eventually gave rise to the Presbyterian Conflict.

As the years passed and the conflict developed within the Presbyterian Church, those who were of a more radical bent, i. e., the faculty of Union Seminary, were pushing ideas that were increasingly seen by many as contrary to the tenets of the Reformed Faith as enshrined in the Westminster Confession of Faith, the historic creed of Presbyterianism. Walter Nigg contends that even the heretic falls within the tradition that he militates against (Nigg 1962:8-15). Were these dissenters, then, also part and parcel of the Presbyterian Tradition? This query forces us to look at another aspect of the Presbyterian Controversy: where does the role of tradition enter into the discussion of development of doctrine? This is also something that was not readily agreed upon.

During the period from Briggs to Machen (1890-1936), the Presbyterian Church moved steadily away from the doctrinal definitions and polity that had historically characterized her. Many of those things which had made the Presbyterian Church distinctive were slowly and methodically abandoned. It is necessary in this study, then, to inquire as to what these distinctions were, and why they were important for some and not for others. William Weston contends that loyalty to the institutional framework in which the Presbyterian Church was cast was sufficient to call one's self a Presbyterian (Weston 1997:111 & 131-133). Contrariwise, for J. Gresham Machen, the Presbyterian Church was characterized by the Reformed faith as it was enshrined in the Westminster Confession, that Church's historic credal standard (Machen [1923] 1946:162-163). Between these two perspectives there is a world of difference.

Some saw the changes that occurred in the period before us as building on the church's historic position. Others saw these changes as a complete repudiation of that position. The bulk of this study, therefore, will be a discussion of this matter. In chapter one, however, the issue of doctrinal development, both its nature and how it was understood by the participants in the Fundamentalist/Modernist Controversy, will first be looked at. In chapter two the concept of "Modernism" will be investigated, both in terms of its appearance within the church at large and its reception within Presbyterian circles. The rest of this monograph will then seek to interpret the events of the Fundamentalist/Modernist Controversy in terms of this structure. Was there doctrinal development taking place in the Presbyterianism during the course of the Fundamentalist/Modernist Controversy? Did the combatants on either side in this controversy seek to maintain the historic traditions of the Presbyterian Church? Or was this tradition expendable? These are the questions I will attempt to answer in the pages that follow.

This dissertation was originally submitted (June 1999) to the Faculty of Theology at the University of South Africa in fulfillment of the requirements for the degree of Master of Theology. I wish to thank my supervisors in this regard, Professors GL Frank and RJ Mouw, for all the effort they put into this work on my behalf. Any mistakes, however, are my own.

On a Personal Note

There is one disclaimer I would like to make at the outset. In the following pages the group I identify as 'Centrists', to use Murray's categories, are the ones who have held to historic Presbyterianism better than any of their antagonists. While I believe these were people of integrity, many of whom sought to be 'Reformed' in the true sense of the word, this does not mean that I would align my own doctrinal position with theirs. One example will undoubtedly suffice: Efforts to change the Westminster Confession in 1903 came from all corners of the Presbyterian Church. And, while the final results were undoubtedly of a 'Centrist,' disposition, I personally believe, contra Benjamin Warfield, that these changes did indeed detract from the historic position of the Presbyterian Church. The changes given confessional status in the Presbyterian Church in 1903 were in many ways similar to changes enacted in the Christian Reformed Church at the Synod of Kalamazoo in 1924. For a detail analysis of these changes and their history in the Christian Reformed Church, see my: *Herman Hoeksema: A Theological Biography* (also available from Amazon.com).

Chapter 1

Doctrinal Development, Tradition and Historicism

Our discussion of the controversy that consumed the Presbyterian Church at the turn of the century begins with a look at the idea of the development of doctrine. It is my contention that a proper understanding of doctrinal development, and its relationship to tradition and historicism, is essential to a proper interpretation of the events of this period. To achieve this end, a clear definition and a proper understanding of these three important themes is imperative. This task in itself is no easy matter simply because of the sheer diversity of opinion. Yet, I am convinced that with a proper understanding of the concepts of development, tradition, and historicism, the history of the period more naturally falls into place. I do not claim herein to have a corner on truth, nor do I claim to have solved all the difficulties related to the period under discussion. But I do hope that by taking a fresh approach new light may be shed on some truly significant events.

1.1 Doctrinal Development

In the early 1960s Roman Catholic theologian and scholar John Courtney Murray gave a series of lectures entitled *The Problem of God* (Murray 1964). In this lecture series he outlined in detail, especially in the first and second lecture, his understanding of doctrinal development. This series of lectures, and the categories of doctrinal development which he established in them, have, in a sense, set the tone for any discussions on the development of doctrine from that time forward, both Protestant and Catholic. And so our discussion of doctrinal development in the Presbyterian Church in the USA during the course of the Fundamentalist/Modernist Controversy from the 1890s to the 1930s, or, more specifically, from Charles Augustus Briggs (1841-1913) to J. Gresham Machen (1881-1937), begins with Murray's structure as our informed guide.

The purpose of Murray's essay is 'to set forth a theological understanding of the problem of God as it has appeared in successive historical phases' (Murray 1964:3). It is in the course of fulfilling this stated purpose that he presents us with a vivid picture of doctrinal

15

development as it occurred in the early church. He proceeds to analyze in intricate fashion the problems created by the knowledge of God in successive epochs of Hebrew and church history. It is not necessary to follow him through the early days of the Hebrew religion, i.e., the history of the patriarchs, the exodus and the giving of the law at Sinai. Close attention, however, must be paid to his discussion of the Arian heresy in the early centuries of the Christian era, which became the catalyst for a new theological understanding. It is in this connection that Murray analyzes the continuity and change in theological formulation that resulted from the decisive Council of Nicaea in 325 AD (Murray 1964:33-66). In addition, Murray tells us that his method will be both descriptive and historical (Murray 1964:3). I propose to follow Murray in his method as well since it suits this inquiry nicely.

The Arian controversy of the fourth century brought into consideration a new question for which there appeared to be, initially at least, no satisfactory answer. The question asked 'was new in the form and mode of thought in which Arius raised it' (Murray 1964:40). In some respects maybe even the question posed by Arius was development upon that theological understanding which preceded it, although this idea is novel at best. Yet, 'if Arius did not ask it, someone else would have' (Murray 1964:41). This alone attests to the inevitability of the question (Murray 1964:41).

Until the time of the Arian controversy, questions of a phenomenological nature (Murray 1964:41) occupied the energies of the young church. That is to say, questions were posed of God from a relational standpoint. This relational inquiry involved Jesus Christ as the Son of God and second person of the Trinity and the church on earth both in its corporate manifestation and individually. What is God's relationship to humanity? What does God mean to us and to our experience? These were very real questions with very real metaphysical and ethical answers, but still very much within the realm of phenomenology. They were concerned mainly with the problem of 'what does God mean to me?' The inevitability of the questionings of Arius is in part just the functioning of the human mind, which, by nature, moves from phenomenology to ontology. Addressing the inevitability of the question, Murray sees this progression as part of 'the essential dynamism of human intelligence.' He continues:

> When it functions without any bias induced by faulty
> or prejudicial training, the mind moves inevitably from

the question of what things are to us (the phenomenological question) to the deeper question of what things are in themselves (the ontological question). The human mind moves from description to definition. In this case, it moves from inquiry into the reality of God's presence to inquiry into the reality of the God who is present. The biblical question, whether God is with us, is organically related to the patristic question, what is the God-who-is-with-us *is*. (Murray 1964:41.)

Arius's inquiries were of a truly revolutionary nature. He sought to probe the very nature of the Godhead. As a result of the questions and subsequent conclusions of Arius, the church was thrown into a state of confusion (for a comprehensive treatment of the Arian controversy see Hanson 1988). Many people, with church officials and clergy in large numbers, sided with Arius, believing that his position resided in the train of the strictest orthodoxy. Out of concern 'to express in the sharpest possible terms the fundamental distinction between the absolute God and all that is not absolute God' (Cunliffe-Jones1978:94), Arius posed a sharp distinction between the nature of the Father and the nature of His Christ. According to Cunliffe-Jones, his reasoning along these lines was born out of his rejection of the

> Origenistic theory of one and the same divine essence broadening down, as it were, so to subsist at different, hierarchically graded levels. Consequently he repudiated the idea that the Logos occupies an intermediate position, in the sense that the Logos is a second divine principle perfectly reflecting the transcendent Father and transmitting to the world of creatures the image by which alone the Father can be known and described. (Cunliffe-Jones 1978:94.)

It would appear that Arius was subject more to the limitations imposed by his age than any overt desire to prejudice prevailing notions about the being of God. His rejection of the explanations provided by Origen was not in itself a vote for orthodoxy, for 'orthodoxy' did not truly exist yet. The question of the relationship of the Father to the Son, a question centering on who and what God is, His ontology, was not a settled one. How the Son was related to the Father was not only a

17

question of relationship but one of being, since the Son was also seen as God. Others besides Arius had attempted to sort out this problem. Murray tells us that,

> In the East, Origen, the greatest genius of the third century and perhaps of any century, attacked the problem in higher terms. He made use of a concept borrowed from the most popular contemporary philosophy, Middle Platonism. It was the dyadic conception, derived from Plato himself. There is the One, the Goodness that is divine. There is also the Logos, which emanates from the One and participates in the One as the Image of the divine Goodness. The Christian doctrine of the Father and his Logos is then interpreted in terms of this Platonist scheme. The Father is *the* God; only of him does Origen use the definite article. The Logos is not *the* God; he is simply God, and he is God by emanation and participation in a Platonist sense. Therefore, he is a God "of the second order," as Origen calls him. He is a diminished deity, since emanation, in Platonist thought, involves some measure of degradation in the order of being. (Murray 1964:37.)

Even with all his genius, 'the best philosophical instrument of understanding within Origen's reach—the Middle Platonism theory of the emanation of the logos from the One—broke in his hands' (Murray 1964:38). Subordinationism was the inevitable result. The Logos, the Son was somehow less than God.

Even though history has inveighed heavily upon Arius, Hubert Cunliffe-Jones helps us put things into their proper perspective. 'Although Arius is often misunderstood as having simply denied the deity of Christ,' writes Jones, 'he was far from asserting, in the ordinary modern fashion, that Jesus was a mere man (and therefore not God). On the contrary, Arius maintained that Jesus was God, and not fully man; but that he was *created* God' (Cunliffe-Jones 1978:94).

Arius's staunchest opponent in this matter was the celebrated Athanasius of Alexandria. Athanasius contested the Arian theological formulations throughout much of the fourth century. In contrast to the Arians, Athanasius taught 'the eternal Sonship of the Logos ...and the redemption of the world and men by God in Christ' (Douglas 1978:81). In this Athanasius stood seemingly against the world. He was one of a

18

few solitary figures standing against the growing tide of acceptance accorded to the Arian position. Part of the reason for the astounding success of the Arian position was that the questions being asked by Arius were not directly answered in the Scriptures, at least not in the mode in which they were being asked (Murray 1964:46). Arius, in fact, was reinterpreting 'the Christian faith in terms of contemporary philosophies' (Murray 1964:54). 'In the adjective *homoousion* (one essence-PB),' Murray tells us, 'the Nicene problem of God found its definitive answer. ...Nicaea did not describe; it defined' (Murray 1964:45). The questions were in a new mode, so the answer, to be effective, also had to be in this new mode. On this point Murray concludes that

> The Nicene dogma was new, however, in that it stated the sense of the Scriptures in a new mode of understanding that was not formally scriptural. ...The alteration in the mode of understanding does not change the sense of the affirmation, but it does make the Nicene affirmation new in its form. ...The Fathers had, therefore, to go beyond the letter of the scriptural formulas to their sense. They stated the sense of the new formulas, "out of the substance of the Father," "consubstantial with the Father." (Murray 1964:46.)

In its finalized form the famous symbol of Nicaea begins

> I Believe in one God the Father Almighty; Maker of heaven and earth, and of all things visible and invisible. And in one Lord Jesus Christ, the only-begotten Son of God, begotten of the Father before all worlds [God of God], Light of Light, very God of very God, begotten, not made, being of one substance [essence] with the Father; by whom all things were made; who for us men and for our salvation, came down from heaven.... (Schaff (1931):58-59.)

Although the Arian party seemed willing to accommodate itself to all previous doctrinal formulations (Murray 1964:44&46), this new formula, defined by *homoousion*, 'would not bear the Arian understanding' (Murray 1964:46). This word, this concept, whether it be borrowed from neo-Platonism (Murray 1964:55), as some think, or not, eventually ended the Arian conflict on the side of Athanasius. In the process, Athanasius took Christian doctrine a step further. He developed it. He took the words of the Scriptures and the trajectory to which they pointed and developed them logically to answer questions that had neither been asked before nor were they answered by the Scriptures alone.

This firestorm of controversy brought to prominence three specific factions based on their differing theological orientation. Murray refers to them as the *Archaists*, the *Futurists*, and the *Centrists*. Led by the famed church historian Eusebius of Caesarea, the *Archaists* (dealt with in detail by Murray 1964 on pages 48-49) were essentially practical men and not scholars. Comparable in many ways to modern right-wing religious, or fundamentalist thought, they wished to say only 'what the Scriptures say and have done with it' (Murray 1964:48). Any change was abhorrent by its very nature, whether it furthered the understanding of the faith to which they clung or not. Without intending to degrade some very sincere Christians, it is not vain to say that the views of the Archaists were obscurantist. As Murray says:

> At the root of the fallacy is the rejection of the notion that Christian understanding of the affirmations of faith can and indeed must grow, at the same time that the sense of the affirmations remains unaltered. Archaist Eusebian thought wanted to cling to the earlier stage of understanding contained in the letter of Scripture.... The trouble is that one cannot thus put back the clock of thought. (Murray 1964:48.)

This means that one cannot turn back the clock to the time before Arius asked his new question. By doing so he forever changed the terms on which discussion has been carried out. Discussion cannot be carried out any longer in the dimension that the Eusebians found so accommodating. While the assumptions needful for current and fruitful discussion and agreement had been transformed, the Eusebians refused to rise to this new level of theological discussion. 'The Eusebians were trying to meet today's question with yesterday's answer,' concludes Murray, 'but the question of the day was new' (Murray 1964:49).

At the opposite end of the theological spectrum in the Arian controversy were those whom Murray calls *Futurists* (Murray 1964:49-50). Futurism is a necessary corollary of Archaism, since Archaism of necessity breeds Futurism as both are open ended (Murray 1964:49). Murray describes the Futurist fallacy as resting

> on the notion that the affirmations of the Christian faith never have a final sense. They are constantly subject

to reinterpretation in terms of any sort of contemporary philosophical thought. Development in the understanding of them is altogether open-ended. It may move in any direction, even to the dissolution of the original sense of the Christian affirmations. (Murray 1964:49.)

Before delving into the Centrist category, Murray's last, I would like to digress a bit and discuss development of doctrine from a slightly different slant with a more contemporary perspective.

Any theology contained in the writings of the New Testament, contrary to certain popular conceptions, is not systematic theology. The Bible does not present us with a neat, systematic treatise on God, or us. If it did, many of the problems and divisions of the modern church probably would not exist. But, alas, it does not. It is rather, as Geerhardus Vos pointed out so nicely in his inaugural address to the chair of Biblical Theology at Princeton Seminary, a book 'of history, the parallel of which in dramatic interest and simple eloquence is nowhere to be found' (Vos 1894:37-38). More specifically, it contains commands, questions, exhortations, as well as simple declaratory statements, all of which are to be studied, assimilated, digested, meditated upon and corrected from time to time as our meditations yield new understanding. Is this not the meaning of the scriptural exhortation in the Second Epistle of Paul to Timothy that 'All scripture is given by inspiration of God, and is profitable for doctrine, for reproof, for correction, for instruction in righteousness: that the man of God may be perfect, thoroughly furnished unto all good works' (2 Timothy 3:16-17 [AV])? Elsewhere, the people of God are simply commanded to meditate on God's word and keep its precepts, with success promised to those who do so (Joshua 1:8 [AV]).

This book of dramatic interests, interwoven as part and parcel of the history, gives the self-revelation of God to His constituent people. Countless times throughout the centuries this self-revelation has been probed, reworked, and made more assimilable to the human mind. The results of these efforts have come to be known as creeds and, especially since the Protestant Reformation in the Sixteenth-Century, as systematic theologies or 'Common Places.' What these human constructs in fact do is to systematize, or group under specific *loci* all that the Bible has to say on certain topics. This is done, at least it was so in the past, by diligent study and meditation on the contents of Scripture and then the systematic and topical arrangement of the results. To be specific, 'up until Bonaventura and Aquinas theology as a body of knowledge was equated with the contents of scripture. It was only after them that theory was adjusted to practice and theology was seen as a body of knowledge resulting from the *study of* and *reflection on* scripture' (Gaybba 1988:1).

These results of theological reflection that have found their way into the great theological systems have not remained the same over the centuries of the Christian era. In the first place, as Gaybba testifies to, the content itself has undergone a metamorphosis. While in the early church and the early medieval periods of church history the content of theology was largely synonymous with the Scriptures, the beginning of the high middle ages brought with it a change in this content to include human reflection on the Scriptures as well in its results.

The second change, following closely upon the first, was simply the growth in the physical size of the subsequent theological systems. And this has been true right up to and including the present. There just seems to be more that needs saying today than there was in the past, even the recent past. And even a cursory glance at some of the multi-volume works of dogmatics by twentieth-century theologians such as Karl Barth, G. C. Berkouwer, or Hans Urs von Balthasar, works that makes their predecessors in previous generations pale by comparison, will bear this out. John Robbins estimates the size of Karl Barth's massive, but unfinished *Church Dogmatics* to be 'nine times as long as Calvin's *Institutes* and twice as long as Thomas' *Summa Theologica*' (Robbins 1998:1). A closer inspection of the individual volumes in any of these sets reveals a plethora of footnotes. Famous, and not so famous, names from every age of the church's history are plentiful. Church Fathers, theologians of the Middle Ages, and Reformers are all consulted for their views. The authors of these multi-volume works unabashedly build upon those who have gone before. The older works are criticized, analyzed, and mined judiciously for their singular and telling insights. They really become the foundation upon which these more modern tomes are then constructed. In this way the contemporary theologian builds upon those who have preceded him in the faith.

It is only natural that these contemporary works will contain insights not found in their forebears. This process is known as development. Each generation learns from the former and builds upon it, which, in turn, is the legacy that it leaves. We could say, then, that development of doctrine is rather a pattern or even a trajectory, if you will; a trajectory that, nevertheless, follows a specific and defined course from a given source. In this case the source is the self-revelation of God in the Scriptures, the space through which it proceeds is the history of the church, and the wake that it leaves is the tradition of a given church, about which more will be said later.

In a recent essay, Dominican J. M. R. Tillard complained about the use of the word *development* in these instances, preferring instead to speak of 'unfolding.' His reasoning for this is that '"development" is usually associated with the idea of progress, of stepping forward to increase the precision of the former steps. "Unfolding" means only the spreading out or unfurling of a rich reality that is already realized.' (Tillard 1996:176). In the same vein, he says that 'it is evident that the knowledge people have of this reality is increased even when the reality itself does not change. This is why we believe that the idea of *unfolding* is more in harmony with the nature of Christian truth than the idea of development as it is usually defined' (Tillard 1996:176). These statements make it quite clear that his opposition to the word 'development' is due solely to its 'association' with the idea of progress.

Actually, the matter might become less complicated if progress is understood to be in the eye of the beholder. One person's progress is another person's regress. It may seem to some that this position advocates either a futurist view of truth as open-ended or a post-modern view of a multiplicity of traditions, each valid within its own framework. Neither alternative is intended. It is merely an attempt to recognize that there are different traditions which have many and varied devotees. No attempt is made to judge the validity any of these traditions. Additionally, this should not be construed to mean the acceptance of a post-modern view of the nature of truth. It is merely an attempt to recognize what is.

Frank Thayer, writing on twentieth-century history, offers an interesting assessment of the popular view of history in general and its relation to the notion of progress. He contends that 'modern civilization suffers from the "inclined plane" theory of history—the view that finds only negative lessons in history and holds that what is, is the best that has ever been' (Thayer 1998:46). We would not insinuate that Tillard sees only negative lessons in history, but he certainly is trying to counter the popular notion described by Thayer as the 'inclined plane' view of history, at least as it applies to Christian doctrine.

23

Does this 'inclined plane' apply to Christian doctrine in general? I think not. While many ordinary people would hold the 'inclined plane' as descriptive of the modern world, technological advancement and the resulting modern conveniences are usually foremost in their thoughts. Although even this area is coming increasingly under fire (see Sorokin 1941 & Armington and Ellis 1984). In the realm of theology, opinion is tremendously variegated. This means that what one individual considers progress is repudiated by another. If we consider one of the multi-volume dogmatic works mentioned earlier, that of the Swiss theologian Karl Barth, the same diversity of opinion exists as to its worth. That Karl Barth built studiously upon his predecessors, both Protestant and Catholic, is undeniable. His erudition was enormous. Yet there exist sharp divisions of opinion regarding the value of what he wrote, and this is true within the Protestant Churches alone. The assessment of Cornelius Van Til, late professor of Apologetics at Westminster Seminary in Philadelphia, was particularly hostile. He writes:

> The Theology of Crisis (another name for the theology of Barth and Brunner-PB), with which we have been concerned, has shown itself in all fundamental respects to be the same as the Modernism of Schleiermacher and his school. Barth and Brunner have what is, basically, the same sort of view of reality and of knowledge as marks the work of Schleiermacher or Ritschl. Fundamental to everything they say about individual doctrines is the fact that they have, throughout and with vigor, cast away as a filthy garment that on which everything in the field of historic Christianity rests, the notion of the self-contained or absolute God. (Van Til 1947:371-372.)

Philosopher and Reformed theologian Gordon Clark purposes to analyze the theological method of Karl Barth specifically. His conclusions are not as harsh as the professor from Philadelphia, yet his dissent is no less obvious. 'The result is that Barth's theology is self-contradictory', Clark concludes. 'He operates on the basis of incompatible axioms, and against his hopes and aims arrives at an untenable or irrational position' (Clark 1963:224). More recently, Clark protégée John Robbins, in analyzing Barth's social and political teachings, concluded that 'Barth qualifies as a socialist in either case, and as a Christian in neither' (Robbins 1998:3). A more positive view of Barth, however, comes from evangelical Protestant Gregory Bolich. Speaking specifically about

Biblical authority, an area where Barth is continually assailed by evangelicals, he admits that 'Barth has proven helpful to me and to others in coming to terms with this and other issues. My own fruitful interactions with Barth compel me to advocate developing a dialog with him far more substantial than what has occurred in the past' (Bolich 1980:207). Again, contrary to some of the criticism that borders on condemnation, Göttingen theologian Otto Weber believes that,

> The physical weight of this work (Barth's Church Dogmatics-PB), however, is only the most obvious side of its real, intrinsic weight—something no one seriously disputes. For here an inquiry is made concerning the "substance" of Christian doctrine with an urgency and devotion such that no one can disregard it, no matter what position he may take to the whole or the particulars. In fact, this dogmatic work is at once a document of church history, something that has fallen to the lot of few of its predecessors. It has not been apart from the life of the Church of Jesus Christ but actually in a constant reference to it. (Weber 1953:15.)

None of the four theologians quoted above say that Barth's writings are just a repetition of what has gone before. If anything, just the opposite is true. The tremendous burden of just reading the Barth corpus is a strain to many of his critics. Peter Monsma, in a review of Van Til's *The New Modernism* (1947), criticizes the Westminster Seminary professor for a less than thorough job: 'an important passage from Barth is freely translated with the result that statements are ascribed to him far different from those he actually made. One wonders,' he concludes, 'how carefully Dr. Van Til has read Barth' (quoted by Bolich 1980:70). Similar criticisms are directed against Van Til from Swiss Catholic theologian Hans Urs von Balthasar (von Balthasar 1971:45).

If all that Barth said was common to all, or if he said nothing new in the way of Christian doctrine, these heated discussions and dissensions would not have occurred. How could one misrepresent what was common to all? This is hardly the case. The common complaint seems to be, from both friend and foe alike, is that Barth says too much. What he says, moreover, is too new and thus controversial; hence, the reason for the often intense disagreement. All this disagreement, however, has not taken place in a vacuum. Each criticism, regardless of how vehement or whether it is substantiated or not, has a point of reference from which it comes. That point of reference is tradition, and the criteria used by each critic, friendly or otherwise, comes from their respective traditions. The tradition of each, then, is the criterion for their respective evaluations. As I said, I will have more to say about tradition later.

The final group to emerge from the Arian conflict in the fourth century is dubbed by Murray as the *Centrists* (discussed by Murray 1964 on pages 49-50). The leader of this faction was the famed Athanasius of Alexandria. Athanasius and those who stood with him were in the end, after much hardship, vindicated in their views. Murray sees these Centrists as the keepers of the flame of orthodoxy. Athanasius and his followers stood against the prevailing tide of opinion, which is why Athanasius is usually depicted as 'Athanasius contra mundum.' Their position, neither Archaist nor Futurist, was one that held the assumption that doctrine was not open ended. Murray believes this to be the genius of their contribution. He writes:

> It was the merit of the Athanasian Center that it saw how dangerous the archaism of the Eusebians was. The Athanasians perceived that it opened the way to the futurism of Arius, who reinterpreted the scriptural affirmations... in terms of a rationalistic dialectic to the destruction of the sense of the scriptural faith. (Murray 1964:49.)

This means that the Futurists, by their essentially rationalistic approach to the faith, came away with the conception that doctrine is of an open-ended nature, having no fixed point of reference, or truth, as some would describe it. In a certain sense the Archaists, by their stranglehold on an outmoded or a 'Scripture alone' terminology, ended up in the same place as the Futurists. While the Futurists openly propagated the mutability of truth (also a post-modern view), the view of truth held by the Archaists led inevitably to the same conclusion. Futurism is open-ended with respect to doctrinal truth. Archaism, because of its near paranoid insistence on the very words of the Scriptures belies the same open-ended view. It is believed by these that unless the very words of the Scriptures, seen as 'sacred words,' are retained, doctrinal truth will not coincide with God's revelation and will tend to fly off in every direction, changing even the very sense of the Scriptural affirmations. Thus, abandoning these essential words leaves doctrinal truth both open-ended and mutable. Futurism and Archaism, while seemingly at opposite ends of the theological spectrum, actually hold views regarding doctrinal truth that lead inexorably to the same conclusion, doctrinal mutability. There was really no way to halt an open-ended view of theology or doctrine based on the assumptions of these two positions.

Athanasius, on the other hand, recognized that just because the word was not contained in the Scriptures, it did not necessarily negate its validity for use in theological discussion and subsequent theological definition. His Centrist approach did not leave doctrine in the position to be viewed as open-ended but, at the same time, it did recognize a development, or a distinct progression, that built squarely on the revelation that all agreed was given by God, even if it did not use what others deemed as sacred words. According to Murray,

> The Nicene homoousion avoids both fallacies, archaism and futurism. It transposes the scriptural affirmations concerning the Son into a new mode of understanding... —from the descriptive, relational, interpersonal, historical-existential, scriptural mode, to the definitive, absolute, explanatory, ontological, dogmatic mode. ...Between the two modes there is harmony, even homogeneity. The sense of the affirmation, as made in both modes, is identical. ...The tradition is maintained. But there has been progress within it, growth of understanding in it. (Murray 1964:49-50.)

The Centrists showed, in contrast to the Archaists, that there were no such 'sacred words,' but that truth could be stated in any combination of words that correctly carried the *sense* of what revelation taught. In contrast to the Futurists, Centrism demonstrated that revelation was a once-for-all event, contained in God's self-revelation in both the Scriptures and in Christ. This revelation is, however, neither changeable in its essence nor is it limited by the limitations imposed by human language. The limitations of human language would probably be better designated the limits of human understanding, but this, although correct, would also be agreed to by the Futurists. To distinguish: while the truths of the faith are not limited by the boundaries of either human language or understanding, they are limited by God's own self-revelation. The truths of God's revelation are the realities and their meaning which

27

underlie the words of Scripture. The words used to describe and communicate the meaning of these realities are constantly subject to change, while the realities themselves and their meaning are immutable. Human understanding of the meaning of these realities is also subject to change. What was uncertain yesterday may be crystal clear today. As our understanding broadens and deepens, new words are sought to further define old truths. One generation builds on the understanding of a former generation, carrying it a step further. And while new words are employed, the meaning of the realities to which the words point can, nonetheless, remain the same. Doctrinal development, then, is development in the human understanding of the meaning of realities given in divine revelation. Hence, it is better definition; it is clarification; or it is more astute application, but it is not some new thing. This is essentially the point made by Russell Dykstra when he says that 'The truth develops *beyond* the confessions—not *outside the boundaries*, understand, but beyond in the sense that it is better defined, becomes sharper, more in focus' (Dykstra 1998:38). I believe this is also the thrust of that much maligned statement of Princeton's Charles Hodge 'that a new idea never originated in this Seminary' (Hodge 1881:521). It is at this crucial point that the Centrists differed from the Futurists. The Centrists believed in old truths regardless of the newness of the form in which they were presented. The Futurists, consistent with their open-ended view of Christian doctrine, believed in the mutability of truth itself. There were no 'truths' per se, only one's perceptions. What was true today may not necessarily be clearer tomorrow; it may be false. Therefore, it is not just the words that are subject to revision, but the faith itself. It can become something entirely new, unrecognizable to those who knew it well.

Some may say at this juncture that all development requires a certain amount of new constructs. How then does this differ substantially from the Futurist position? There is indeed a fine line between the Futurist and Centrist positions, especially since, in this day and age they are both concerned with development and both have revered traditions. This is especially true of the period between Briggs and Machen in the Presbyterian Church. The key word here, however, is tradition. The Archaists, the Futurists, and the Centrists could be viewed as three separate and distinct traditions, which, essentially, they are. They are analogous, in a certain sense, to the Fundamentalists, the Liberals, and the more amorphous Confessionalists. Before we look more closely at the concept of tradition, a few words about the study of development itself are in order

This idea of doctrinal development did not originate with Father Murray, whose scheme we will be more or less following in this dissertation. Even Athanasius, although seeing orthodoxy through the troubled times of the Arian Controversy and the subsequent council at Nicaea, did not focus his energies on a full blown theory of development either. While orthodoxy and heresy have contended throughout the nearly two-thousand year history of the Christian Church, theories of doctrinal development are in comparison of a comparatively recent origin. Cambridge scholar, Owen Chadwick discusses at length the idea of doctrinal development, but unfortunately he only traces it back to 1688 when the 'mighty Bossuet' spoke of variation in the faith (Chadwick 1957:1). Actually, his intention, as made plain by the amount of space accorded the various stages of development, is really to relate the idea of doctrinal development as it was put forth by John Henry Newman in the 1840s. For it was Newman's *Essay on the Development of Doctrine* (Newman [1878] 1949) which actually carried the discussion of development, begun years earlier in a more off-handed fashion, to new heights. Newman, tracing the history of the development of Christian doctrine both in his *Essay on Development* and his book on the *Arian Controversy*, attempted to show that doctrine was in its earliest stages in a seed or embryonic form and, as the centuries passed, with controversy as the catalyst, it developed. As Newman himself says:

> ...from the nature of the human mind, time is necessary for the full comprehension and perfection of great ideas; and that the highest and most wonderful truths, though communicated to the world once for all by inspired teachers, could not be comprehended all at once by the recipients, but as being received and transmitted by minds not inspired and through media which were human, have required only the longer time and deeper thought for their full elucidation. This may be called the *Theory of Development of Doctrine*.... (Newman [1878] 1949:28.)

In this theory Newman did not depart significantly from Bossuet or anyone else whom Chadwick discusses. Newman, however, believed that certain doctrines unique to the Roman Catholic Church were indeed in seed form in the original revelation, only in unrecognizable form. To those who would suggest that Newman would have condoned addition to the original revelation, Chadwick retorts,

According to Newman's theory it was necessary to assert that *doctrines* which did not form part of the revelation had been added by the Church. But these doctrines were the formulated expressions of an original experience or feeling which did form part of the original revelation; and in this context he was saying no more than when he wrote that external circumstances had assisted the process of doctrinal formulation. In expressing her (partly wordless) feeling or experience, the Church, needing human language, turned to the philosophy of the age to discover the best method of explaining the revealed datum. (Chadwick 1957:159.)

Probably the best way to explain the differences in doctrine advocated by Newman as part of the Roman Catholic Church and some of his Protestant counterparts is again contained in the word tradition. It is to this discussion that we will now turn in the next section.

In summary: doctrinal development is essentially development in the human understanding of the realities and meaning of God's self-revelation. It is from this perspective that we will be critiquing the Fundamentalist/Modernist controversy. To aid us in our assessment, we have adopted the structure of development developed by Catholic scholar John Courtney Murray which he based on the Arian controversy. Murray has identified three factions: 1) Archaists, or those who would not agree to a formulation to counter Arius unless the words were also the words of Scripture, 2) Futurists, a faction, headed by Arius himself, who were determined to reinterpret the Christian faith in light of contemporary philosophical insights, 3) Centrists, led by Athanasius, who believed in the immutability of truth, while, at the same time, allowing for constant development in both understanding and human language. These three factions, which are really three different competing theological traditions, were, as we shall see, also visible in the Presbyterian controversy.

1.2 Tradition

According to Ferdinand Deist, the term 'tradition' refers to a 'a fairly consistent body of knowledge, customs, doctrines, opinions, political and/or religious views, etc. passed on from one generation to the next by word of mouth or in writing, usually in characteristic phraseology. A tradition may consist of several transmissions' (Deist 1990:262). In the opinion of John Courtney Murray, the main difference between the Protestant and Roman Catholic traditions center on their acceptance, or lack of acceptance, of the idea of doctrinal development. He says that 'leaving aside the issue of what Catholic and Protestant respectively mean when they say, "Credo," I consider that the parting of the ways between the two Christian communities takes place on the issue of development of doctrine' (Murray 1964:53). This is the same conclusion drawn by former Protestant (now Orthodox) church historian Jaroslav Pelikan (Pelikan 1969:1). John Henry Newman, in his assessment of doctrinal development as it related to Protestantism, was even more dismissive. In fact, he was prone to sideline Protestantism altogether, rather than to give it a place among the descendent of the ancient church. In his analysis of Newman's views on development, Owen Chadwick writes that

> ...for prolonged historical investigation into the ancient church proved that none of the present bodies, claiming to be churches, precisely resembled the ancient Church. Newman did not argue that the Protestant bodies were not true images of the ancient Church. He assumed it, regarded it as a matter which needed no proof, since the Protestant had discarded so much which the church of antiquity valued, from fasting to the real presence. If any proof were needed that Protestantism is not 'historic Christianity', we may observe that the Protestants have jettisoned a thousand years of Christian history... "Whatever be historical Christianity, it is not Protestantism." (Chadwick 1957:139.)

Newman's proclivity to sideline Protestantism in regard to doctrinal development, effectively denied them a tradition, at least one that could be traced back further than the Reformation of the Sixteenth-Century. This is true because, as Günther Biemer says, the heart of Newman's doctrine of tradition 'is dominated by the thought of development, as is Newman's whole theology' (Biemer 1967: 134). Elsewhere, though, Biemer concedes that Newman's doctrine of tradition almost defies definition (Biemer 1967:138). Yet, in the process he does distinguish two important elements of Newman's concept which

31

he calls *locutio* and *scriptio* (Biemer 1967:140). *Locutio* refers exclusively to oral transmission, whereas *scriptio* takes in the inspired writings, oral statements, and records of the words and writings of the Apostles (Biemer 1967:140). These two components together, according to Newman, form the tradition of the church, albeit in a very wide sense (Biemer 1967: 140-141 & 168). The result is that,

> In light of these obvious criteria each developed Christian doctrine can be seen in its intrinsic connection with the original "idea" of Christianity. Thus, for instance, the cult of the saints appears as a straightforward development from the central truth of the Incarnation, under the aspect of mediation. It leads in direct consequence to the veneration of relics, blessings etc. The sacraments are also a direct consequence of the central idea, under its sacramental aspect, that matter can be a vehicle of grace; thus baptism can be seen to be legitimate, from which in turn developed confirmation on the one hand, and the sacrament of penance, the doctrines of purgatory and indulgences on the other. (Biemer 1967:133.)

Raymond Brown also sees these same results of development as part of the Roman Catholic tradition. In his work on *Biblical Exegesis and Church Doctrine* (Brown 1985), he lists them under three separate headings depending upon their substantiation in the Scriptures: doctrines for which there is abundant but incipient basis in Scripture (Brown 1985:31), doctrines for which there is slender basis in Scripture (Brown 1985:34), and doctrines about which the Scriptures are virtually silent (Brown 1985:40). Speaking in the context of the 'results of Catholic historical-critical exegesis and a nuanced understanding of Catholic dogma' (Brown 1985:17), it is what Brown says by way of inference that is truly significant concerning church tradition. He writes:

> Therefore, it is perfectly possible to claim that the Bible, historically-critically considered, does not offer sufficient proof for a doctrine and still think the dogma must be accepted as infallibly taught because of church tradition. Sometimes such an approach has been dismissed as fideism. It would be fideism if one held that the church teaching was to be maintained even though the biblical evidence denied the dogma, or if there was no

intelligible argument for a position of the church which goes beyond the biblical evidence. But in the examples I am thinking of, Catholic exegetes are not suggesting that the limited biblical evidence contradicts church dogma or that the church has no reason for going beyond the biblical evidence. They are simply placing the responsibility for the dogma where it belongs, not in the Scriptures, but in the complementary developments of subsequent church tradition—developments that stem from reflection upon the Scriptures in the context of church life.... Rather, literalists who attack such exegesis as undermining the faith are often identifying the dogma with their own understanding of it. (Brown 1985:17.)

That Brown himself is arguing from the standpoint of a given tradition is evident by what he considers development of doctrine to be. It contains many things for which the Scriptures may only give marginal support. Positions which both Newman and Brown see as essential to the doctrinal corpus of the church, however, are sternly challenged by the nineteenth-century Scottish Presbyterian, William Cunningham. In an article written specifically in response to Newman's *Essay on the Development of Doctrine*, Cunningham criticized Newman's use of logical sequence as a test for development of doctrine. This is the very test used with such confidence by Biemer and Brown above. Cunningham writes:

We were rather surprised to find a valid and precise test like this thrust into the middle of so many that are unsatisfactory and indefinite; and on turning to the section where its application is illustrated, we found an attempt to prove, that the scriptural doctrine of our Lord's divinity developed, *by logical sequence*, into "the worship of angels and saints,"—"the deification of the saints," and "the deification of St. Mary,"—and that the scriptural doctrine of baptism for the remission of sins developed, by logical sequence, into infant baptism, penance, purgatory, and the monastic rule! When "logical sequence" is made to play such "fantastic tricks," we need not wonder at anything that may be brought out of "continuity of principle," "power of assimilation," or "preservative additions." (Cunningham [1863] 1991:71.)

In addition to logical sequence, Cunningham also looks with scrutiny at another of Newman's tests for development, namely, the preservation of the original type. He concludes, rather sarcastically, that

> From some cause or other, certainly not for want of courage, ...Mr. Newman seems to have shrunk from attempting to show that the Romish worship of the saints, angels and images, preserved the type, or idea, of the scriptural restriction of all religious worship to God alone; that the Romish reliance upon the merits and intercession of creatures preserved the type, or idea, of the scriptural principle of relying exclusively upon the merits and intercession of the divine Redeemer; that the sacrifice of the Mass preserved the type, or idea, of the scriptural doctrine of the perfection of Christ's one sacrifice; or that the seven sacraments, with a load of ceremonies, preserved the type, or idea, of the two simple ordinances of the New Testament. Instead of attempting this, he merely skims over the history of the first six centuries, and collects a few points, bearing solely upon the general external aspects of the Church,—points of a very vague and incidental description,—and holds up the modern Church of Rome as preserving the type, or idea, of these things. (Cunningham [1863] 1991:71-72.)

I deliberately chose these two quotes from Cunningham, not for the purpose of disparaging Newman, Biemer, or Brown, or Cunningham for that matter, but to illustrate the vast chasm that exists between these two perspectives concerning the idea of doctrinal development. This disagreement is especially acute in those churches which hail from the Reformation of the Sixteenth century; more specifically the Reformed and Presbyterian denominations.

In spite of this obvious tension between the Roman Catholic and Reformed positions, Otto Weber states categorically that 'the Reformers had much more respect for tradition than they are generally given credit for' (Weber 1983:133). But how can this be in light of the obvious differences that we have encountered? It seems that Alister McGrath, building on the solid foundation laid by Heiko Oberman, may be on to something when he distinguishes what he designates as 'Tradition 1' and 'Tradition 2.' This distinction, while similar, does not bear an exact correspondence to the divisions advocated by Newman above. McGrath's thesis is that,

> In response to various controversies within the early church, especially the threat from Gnosticism, a "traditional" method of understanding certain passages of Scripture began to develop. Second-century patristic theologians such as Irenaeus of Lyons began to develop the idea of an authorized way of interpreting certain texts of Scripture, which, he argued, went back to the time of the apostles themselves. Scripture could not be interpreted in a random way; it must be interpreted within the context of the historical continuity of the Christian church. The parameters of its interpretation were historically fixed and "given". Oberman designates this understanding of tradition as "Tradition 1". "Tradition" here means simply "a traditional way of interpreting Scripture within the community of faith". In the fourteenth and fifteenth centuries, however, a somewhat different understanding of tradition developed. "Tradition" was now understood to be a separate, distinct source of revelation, *in addition to Scripture*. Scripture, it was argued, was silent on a number of points. But God had providentially arranged for a second source of revelation to supplement this deficiency: a stream of unwritten tradition, going back to the apostles themselves. This tradition was passed down from one generation to the next within the church. Oberman designates this understanding of tradition as "Tradition 2". To summarize: "Tradition 1" is a *single-source* theory of doctrine: doctrine is based on scripture, and "tradition" refers to a "traditional way of interpreting Scripture". "Tradition 2", by contrast, is a *dual-source* theory of doctrine: doctrine is based upon two quite distinct sources, Scripture and unwritten tradition. A belief which is not to be found in Scripture may thus, on the basis of this dual-source theory, be justified by an appeal to an unwritten tradition. ...it was against this dual-source theory of doctrine that the reformers primarily directed their criticisms. (McGrath 1993:135-136.)

The Reformation of the Sixteenth-century was, to use McGrath's schema, a reevaluation of 'Tradition 2' in the light of a rediscovery of Holy Scripture. The battle cry of the Reformation thus became *'ecclesia reformata quia semper reformata est'* (DeMar 1994:x), with its formal principle being: *'sola scriptura.'* George Marsden calls Protestantism in general 'the religion of sola scriptura' (Marsden 1991:37), although this is probably more true of the Reformed and Presbyterian denominations than others. On the Reformed principle of sola scriptura, McGrath has this to say:

> "The Bible", wrote William Chillingworth, "I say, the Bible only, is the religion of Protestants." These famous words of this seventeenth-century English Protestant summarize the Reformation attitude to Scripture. Calvin stated the same principle less memorably, if more fully, thus: "Let this then be a sure axiom: that nothing ought to be admitted in the church as the Word of God, save that which is contained, first in the Law and the Prophets, and secondly in the writings of the Apostles; and that there is no other method of teaching in the church than according to the prescription and rule of his Word." For Calvin... the institutions and regulations of both church and society were required to be grounded in Scripture: "I approve only of those human institutions which are founded upon the authority of God and derived from Scripture." Zwingli entitled his 1522 tract on Scripture *On the Clarity and Certainty of the Word of God*, stating that "The foundation of our written religion is the written word, the Scriptures of God." Such views indicate the consistently high view of Scripture adopted by the reformers. This view... is not a novelty; it represents a major point of continuity with medieval theology, which—certain later Franciscan writers accepted—regarded Scripture as the most important source of Christian Doctrine. The difference between the reformers and medieval theology at this point concerns how Scripture is *defined* and *interpreted*, rather than the *status* which it is given. (McGrath 1993:140.)

The Reformed insistence on the Scriptures as the only 'rule of faith and life,' as stated in the Westminster Confession of Faith (Schaff [1931] 1985:602), does not oppose the concept of tradition as some have supposed. On the contrary, these two concepts are compatible. 'In fact,' writes Otto Weber,

> the churchly tradition was of much more importance to the Reformers ... than would usually be assumed. This was partly due to the fact that the fathers were appealed to in support for their views (we think of Augustine), and partly to the necessity of dealing with the traditional proofs introduced by their opponents. Works like Calvin's Institutes or John Gerhard's Loci communes theologici are veritable gold mines of patristic and patrological learning. ...The Church of the Gospel did not understand itself as being something new, but rather as being the old Church rightly understood. (Weber 1981:275-276.)

Elsewhere Otto Weber tells us that 'the Reformers generally pursued the directions which had been passed down to them from earlier generations' (Weber 1983:132-133). This was, however, no easy matter for either the Reformers, or those whose views they militated against. While Calvin was of a surer nature (Weber 1983:133), Luther agonized long and hard over the situation. He wondered whether he was the purveyor of something new or whether he had indeed rediscovered the truth. As Wilhelm Pauck relates:

> He (Luther) was often sorely beset by the thought that he as a single individual had dared to stand against the authority of the Roman Church. Indeed, he asked himself the question: "Do you think that all earlier teachers knew nothing? Why should you regard all our fathers as fools? Have you alone been preserved as the seed of the Holy Spirit in our time? Should it be possible that God should have left his people in error for so many years? (Pauck 1950:380.)

The tradition which the Reformers promoted and Luther anguished over was what Alister McGrath has previously defined as 'Tradition 1.' It was a recapturing of the singular significance of the Scriptures for the church, along with those traditional interpretations of Scripture which, as Calvin states, 'agree with the rule of the Word' (quoted by McGrath 1993:142). In similar fashion, McGrath writes:

...the decisions of bishops (and also of councils and popes) are authoritative and binding to the extent that they are faithful to Scripture. Where catholics (sic) stressed the importance of *historical* continuity, the reformers emphasized equally the importance of *doctrinal* continuity. While the Protestant churches could not generally provide historical continuity with the episcopacy (except, as in the case of the English or the Swedish reformations, through defections of catholic bishops), they could supply the necessary fidelity to Scripture— thus, in their view, legitimating the Protestant ecclesiastical offices. There might not be an unbroken historical link between the leaders of the Reformation and the bishops of the early church, but, the reformers argued, since they believed and taught the same faith as those early church bishops (rather than the distorted gospel of the medieval church), the necessary continuity was there none the less The *sola scriptura* principle thus involved the claim that the authority of the church was grounded in its fidelity to Scripture. (McGrath 1993:143.)

Thus those externals rites and rituals and even oral tradition (Tradition 2) by which Newman et al determined the continuity of the church of the present with the church of the past were of little interest to the churches of the Reformation. Doctrinal continuity was what held sway in these circles (Tradition 1), doctrinal continuity that was based on a fidelity to the Scriptures. It was this and this alone that made up the heritage, or legacy of the Reformation. And this is what the reformers strove for in their radical break with the existing church of the day. The Second Helvetic Confession (1566) begins by framing the rationale given by the Reformation for its radical reliance on Scripture alone (Tradition 1). It states, under the heading: Of the Holy Scriptures Being the True Word of God:

We believe and confess the Canonical Scriptures of the holy prophets and apostles of both testaments to be the true Word of God, and to have sufficient authority of themselves, not of men. For God himself spake to the fathers, prophets, and still speaks through the Holy Scriptures. And in this Holy Scripture, the universal Church of Christ has all things fully expounded which belong to a saving faith, and also to the framing of a life acceptable to God; and in this respect it is expressly commanded of God that nothing be either put to or taken from the same (Deut. iv. 2; Rev. xxii. 18, 19). (Leith 1982:132.)

The confession elsewhere adds to this insistence on Scripture alone other carefully selected statements detailing how this belief is integrated with a critical view of, but not a jettisoning of, the past to produce a positive tradition (Tradition 1).

Furthermore, we teach that great care is to be taken wherein especially the truth and unity of the Church consists, lest we either rashly breed or nourish schisms in the Church. It consists not in outward rites and ceremonies, but rather in the truth and unity of the Catholic faith. This Catholic faith is not taught us by ordinances or laws of men, but by the Holy Scriptures, a compendium and short sum whereof is the Apostles' Creed. And, therefore, we read in the ancient writers that there were manifold diversities of ceremonies, but that those were always free; neither did any man think that the unity of the Church was thereby broken or dissolved. We say, then, that the true unity of the Church does consist in several points of doctrine, in the true and uniform preaching of the Gospel, and in such rites as the Lord himself has expressly set down. (Leith 1982:149.)

That this confessional statement contains a positive view of tradition within certain parameters is undeniable. Yet it may still be argued that the Reformers rejected tradition in general in favor of 'the scriptural witness alone' (McGrath 1993:144). Alister McGrath counters this view by saying that

...the reformers were concerned with the elimination of human additions to or distortions of the scriptural witness. The idea of a "traditional interpretation of scripture"—embodied in the concept of "Tradition 1"—was perfectly acceptable to the magisterial reformers, *provided that this traditional interpretation could be justified.* (McGrath 1993:144.)

39

Otto Weber confirms this opinion by judging that one of the duties of the church as an institution is 'to preserve the tradition, to recognize and to fix what is valid in it, and to provide the obligatory interpretation of Scripture' (Weber 1981:279). I do not think that it would distort Weber's meaning to any degree to say that the church preserves the tradition and fixes what is valid in it by providing the obligatory interpretation of Scripture. And it is this obligatory interpretation of the Scriptures which make up the contents of the confessions of the Reformation and post-Reformation period in Protestant church history. The well known Dutch theologian G. C Berkouwer agrees that 'the teaching and tradition that must be preserved is sound doctrine (Titus 1:9)' (Berkouwer 1976:227). The preservation of this continuity of doctrine takes place in an organic, growing fashion in the successive credal formulations of the church. As Otto Weber says:

> ...each new confession does not abolish its precursors, but incorporates them. Thus, for example, the Reformation confessional statements expressly acknowledge the symbols of the ancient Church. The Church preserves its tradition in that it does not become fossilized in it. (Weber 1981:31.)

It is in these creeds that the living faith of the Reformed church is expressed. It could even be said that these statements of faith are the life's blood of the church. They are indeed the Church's tradition. But creeds are made up of doctrine; doctrine that is derived solely from the biblical record. At the outset of an article on doctrinal development J. Gresham Machen believed it imperative that his readers harbor no false notions as to just what doctrine is. 'Christian doctrine,' he wrote, 'is just the setting forth of what the Bible teaches. At the foundation of Christian doctrine is the acceptance of the full truthfulness of the Bible as the Word of God' (Machen 1973:150). Machen said all this in an article on 'The Creeds and Doctrinal Advance,' in which he sought to analyze doctrinal development within the confines of a church governed by a credal formula, i.e., the Westminster Confession of Faith. But I am sure that some would object saying: How could one believe in doctrinal development and still adhere to a human credal formulation; moreover, one that was written at a certain point in the church's history? Machen shows how this is possible by stating that,

> For one thing, all real doctrinal advance proceeds in the direction of greater precision and fullness of doctrinal

statement. Just run over in your minds again the history of the great creeds of the church. How meager was the so-called Apostles' Creed, first formulated in the second century! How far more precise and full were the creeds of the great church councils, beginning with the Nicene Creed in A. D. 325! How much more precise and how vastly richer still were the Reformation creeds and especially our Westminster Confession of Faith! This increasing precision and this increasing richness of doctrinal statement were arrived at particularly by way of refutation of errors as they successively arose. At first the church's convictions about some point of doctrine were implicit rather than explicit. They were not carefully defined. They were assumed rather than expressly stated. Then some new teaching arose. The church reflected on the matter, comparing the new teaching with the Bible. It found the new teaching to be contrary to the Bible. As over against the new teaching, it set forth precisely what the true biblical teaching on the point is. So a great doctrine was clearly stated in some great Christian creed. ...You cannot set forth clearly what a thing is without placing it in contrast with what it is not. All definition proceeds by way of exclusion. ...The historic creeds were exclusive of error; they were intended to exclude error; they were intended to set forth the Biblical teaching in sharp contrast with what was opposed to the Biblical teaching, in order that the purity of the church might be preserved. (Machen 1973:151-152.)

Machen not only believed in the possibility of doctrinal development, he gave what he believed to be the necessary conditions for it to take place. 'If there is to be any doctrinal advance,' Machen argued,

we must believe that doctrine is the setting forth of what is true, not a mere expression of religious experience in symbolic form; we must believe, in the second place, that doctrine is the setting forth of that particular truth that is contained in the Bible, which we must hold to be truly God's Word and altogether free from errors found in other books; we must endeavor, in the third place, not

41

to make doctrine as meagre and vague as possible in order that it shall make room for error, but as full and precise as possible in order that it shall exclude error and set forth the wonderful richness of what God has revealed. Ignore these conditions, and you have doctrinal retrogression or decadence; only if you observe them can you possibly have doctrinal advance. (Machen 1973:155-156.)

The creeds, i.e. the traditions of the Presbyterian and Reformed church world, are, therefore, not incompatible with the idea of doctrinal development. In fact they presuppose it. They are, therefore, also not incompatible with the idea of *sola scriptura* as embodied in the Reformation understanding of 'Tradition 1.' I believe that this is essentially what Machen was trying to show; that there is no antagonism inherent in these concepts from a historic Reformed perspective. Showing this conceptual compatibility is not exclusive to the pen of J. Gresham Machen, nineteenth-century Scottish Presbyterian James Bannerman was even more precise and forceful in his analysis of these seemingly disparate themes.

Creeds and confessions are objected to by not a few as hindrances to the progress and development of theological science, as based upon the assumption that all revealed truth can be fully comprehended by any body of uninspired men, and stereotyped for all time in a merely human summary. Now, such objections as these proceed upon a total misapprehension of the true state of the case. We do not say that the statements of the Westminster Confession, for example, comprise the whole truth of God: what we do say is that we believe them to be true— to be a true expression of the revealed mind and will of God, so far as they go. Let any part of them be proved from Scripture to be false, we give it up; for we hold them only because, and in so far as, they are true. We invite every man to go beyond them if he can. We encourage and call upon every student of God's holy Word to press forward to fresh discoveries of the truth, and to open up new views of the meaning of Scripture. "There remaineth yet much land to be possessed." Those who have studied their Bibles longest and most prayerfully are most convinced of that. But here, we believe, in this form of ancient and sound words, is so much of the good land and large already so far explored and taken possession of. Here is so much of truth made good, and rescued from the tumult of error and ignorance, and fenced round with enduring bulwarks which have many a time already turned battle from our gates. As well might you ask the men of Holland to throw down the dykes (sic) that guard their shores from the assault and inroads of the sea, and that were reared at such cost and pains by those that went before them, as call upon us, unless with far more weighty arguments than have ever yet been offered, to yield up the territory won for us by the sanctified learning, the insight, and the prayers of our forefathers. (Bannerman [1869] 1991:320.)

Not every proposition in the confessions of the Reformed and Presbyterian Churches was stated plainly in the Scriptures themselves. This was the case with a number of doctrines held dear, most notably: the doctrine of the Trinity and even the concept of *sola scriptura* itself. It was believed that while these doctrines were not explicitly stated in the Bible, nevertheless, their implicit testimony was so great as to have them accorded the status of doctrine. This implicit testimony is what is alluded to in the Westminster Confession of Faith (chapter 1, section 6) when it defines the Scriptures as: 'The Whole counsel of God, concerning all things necessary for his own glory, man's salvation, faith and life, is either expressly set down in Scripture, or by good and necessary consequence may be deduced from Scripture' (Schaff [1931] 1985:603). These doctrines for which there is only implicit testimony in the Scriptures are known as doctrinal constructs or consequent doctrines (Muller 1994:75). Writing on the covenant of works in Reformed theology, Richard Muller submits that

The doctrine of the covenant of works, which occupied a place of considerable significance in the reformed theological systems of the seventeenth century, is an example of a doctrinal construct, not explicitly stated in Scripture but drawn as a conclusion from the examination and comparison of a series of biblical loci or *sedes doctrinae*. The concept of a covenant of works belongs, therefore, to a secondary or derivative albeit still fundamental category of doctrine.... (Muller 1994:75.)

Muller adds the covenant of works to the list of implicit doctrines and, at the same time, he attests to their fundamental nature as doctrines of the Christian Faith. This idea of a doctrinal construct, or consequent doctrine, consists in those things that history has had a hand in establishing. In the Presbyterian and Reformed tradition these doctrines are included under the rubric of 'tradition 1;' for some other branches of the Christian church 'tradition 2' might be a more accurate category. Doctrinal constructs are, however, present in every branch of the church of Christ. They are the result of the historical evolution of the church through the centuries, better known as development. Biemer calls it the 'prophetic tradition,' a term he uses to 'evaluate the dynamic or evolutionary element in the transmission of Christian doctrine' (Biemer1967:50) which, in turn, is the result 'of an "increase of light in the Church"' (Biemer 1967:49). This development in understanding has taken different paths in the different segments of the church. Hence it manifests itself differently depending upon which branch of the church is studied. It is not our intention to pass judgment on the validity or correctness of any of these constructs, but simply to attest to their presence throughout the modern church. Different manifestations in understanding of different scriptural truths are the work of development in history. These manifestations make up the foundations of the varying Christian traditions. These traditions, expressed in credal formulations in the Reformed and Presbyterian Churches, in turn have tended to define and to control further manifestations of doctrinal development as they have occurred. Speaking of this close, almost intimate relationship between development and tradition, Yves Congar asserted that 'tradition acquired its "inner dimension" in the idea of development' (quoted by Pelikan 1984:39). Tradition, then, in the form of a creed, reflecting the labor and sentiments of the past, has tended even within Protestantism to define later doctrinal developments. This, however, has not always been the case, and, thus, the controlling function of tradition was precisely the nub of the conflict in the Fundamentalist/Modernist dispute.

The doctrinal development of the church is known as 'dogma.' According the Protestant Reformed theologian Herman Hoeksema, 'dogma' is 'a doctrine elicited from Scripture, defined and officially established by the church' (Hoeksema 1966:4). Without wasting any words in defining dogmatics, Hoeksema synthesizes the ideas of doctrinal development, dogma, sola scriptura, and tradition. In contradistinction to the more generic 'theology,' he writes:

> Dogmatics is that theological discipline in which the dogmatician, in organic connection with the church in the past as well as in the present, purposes to elicit from the Scriptures the true knowledge of God, to set forth the same in systematic form, and after comparison of the existing dogmas with Scripture, to bring the knowledge of God to a higher state of development. (Hoeksema 1966:5.)

Such dogmatics are the stuff of which creeds are made. While they require the official sanction of the church for acceptance, they are ultimately subject to the authority of the Scriptures themselves. They are 'not formularies which we place above the Bible,' wrote nineteenth-century Presbyterian Samuel Miller, 'but simply those which ascertain and set forth how we interpret the Bible' (Miller 1839:110). In the course of defining 'dogmatics,' Hoeksema also reveals the distinction between theology and dogma. Theology is doctrine elucidated from the Scriptures, as is dogma. But dogma has the official sanction of the church—in our case the Presbyterian Church—whereas theology does not. To illustrate: there are several different schemes of eschatology, the doctrine of last things, which hold sway in various quarters of the church of Christ. Yet none of these doctrinal constructs have, at least to my mind, ever received the official sanction of the church, and one will search the creeds of the Reformed and Presbyterian Churches in vain for their mention (Bahnsen 1988:xi). Admittedly, the creeds do mention the resurrection of the dead, the judgment, and the life of the world to come, but no specific cosmic eschatological paradigm is advanced above another.

The purpose of officially sanctioned dogma in a credal statement is at least two-fold: for the unity of a given branch of the church and for its protection. As Samuel Miller has said, 'Without a Creed explicitly adopted, it is not easy to see how the ministers and members of any particular church, and more especially a large denomination of Christians, can maintain unity among themselves' (Miller 1839:8). A creed, it seems, creates solidarity, cooperation, and a unity of purpose which really cannot be sustained in any other way. Various churchmen of the Reformed and Presbyterian tradition have insisted that in addition to a union which is beneficial there is also a union which is harmful. So, while a creed makes unity possible, as Miller suggests, it also makes separation necessary for the protection of that union. With a bit of vitriol, Herman Hoeksema outlines this facet of credal function in detail. He says at length:

> Many there are in our day who find the cause of all the dissension and division in the church in too much doctrine and in the creeds that are too specific in their doctrinal declarations. Hence, they advocate that all these specific declarations of faith by which each church erects a wall of separation around itself be forgotten, erased, eliminated, that the confessions be broadened, generalized, and that on the basis of this broad declaration of general principles the various denominations merge, and thus realize the unity of the church. However, it should be evident that in this fashion an outward unity may indeed be effected, but only at the expense of the truth, at the cost of the church's faith, which is the same as saying that it is a unity without the Christ of the Scriptures. ...The question, therefore, is urgent: what must be our attitude? What is the proper Scriptural position to assume in this situation? Must we take the stand of those who would have the various churches simply break down the confessional walls of separation, forget their differences, and unite on a very broad platform of a few general principles, hardly expressive of the true Christian faith? Such, indeed, is the attitude of many, in fact of the majority, of those that still call themselves church in our so-called ecumenical age. But such an attitude can be taken only by those churches and by those believers who have long forgotten to take their own confessions seriously. They are ready officially to relinquish their doctrinal standards, which for them are no more than dead traditions, that no longer have a place in their conscious faith and practical spiritual life. No church that takes its confessions seriously could lend its support to such a movement, or assume such an attitude. ...The unity of the church is centered in Christ. If the church is to grow in this true unity, she must grow in Christ. She must not have less of Christ, but always more. And her Christ is in the Scriptures. Hence, she must

appropriate the Christ of Holy Writ. And that means that she must instruct and be instructed in the truth. She must not seek union in the way of less, but rather in the way of more and richer doctrine. She must put aside all doctrines of men, to be sure; but she must ever grow in the doctrine of Christ. Let the true church be ever so small in the world, she dare not seek the realization of her unity in any other direction than that of growing in the knowledge of Christ her head, "till we all come in the unity of the faith, and of the knowledge of the Son of God, unto a perfect man, unto the measure of the stature of the fulness (sic) of Christ." Only they that strive to approach that stature are really working for the manifestation of the unity of the church, and whatsoever is more than these is of the evil one. (Hoeksema 1966:606-607, 618.)

It is for these two seemingly disparate purposes, unity and separation (for reasons of protection), that creeds or confessions have historically been adopted. These two purposes are also, therefore, the theological significance of credal formulations in general within Reformed and Presbyterian thought. In this respect creeds are really distillations of what a given group or denomination believes the message of the Bible to be. Hence, creeds contain officially accepted interpretations of the whole, or various parts of the Scriptures (Miller 1839:58), i.e. 'Tradition 1.'

During the course of the Fundamentalist/Modernist controversy the observance of the historic formulas of the faith was an issue that was in the forefront of debate. J. Gresham Machen complained bitterly that the approach to the Scriptures advocated by Charles Briggs of Union Seminary in New York City, and those of his persuasion, was laying the groundwork for a totally new religion that occupied a separate and distinct class from historic Christianity. This was the central theme of Machen's popular work *Christianity and Liberalism* (Machen [1923] 1946), published at the height of the Fundamentalist/Modernist controversy. While Machen may have classified the emerging Liberalism in the Presbyterian Church as an entirely new religion, he was in fact witnessing the creation of two separate and distinct traditions. One, his own, which honored and adhered to the historic symbols, or credal statements, of the Reformation, and one which, primarily because of a new methodology, refused to do so. These two traditions had grown together for many years. They had grown apart for almost as many. This time of struggle in the Presbyterian Church was a time of birth; one tradition was, in a sense, giving birth to a new tradition. And just as natural birth has its moments of anguish and pain, so did the birth of a new tradition.

This new tradition eventually showed itself to be much broader and all-encompassing than its predecessor. Whereas the prevailing version of the Reformed faith, as delineated in the Westminster Standards, was a closely defined set of beliefs and practices. This new tradition, which has subsequently come to be known as Modernism or Liberalism, sought an overall inclusivity. Its definitions were broader and its practices less uniform. Its appearance was markedly different than its progenitor. In its downplaying of historic Presbyterianism's credal stance, it seemed to many in the church that this new tradition, i.e. Modernism, sought a unity based on the lowest common doctrinal denominator (Machen 1973:153-154). In this respect it abandoned as unnecessary, in this quest for institutional unity, the doctrinal protection afforded by many of the earlier doctrinal formulations of Reformed Protestantism.

Even with all the differences between historic Presbyterian and its offspring, the similarity was unmistakable. These differences were as two members of the same family, not as strangers. They were different in personality and temperament, different in appearance and demeanor, even different in belief and practice. While the family resemblance was unmistakable, the reasons for both the similarity and dissimilarity were strangely the same. The main reason for the emergence of Liberalism or Modernism, especially in the Presbyterian Church, was the proliferation, at the professional level, of the higher-critical methodology in biblical study. While many looked upon this method as the salvation of the Christian faith in the modern world, many more did not. Many saw this method as destructive of the supernatural character of the Scriptures, not as an aid to their clarification. This was the view of George Eldon Ladd of Fuller Seminary in California. He said,

> If one's view of history is such that he cannot acknowledge a divine plan of salvation unfolding in historical events, then he cannot accept the witness of the Bible. The point we are stressing is that the historical-critical method denies the role of transcendence in the history of Jesus as well as in the Bible as a whole, not as a result of scientific study of the evidences, but because of

48

its philosophical presuppositions about the nature of history.... The historical-critical method excludes by definition that which I believe.... (quoted by Lindsell 1976:82.)

Commenting on Ladd's remarks, Harold Lindsell, another former member of Fuller's faculty, had this to say: 'Ladd is correct in his assertions that the use of the historical-critical method... is based on presuppositions that destroy historic orthodoxy. Orthodoxy and the historical-critical method are deadly enemies that are antithetical and cannot be reconciled without the destruction of one or the other' (Lindsell 1976:82).

By this standard, adoption of the historical-critical method in the Presbyterian Church undermined a belief in the Bible as the only source for faith and practice. Gradually history began to take the place of the Bible as the source for truths of the faith. Historicism, as will be discussed in the following pages, looked for its doctrinal content within the confines of human history exclusively. This, strangely enough, is also the reason why Liberalism or Modernism bares such a close resemblance to historic Presbyterianism. In seeking Christian truth in history, Liberalism turned to the history of the Christian Church, which, in turn was saturated with Scriptural truth. It is only natural that Liberalism's embrace of this biblically saturated history would yield a biblically saturated church, despite their askance view of the Scriptures as a whole. With their embracing of history in addition to the Scriptures as the source of the faith, Liberalism more readily resembled medieval Catholicism with 'Tradition 2' as its source of truth (McGrath 1993:135-136 & 142-147).

1.3 Historicism

In considering the changes that were taking place as this new tradition was being born, Ki-Hong Kim, in his thesis, hints at something very basic to an understanding of the conflict that ensued, something that was also very subtle. Unfortunately, however, he stops short of any detailed analysis, calling this phenomenon simply 'the particular theological situation of the age' (Kim 1983:127). Was this particular situation, a product of the early twentieth century, a fad or passing fancy? Actually, 'particular situation' could be more accurately designated as 'epistemological change,' with origins traceable to the Enlightenment's awakening to the importance of human reason (Cauthen 1962:7-8). In discussing the shift that took place in epistemology, Kenneth Cauthen has drawn the following conclusion:

> A distinction can be made between a concept of religious knowledge based on human reason and experience and one based on a given revelation of God which stands over against the reasoning, experiencing subject. These two approaches to religious knowledge are by no means mutually exclusive, and theologians generally have tried to include both reason and revelation in one way or another. Nevertheless, the emphasis usually falls on one side rather than on the other, and liberalism differs significantly from Protestant orthodoxy in the way it deals with this issue. Within this context the principle of autonomy means that liberal theologians rejected any arbitrary appeal to external authority and insisted that all religious affirmations must be grounded in, or at least subject to confirmation by, the data of religious experience or the conclusions of reason. All liberals adhered to this general principle, although they varied considerably in the extent to which they retained belief in a normative historical revelation. (Cauthen 1962:12.)

Cauthen proceeds to give this Liberal perspective both an objective and a subjective side. 'Some liberal thinkers were subjectivistic,' he writes, 'in that they pointed to certain inner experiences as being the most relevant source of religious knowledge. These men emphasized feeling, intuition, and the immediate awareness of the divine presence and power. By comparison some Liberals were objectivistic in that they stressed the role of sensory observation, scientific method, speculative reason and other such factors' (Cauthen 1962:12). These two characteristics, the objective and the subjective, complimented each other well even as they combined to form the Liberal outlook as a whole. The conflict in the Presbyterian Church from the 1890s to the 1930s was marked by both the objective and the subjective natures of Liberalism simultaneously. On the one hand, the objective side showed itself primarily in the historical criticism of the Bible; a tool indispensable to the Liberal epistemology. On the other hand, history itself came to be viewed subjectively, as something left to the eye of the beholder. The truth of history, or its lack thereof, increasingly came to be seen as a subjective assessment, left for the most part to the judgment of the historian. The presuppositions, perspectives and even biases of the reviewer, rather than the historical data itself, were increasingly given larger scope in determining what was true in a historical situation. In his 1935 publication *Everyman His Own Historian*, noted historian Carl Becker brought out the truly subjective nature of this approach. He said that 'the old idea of using scientific means to discover the fixed facts of history was an illusion. Rather, what were considered "the facts" varied with time, the place, and the perspective' He goes on to say that, 'left to themselves, they (the facts) do not exist, not really, since for all practical purposes there is no fact until someone affirms it' (quoted by Marsden 1991:190-191). For Machen, the Liberal theory of factuality was really fantasy. He wrote that 'the facts of the Christian religion remain facts no matter whether we cherish them or not: they are facts for God; they are facts both for angels and for demons; they are facts now, and they will remain facts beyond the end of time' (Machen 1925:249).

These two perspectives, the objective and the subjective, combined in the Liberal schema to undermine what the orthodox held to be the foundations of the faith. Having given 'up any appeal to historical revelation' (Cauthen 1962:12), Liberalism was left with reason and experience alone as materials for the building of the faith. To them, however, this was not something to be lamented. 'The question,' according to the nineteenth-century liberal Roman Catholic theologian, Alfred Loisy, 'which lies at the bottom of the religious problem to-day is not whether the pope is infallible, or whether there are errors in the Bible, or even whether Christ is God, or whether a revelation exists—all these problems are either obsolete or have changed their meaning, and they all depend upon the one great problem—but whether the universe is inert matter, empty, deaf, soulless, pitiless; whether man's conscience finds in it no echo truer and more real than itself' (quoted by Sabatier 1908:30). Experience thus became an authority in religious belief (Cauthen 1962:11-12), and the collective experience of the church took on the cloak of authority in matters of doctrine, a position reserved in other traditions for the Bible alone. A new tradition was in the making. Pelikan says that 'among the most permanent results of liberalism none is more important than the discovery that the Bible and the Church have been conditioned by history' (Pelikan 1962:ix). And it is in this history that both development of doctrine and tradition find their origin. Herein lay the assumptions of the historicist approach to history, and by association, to doctrine.

Historicism was a new understanding of the very nature, and especially use, of history. 'Historicism emerged as a world view that saw all of reality as a historical stream in which social institutions, intellectual constructs, and even logical categories were immersed.' argues Mark Massa in a recent study.

> The new historicist world view (and the historical-critical methods that its adherents applied) argued that the history of any phenomenon was a sufficient explanation of it, and that all social institutions and belief systems could be understood and evaluated through the discovery of their historical origins and development. Herder, as close to being the "founder" of this new world view as anyone, offered a *Weltanschauung* in which life and reality were synonymous with history and history alone, and all notions of truth and value, even those ostensibly claiming transcendental warranty, were seen as products forged within the historical process. (Massa 1990:5.)

Ferdinand Deist largely agrees with Massa that '(historicism is) the conviction that knowledge must always be judged in the context of historical development and change and that the history of anything sufficiently accounts for its nature or value' (Deist 1990:115). The Italian philosopher of history, Benedetto Croce, explains things a bit differently, delving into the distinction between history per se and historicism. He writes that

> "Historicism" (the science of history), scientifically speaking, is the affirmation that life and reality are history and history alone. ...the ideas or values which have been taken as the measure and the models of history are not universal ideas and values but are themselves particular and historical facts clumsily elevated to the rank of universals. ...The moral ideas were but the rules and qualities which had been formed by ancient civilization or by early or later Christian civilization. ...it recognizes no other revelation than that which thought gives to thought by means of criticism, no other mystery than the perpetual conquest of mystery by thought, no agnosticism save by way of convalescence from ignorance, and no reality beyond history which is absolute immanence. (Croce 1955:63-65.)

Historicism, thus defined, is a state of mind, a focus that is applied logically to the historical data. It sees all mores, beliefs, and traditions as part and parcel of that progressively unfolding course of events that is history. Their meaning and importance are perceived as bound inextricably to the history in which they come down to us. Apart from its history, therefore, any belief or tradition is thoroughly unintelligible to this modern scientific world view.

The salient feature of this historicist understanding of history is that all religious doctrine is historically bound; bound to the thought patterns and culture in which it finds its origin. Historical criticism as a tool is thus needed to free Christianity from its historical bondage, in order to make it relevant to a more modern scientific culture. The same is true of all credal statements which have also been bequeathed to us from the past. They are the now just the outdated responses of our forebears to the Christian faith, valid only in a specific place and time. The modern response need not agree materially with a formula of belief derived from the past since there now exists a different context altogether with entirely different needs. A twentieth-century response to the dictates of the faith may well be decidedly different from that of the first or even sixteenth centuries. As doctrinal understanding develops, new insights are revealed. As these new insights come together in the Christian community, a new understanding of the faith will inevitably develop. This new understanding will become part of the emerging tradition which will, in turn, develop new statements of faith, i.e., credal formulations.

While historicism sees any doctrine as evolving out of the process of history, the history to which it directs our attention is still the history of the Christian Church. And since this history is so saturated with Christian principles, it is only natural that any doctrine or theology arrived at in this manner would have a distinctly Christian character. Not to be neglected, the Scriptures were still an integral part of this process. But to the historicist understanding, and the historical-critical method it generated, Scripture is a record of Hebrew and early Christian religious experience, needing only to be supplanted by more current experience. The tradition, while still formed in the wake of development, was now beginning to expand exponentially because of the addition of new source material, material that previously had never been considered authoritative, i.e. experience. In historic Protestantism, experience was understood as being based on doctrine, not determinative of it. As Cauthen says: 'the focusing of attention upon feeling and personal experience significantly shifted attention from doctrine to life, from past, written revelation to present, experiential knowledge' (Cauthen 1962:19).

I will return to the discussion of the Liberal attitude towards history in more detail in the following pages. For now, the important point is that Liberalism tended to adopt a historicist approach to the self-revelation of God in the Scriptures. This historicist approach manifested itself most consistently in the application of the historical-critical method to the Scriptures. Doctrines were judged not so much to be found in the Scriptures themselves, but were increasingly seen as being products of history. Thus, compatible with their insistence on the primacy of reason and experience, Liberal theology sought meaning and religious truth in history rather than exclusively in the biblical texts. Any and all doctrines were understood to have evolved out of the historical situation, and, in turn, were subject to the light of historical criticism. It was precisely here that the new Liberal tradition concentrated its efforts.

1.4 Conclusion

At the end of subsection 1.1 Doctrinal Development, building on Murray's foundation, I drew attention to three factions clearly discernible in the Arian controversy: the Archaists, the Futurists, and the Centrists. The Archaists were of the opinion that unless a doctrinal formulation was limited exclusively to the words provided in the Scriptures, the formulation was invalid. The Futurists, in their quest for relevance, were willing to amend, even change, the historic affirmations of the faith. And the Centrists, while believing in the unchangeable reality of the historic affirmations of the faith, were not stultified by insisting on the very words of the Scriptures. The Centrists alone believed in development of doctrine. Development, I contend, meant further clarification and more precise definition of the existing affirmations of faith, or doctrines, not something new. These three factions from the early church also seem to be visible, under different names, in the Fundamentalist/Modernist Controversy in the Presbyterian Church.

In the section on Tradition, I pointed out that, while tradition has different meanings in different Christian communions, for the Reformed and Presbyterian Churches tradition has usually focused on doctrine to the exclusion of other elements. It was in this regard that I enlisted the aid of Alister McGrath and his categories of 'tradition 1' and 'tradition 2.' According to McGrath, 'tradition 1' simply meant 'a traditional way of interpreting Scripture within the community of faith' (McGrath

1993:136). By way of contrast, 'tradition 2' was 'understood to be a separate, distinct source of revelation, *in addition to Scripture*' (McGrath 1993:136). Hence, the tradition of the Reformed and Presbyterian Churches has usually been referred to as their *heritage*. And that heritage has, for the most part, been doctrinal—inclusive of 'tradition 1' and exclusive of 'tradition 2.' This contention in no way negates doctrinal development since development is seen as a further clarification of the existing affirmations of the faith.

In discussing historicism, I wanted to focus on a seemingly new development, which in reality is much older, that became an issue in the Presbyterian Church during the Fundamentalist/Modernist Controversy. The historicism that developed in the Presbyterian Church tended to focus on 'tradition 2,' something that had not been given a theological place in the Reformed and Presbyterian heritage, or tradition. 'Tradition 2' added another dimension to the Reformed faith, that of history. In downplaying 'tradition 1,' historicism asserted that doctrine was not so much to be found in the Scripture texts, but instead was a product of the historical process. And, since the Scriptures were also a product of history, they were subjected to the historical-critical method, which was seen by many as destructive to the faith. Those who promoted this historicism tended to supplant 'tradition 1' with a form of 'tradition 2,' namely, whatever was considered genuine after the application of the historical-critical method. Thus, I believe, that what we have in the Fundamentalist/Modernist Controversy is traditions in conflict.

Chapter 2

Modernism and Charles Augustus Briggs

The Presbyterian Church in the USA had experienced many dramatic ups and downs prior to the arrival of Professor Charles Augustus Briggs (1841-1913) at Union Theological Seminary in New York in 1874. Yet, he, in his own unique way, eventually became the storm center of one of the most virulent controversies the Presbyterian Church had ever seen. From the very beginning of his long career, Charles Briggs seemed to excel at attracting controversy. And it is to this turbulent career that I would like to direct our attention. But first, I would like to set the stage by discussing the origin of the theological context, known as Modernism or Liberalism, that ran concurrent with Professor Briggs's career; a context with which his name has since became synonymous. Modernism's doctrinal distinctives, however, will be interwoven in the course of the narrative.

'The decade of the nineties,' wrote the celebrated historian of Americana, Henry Steel Commager, 'is the watershed of American history' (Commager 1950:41). It was during this acknowledged period of national change that the Presbyterian Church was itself undergoing a profound internal ideological struggle. New ideas, ideas not in accord with the prevailing religious establishment in the church, were beginning to make their presence known in a broad way. Some called these new ideas 'Modernism;' while others referred to them simply as 'Liberalism.' For J. Gresham Machen, both terms referred to the same reality, although he really liked neither as an accurate description of what he saw as an entirely new religion taking shape unchecked within the confines of the Presbyterian Church (Machen [1923] 1946:2, 6-7). Machen believed this rival to historic Presbyterianism to be especially pernicious 'because it makes use of traditional Christian terminology' (Machen [1923] 1946:2). In most of his writings, though, Machen seemed to prefer the appellation 'Liberalism,' as the title to his popular exposé on the subject, *Christianity and Liberalism* (Machen [1923] 1946), illustrated. Contemporary Protestant church historian George Marsden agrees that both

57

designations are appropriate, but for different reasons, internal within the movement itself. He said that 'A movement of this proportion and which stressed freedom from tradition (hence the term "liberalism") and adjustment to the modern world (hence "modernism") inevitably encompassed wide variety' (Marsden 1991:33). It was in part this wide variety of religious ideas, which tended to go beyond the confines established by the confession, that added to the growing suspicion of those in the church who did not view the church's confessionalism as a burden.

2.1 Modernism

While the concepts of Liberalism and Modernism were not really that well defined in the American mind during the early part of Charles Briggs's career, the situation in Europe was another matter. As early as 1871 Dutch Calvinist Abraham Kuyper wrote a small book entitled: *Het Modernisme een Fata Morgana of Christelijk Gebeid* (Modernism: A Fata Morgana in the Christian Domain) criticizing what he perceived as a departure from the historic Reformed platform. In contrasting the two Kuyper wrote:

> In matters of faith Modernism chooses human authority as its starting point, the very thing against which Protestantism raised its mighty protest. It forfeits the right to adorn itself with the honor of the Reformation if for no other reason than it never knew the desperation, brokenheartedness, and mental anxiety from which Luther cried out to his God. The Reformation sought *redemption* for the troubled heart, Modernism only the *solution* to an ingenious problem. This is why Modernism only knows the reality of visible things and misses the reality of the other kind, which is much higher and much more firmly established, which speaks to us of the "immovable" kingdom of God even in the fact of sin. ...Tell me, with what else but unproven premises and therefore (from their own viewpoint) cheap dogmas does Modernism start in all its preaching? Its confession can be broadly sketched as follows: I, a modernist, believe in a God who is the Father of all humankind, and in Jesus, not the Christ, but the rabbi from Nazareth. I believe in a humanity which is by nature good but needs to strive after improvement. I believe that sin is only relative and

hence that forgiveness is merely something of human invention. I believe in the hope of a better life and, without judgment, the salvation of every soul. (Kuyper [1871] 1998:103-104 & 116.)

As to the origin of this Modernism, Kuyper argued that it 'is not even new. All through the centuries it has brought about sorrow in the church of Jesus and it will continue to ferment till the Day of the Lord' (Kuyper [1871] 1998:98). The contemporary Roman Catholic Church historian, Alec Vidler, understands the origins and meaning of Modernism somewhat differently. He emphatically asserts that Modernism had no relationship to Protestantism whatsoever. 'Modernism was essentially a Catholic movement,' he wrote, 'its object was to revise and revive Catholic, not Protestant theology' (Vidler 1934:234). Additionally,

...the movement, so far from being congruous with, had been consistently opposed to, liberal Protestantism. Loisy had not tried to adapt Harnack's theology in a Catholic sense, but had attacked it root and branch. To the modernists liberal Protestantism had seemed a reduced Christianity, an emaciated religion, which was supported by a prejudiced criticism of Christian origins and by a mistaken reading of history. It was therefore hardly to be expected that modernism, when recognized in its true colours, would commend itself to Protestants, whether orthodox or liberal. (Vidler 1934:235.)

This Modernism, as described by Vidler, had both a political wing, as identified in the Christian Democrat movement in France and Italy (Vidler 1934:xii), and a sociological wing—which he elsewhere refers to as the religious side of the movement. The political wing of this Modernism was separate and apart from the religious wing and hence did not share in its fate. Religious Modernism, however, within the Roman Catholic Church was stoutly condemned by Pope Pius X's encyclical letter *Pascendi Dominici Gregis* in 1907 (Sabatier 1908:231). One of the lights of the movement, Alfred Loisy, called this papal encyclical a 'solemn slander' (quoted by Sabatier 1908:38). Regardless of the objections voiced from many quarters against the papal action, Modernism did not survive. As Vidler says:

The primary outcome of the modernist movement was the completeness of its defeat. The papal acts of condemnation and suppression that it provoked not only affected the modernists themselves, but they imposed on the whole Roman Church conditions which have added to the restrictions on the intellectual freedom of its members, and which have retarded the development of its theology. ...The movement was not only defeated; it was killed, it came to an end. It did not continue as a movement outside the Roman Church, when it had been suppressed inside. It had no schismatic outcome. If it can be said to have survived at all, it is only in the sense that the writings of the modernists have had some influence outside the Roman Church, and especially upon certain High Anglican theologians. (Vidler 1934:216.)

It would seem, based on Vidler's observations, that the 'Modernist' movement in the United States had little relation to the movement of the same name in Europe. This statement is both true and false. The name 'Modernism' properly belongs to that movement in the Roman Catholic Church which Vidler identifies, although Vidler would probably dispute my use of the word 'movement' since he also claims that there was no Modernist school or system per se (Vidler 1934:2). Yet, aside from the technical sense in which Vidler uses the word, I think the name Modernism can definitely be appropriated to apply to the diffusion of ideas that laid the groundwork for the Fundamentalist/Modernist Controversy. This is especially true when one scrutinizes what the papal letter deems as some of the basic assumption of this 'movement.' Modernism is accused of making experience the primary content of the faith. 'For what is laid down as to *experience*,' declares the papal encyclical, 'is applied with destructive effect to *tradition*.... Tradition, as understood by the Modernists, is a communication with others of an *original experience*' (Pope Pius X 1907:256). This accusation is noteworthy because it mirrors, as demonstrated in the previous chapter, the growing tendency among Protestant Liberals to substitute the experience of the church of the past for currently unpopular doctrinal formulations as set forth in the church's creed. This inevitably points to the subjectivity of both groups in their search for the truth, a charge, from which the European Modernists wish to distance themselves. The Pope recognized this desire, and then denied it to them. He realized that they are particularly desirous not to be suspected of any prepossession in favour of philosophical theories which would lay them open to the charge of not being, as they call it, objective. And yet the truth is that their history and their criticism are saturated with their philosophy, and that their historico-critical conclusions are the natural outcome of their philosophical principles. (Pope Pius X 1907:288.)

This criticism of the methodology of Roman Catholic Modernism by Pope Pius X sounds strikingly similar to the critique of the historical-critical method in American Protestantism by George Eldon Ladd, a Baptist biblical scholar who taught at Fuller Seminary from 1950 to the 1970s. He said that the 'historical-critical method denies the role of transcendence in the history of Jesus as well as in the Bible as a whole, not as a result of scientific study of the evidences, but because of its philosophical presuppositions about the nature of history.... The historical-critical method excludes by definition that which I believe' (quoted by Lindsell 1976:82).

A question may be asked: What then, is the origin of this Modernism or Liberalism? Alec Vidler traces its European origin to the Enlightenment (Vidler 1934:15-19). I think that American Protestant Liberalism can also be traced to the same source. In a particularly astute editorial on *Transcendentalism*, Charles Hodge (1797-1878) does just this. In the course of analyzing the philosophy of M. Cousin, Hodge traces his method and presuppositions back to the German rationalism of the Enlightenment. He accuses those who propagate the philosophy of M. Cousin 'of flooding the land with German infidelity and pantheism' (Hodge 1839:93). Speaking of the philosophical principles involved in this thought and its effect on historic Presbyterianism, Hodge ventures that:

It is too plain for argument, that these principles destroy all that is peculiar and valuable in the Sacred Scriptures. The distinctive claim which they put forth, of containing a revelation from God, is set aside by a similar claim on behalf of every man. ...The Gospel of Christ is thus stripped of its high prerogative as a special message from God; and holy prophets and apostles, nay our Savior too, were deceived in supposing that they had any other kind of communication with God, than that which every man enjoys. No special revelation could, according to this philosophy, be accredited to the world. No messenger or interpreter could be furnished for a divine mission among men. The truths revealed to any one man through the operations of his instinctive reason, and by which proclaimed to others, cannot be received except by such as find the same truths in their own spontaneity of reason. And the only way therefore by which God could make known his will, and give it authority among men, would be by enlarging the spontaneous reason of every man. At precisely this point the extremes of flat Rationalism, and the philosophy of the Absolute come together. (Hodge 1839:81.)

Hodge concludes his study of this new German philosophy by saying:

We pretend not, as we have said, to comprehend these dogmas. We know not what they are: but we know what they are *not*. They are not the truth of God; nay, they gainsay that truth at every step. They are, if anything can be, profane and vain babblings, and oppositions of science *falsely so called*. So far as received, they rob us of our most cherished hopes, and take away our God. No one who has ever heard such avowals can forget the touching manner in which pious as well as celebrated German scholars have sometimes lamented their still lingering doubts as to the personality of God. But while these systems rob us of our religious faith, they despoil us of our reason. ...It proves nothing; it determines nothing; or where it seems to have results, they are hideous and godless. ...We do not wish to have a philosophy already effete, long since refuted, and heartily denounced by the best men in the country of its origin; and above all we do not wish to have a philosophy which shall conduct our young scholars into the high road to Atheism. We learn with pain that among the Unitarians of Boston and its vicinity, there are those who affect to embrace the pantheistic creed. The time may not be far off, when some new Emerson shall preach Pantheism under the banner of a self-styled Calvinism; or when, with formularies as sound as those of Germany, some author among ourselves may, like Dinter, address his reader thus, *O thou Son of God!* For the tendency of German philosophizing is towards impious temerity. (Hodge 1839:100-101.)

While Hodge's denunciation of this new rationalism was scathing, it was only selectively heeded. In part, the reason for this selectivity was the distinctly American view of the relation of science and religion. There are a number of fine studies that address this issue, and the more general issue of the effect of the Enlightenment on America (see Commager 1978, May 1976, and even Johnson 1968). George Marsden's explanation, in particular, seems especially valuable. Marsden begins his explanation by showing the different reception that Enlightenment ideas received in Calvinist Holland, represented by Abraham Kuyper (1837-1920), and Calvinist American Presbyterianism, represented by Princeton's Benjamin B. Warfield (1851-1921). While both of these men were of an orthodox Calvinistic bent, they operated on a different epistemological level with regard to the relationship between science and religion (Marsden 1991:122-123). Kuyper advocated a presuppositional approach to all knowledge with the truths of the Bible as a priori. Hence,

> Kuyper denied that there was one unified science for the human race. Rather, he argued that because there are "two kinds of people," regenerate and unregenerate, there are "two kinds of science." The differences in the two sciences, of course would not show up in simple analyses, such as measuring, weighing, or the like; but insofar as any science was a *theoretical* discipline, Christians and non-Christians would reach some conclusions that were different in important ways. Each would be equally scientific, but they would be working from different starting points and frameworks of assumptions. So, said Kuyper, Christian and non-Christian scientific thinkers were not working on different parts of the same building, but on different buildings. (Marsden 1991:122-123.)

Warfield, on the other hand, did not share Kuyper's presuppositional views. In fact,

> To B. B. Warfield, Kuyper's view was sheer nonsense. Warfield was a man of his age at least to the

63

extent of believing that science was an objective, unified, and cumulative enterprise of the entire race. ...In response to Kuyper, he maintained that "men of all sorts and of all grades work side by side at the common task, and the common edifice grows under their hands into ever fuller and truer outlines." ...For Warfield and his colleagues at Princeton, theology was still the queen of the sciences and its truths could be discovered once and for all on the same foundational epistemological principles as the truths of Newtonian physics had been established. ...As long as science was the common task of all people, said Warfield, "it is the better science that ever in the end wins the victory.... How shall it win its victory, however, if it declines the conflict?" (Marsden 1991:123-124.)

These two widely divergent approaches to what is 'true,' Kuyper's presuppositional view with the Scriptures as the ultimate axiom, so to speak, and Warfield's strictly empirical approach, were both resultant from Enlightenment rationalism, one as a reaction and the other as conciliation. Kuyper's outlook was clearly reactionary. The reason being that, 'In Holland the Enlightenment had been associated largely with the secularism that had been on the rise since the seventeenth century' (Marsden 1991:126-127). To the Dutch Calvinist mind, this meant a close association between the French Revolution and the Dutch revolution of the 1790s (Marsden 1991:127). Any collaboration with Enlightenment 'infidelity' was thus out of the question for a 'true' Calvinist from the Lowlands. It was seen as a denial of the truths of God in the face of stiff opposition from those who would elevate the creature above the creator. There was thus no common ground with this 'heresy;' no point of contact upon which to engage in dialogue to seek solutions even in everyday matters let alone matters of faith. For Kuyper, this was the ultimate expression of the Antithesis: that unbridgeable gulf that separates the elect and the reprobate, or the regenerate and the unregenerate, in all areas of life. For Warfield, Kuyper's position was untenable. 'In contrast to the situation in Europe, then,' writes Marsden, 'not only did an important component of the classic Enlightenment outlook survive, it was closely allied with the biblically conservative evangelicalism. What lived was not any explicit commitment to the "Enlightenment" as such, but rather a dedication to the general philosophical basis that had undergirded the empirically based rationality so confidently proclaimed by most eighteenth-century thinkers' (Marsden

1991:129). This commitment went back to the days of the Puritans, and, as such, it had a long history of general acceptance. An example of its outworking among the Puritans was that they 'were so preoccupied with their understanding of God as an orderly lawgiver that they welcomed and fostered investigation of that orderliness' (Marsden 1991:130). This testing of the things of God at the bar of human reason grew as the tools of science, viewed as a part of natural law, grew. 'Because God was the author of all that was,' Marsden concludes, 'what he revealed through natural law would always harmonize with special revelation. The two revelations, indeed, paralleled each other, as Bishop Butler argued. Moreover, as William Paley eventually put it in what became its classic statement, empirical science supported Scripture by providing irrefutable evidence of design' (Marsden 1991:130-131).

The distinction that we have been considering between Abraham Kuyper of the Netherlands and Benjamin Warfield of Princeton is significant because it illustrates in microcosm a trend in the Reformed and Presbyterian world at large. There were those who, following the reasoning of Kuyper, held to the Bible as the a priori source of all truth, from which all else was to be deduced. This 'all else' included those derivative doctrines which, following Richard Muller's lead, were classified as 'consequent doctrines.' (Muller 1994:75). These consequent doctrines are also referred to in the Westminster Confession of Faith, the creed of Presbyterianism, as those things which 'by good and necessary consequence may be deduced from Scripture' (Schaff [1931] 1985:603). In his attempt to reason directly from the Bible, admitting little or no accretions, Kuyper was much closer, it can be argued, to the ideal established by the authors of the Westminster Confession. American Presbyterianism, by contrast, through its overly zealous use of empirical, scientific methods in its quest for a more refined religious truth, left itself open to influences that would eventually undermine the very truths of the confession which it sought to refine.

The ideas which eventually came to characterize the Modernist side of the Fundamentalist/Modernist Controversy were in America, if only in latent form, long before the controversy erupted around Professor Briggs. I have attempted to trace them to the Enlightenment, and the rationalism which flowed so naturally from it. It is also true that the more specific tenets of the higher-critical method originated in Germany, more specifically from the school of Ferdinand Christian Baur

(Harris 1975). The many nuances which make up the Modernist/Liberal religious mind are a source of constant debate. Rather than entering into such a debate, which is outside the scope of this dissertation, the judicious comments of Alec Vidler can suffice to summarize the situation:

> The whole subject is one about which widely different opinions are held. It would be futile to try to trace the ancestry of, and the influences which moulded, a character in history, or the outcome of his activities, unless his identity and the distinguishing features of his life were evident. *A fortiori* this applies to a movement in which many different persons were engaged, and of which the characteristics were anything but simple and coherent. It is therefore necessary to investigate and to understand the character of the movement itself in order to appreciate in what sense, and to what extent, it had, or could be expected to have any specific origins and outcome. Moreover, to follow the course of the movement, and in particular the careers of the two most prominent figures who took part in it, is to go a long way towards discovering the nature of its origins and outcome. (Vidler 1934:xii-xiii.)

Professor Charles A. Briggs of Union Seminary in New York City was not the source of Modernism in the Presbyterian Church; neither was he the originator of the higher-critical method with which his name is forever linked. He was, however, one of higher-criticism's most outspoken advocates (Massa 1990:157), which, in turn, brought an emerging Modernism out of the shadows into the light of public and ecclesiastical scrutiny.

2.2 Charles Augustus Briggs

If Charles Briggs can be said to have had a stormy career, the same can almost certainly be said for the Presbyterian Church as a whole. A nice summary of American Presbyterian structure and history, recounting only those points more pertinent to our discussion, is given by William Weston, whom I shall quote at some length:

> The Presbyterian Church is organized in a hierarchy of courts, in which clergy, representing the pastoral ministry, and elders, representing the laity, are represented

equally. Each congregation has a "session," which sends representatives to the area "presbytery." Presbyteries are represented in a "synod," and all the synods are represented in the national "general assembly." The American Presbyterian denomination organized a presbytery in Philadelphia in 1706, and a synod in 1717. The General Assembly for the new national church was created after the American Revolution in 1788. The constitution of the church consisted of the Westminster Standards: the Confession of faith, The Larger and Shorter Catechisms, the Directory of Worship, and the Plan of Government and Order, as modified by the church. The constitution established what had to be believed and done in the church, and the organization of the church as a system of courts meant that these constitutional standards of faith and practice would be enforced. In 1729, a crucial debate took place between the Philadelphia and New York groups over how strictly ministers should be bound to the Westminster Confession. The Philadelphia group argued for strict subscription to every article, while the northern members opposed being bound to any creed created by humans, preferring to accept only the Bible as the rule for the church. In the "Adopting Act," a compromise was worked out by institutional loyalists, according to which ministers would subscribe to the Westminster Confession "as containing the system of doctrine" found in the Bible; if a candidate had scruples about any part of the Confession, it was left up to the presbytery to decide if these scruples posed a bar to ordination, subject to review by the higher courts. ...The Adopting Act allowed enough room for interpretation that each presbytery could establish standards somewhat different from those adhered to by the others. The strict presbyteries got stricter, and the broad ones got broader. The differences sometimes grew into schisms. In the mid-eighteenth century, there was a seventeen-year separation (1741 to 1758) between the revivalistic, New York-oriented New Side and the confessional, Philadelphia-based Old Side.

At the beginning of the nineteenth century, the revivalistic Cumberland Presbyterians, who did not hold the strict Westminster Confession view of predestination, separated from the rest of the church. In 1837, a separation occurred between the ecumenical, New York-oriented New School and the confessional, Philadelphia-based Old School. By the time of the Civil War, each of these schools had divided into northern and southern churches over questions of slavery, union, and the political role of the church. The southern Old and New schools reunited in 1865 to form the Presbyterian Church in the United States (PCUS), and the two schools in the north united in 1970 to form the Presbyterian Church in the United States of America (PCUSA). (Weston 1997:3-4.)

Only five years after the long awaited reunion of the two dissenting branches in the Presbyterian Church in the USA (northern church), Charles A. Briggs took up his position as a lecturer in Old Testament at Union Theological Seminary in New York. (For details in the following brief biographical outline I have relied largely on Rogers 1964.) Briggs was a product of New York; he was born on Henry Street in Manhattan's lower east side in 1841. His family owned a prosperous barrel company that supplied breweries far and near. As the heir apparent, Charles was tempted and even pressured by his father Alanson to take his place in the family business (Rogers 1964:21). The younger Briggs, however, had other plans. He attended the University of Virginia where in 1858 he experienced what he considered his conversion experience, an event to which he would refer again and again throughout his many and varied literary productions. Throughout all the turbulent events of his stormy career, he always maintained his commitment to the Christian faith because of his experience at Virginia (North 1996:169). He left the university as the rumblings of the Civil War grew in intensity, and he began attending Union Theological Seminary in his home town. Studying under Henry Boynton Smith was exhilarating, but the illness of his father brought him back to the family business while the elder Briggs recovered. Alanson Briggs wished his son would remain at the helm, as the company had prospered under his management (Rogers 1964:21), but this was not to be. When his father had sufficiently recuperated, Charles quit the business, married, and shortly thereafter set out to sample the cutting edge of Biblical scholarship in Germany.

On the recommendation of Professor Julius Muller of Halle, Charles and his new bride took up residence in the center of modern scholarship, the University of Berlin (Rogers 1964:25). The faculty, in retrospect, was renowned. E. W. Hengstenberg occupied the chair in Old Testament (Rogers 1964:26), and, although initially drawn to him by his love of the Pentateuch and the historical books, Briggs found study under him to be tedious (Rogers 1964:27-28). He wrote in his diary in October 1866 that 'His (Hengstenberg) manner is dogmatic--dictatorial. ...I soon became tired of Dr. Hengstenberg on acct (sic) of his dogmatic manner & his peculiar nervous habits & give myself up to Dr. Roediger & Dorner (sic)--with these I have been well pleased especially with Dr. Dorner' (quoted by Rogers 1964:27). His voracious appetite for knowledge thus seemed to be satiated at the feet of Drs. Isaac August Dorner and Emil Roediger. Concerning these, his fovorites, Briggs wrote in the last week of October 1866:

> Dr. Roediger is a cheerful—lively old man—who goes out towards you in his lectures—He is a sharp critic—tinged with Rationalism—he cuts as it were—dissecting his subject & shows the various parts to you. Dr. Dorner is a thorough scholar & a man of the spirit--we listen to him with wrapt (sic) attention--he penetrates to the very soul of his subject & takes you there. He has no superior in any that I have yet listened to. I feel this though as yet I understand the lectures rather imperfectly. (quoted by Rogers 1964:28.)

It was from Dorner that Charles Briggs gained valuable insights into the concept of the church's doctrinal development, or development of dogma, insights that would characterize even his most mature writings. According to Dorner, dogma and its historical development were inseparable because this development took place within the community of faith. Historical development accounted for differences in both theological and ecclesiastical traditions since dogma, as well as the church, were products of a succession of historical events. And since historical events shaped the church, they also shaped the church's confession, i.e. her dogma. Thus, the church and her talk about God—dogma— were both objects for empirical study since both arose from history. For Briggs, all this was not to detract in any way from Christian piety since it was the Spirit of God who was the prime mover in this development. As Dorner himself says:

> The History of Dogmas, as such, has to do, not with the utterances out of which faith springs, i.e., not the objective doctrinal declarations of Christ and His Apostles, but with the faith that is exhibited to the knowledge of men, or developed into Church doctrine.... History of dogmas has to show how the objective testimony concerning Christ, given for all times, is, in the entire fulness (sic) of all its elements, more and more disclosed to the consciousness of the Church in virtue of her work, conducted by the Holy Ghost.... But in spite of this its dogmatic position, the testimony of Christ and the Apostles finds its place also in the History of Dogmas; it forms the *impulse* which must be presupposed in the dogmatico-historical process in the Church. (Dorner 1872:48.)

Yet, methodologically,

> ...we guard against setting forth this impulse, as it operated in the Church, as so dogmatically formed from the beginning, that we shall accredit the Church with the immediate possession of what was the collective property of the Apostles.... Hence the right course will be here to consider somewhat more closely only that form of apostolic doctrine which undoubtedly stands nearest to the Christological standpoint of the primitive Church, and represents the sure as well as sufficient impulse for its dogma framing activity. (Dorner 1872:50.)

This dogma, i.e., theology which has the official sanction of the church, according to Dorner, unfolds in the process of historical development. Yet, whether this dogma unfolds directly out of the history of revelation alone is not clearly spelled out. While it is within the sphere of the church that this development takes place, it appears that the church as part of the historical situation and as thinking subject in this process adds to the content of the dogma in ways other than providing clearer and more precise definition. This process was referred to by Dorner as the church's 'dogma framing activity.' The significance of this definition has not eluded the contemporary historian, Claude Welch; he considered it a 'Socratic turn to the self.' He writes:

It (Dorner's idea of the church's dogma framing activity) meant a new kind of self-conscious and systematic recognition of the involvement of the religious subject—his point of view, his cognitive act, his interest, his willing and choosing, with which theological reflection has to begin. Consciousness of the truth of the religious object was peculiarly one with self-consciousness. An ineradicably subjective (though not subjectivist) viewing of the religious object emerged. Significant talk about God is talk in which the self is concerned. The religious object, God, is present for reflection only in and with the religious subject in his relation to God. Religious truth is not of a disinterested, neutral sort, but irreducibly involves the believer's believing the truth. (Welch 1985:68.)

Elsewhere, Welch, using Dorner's work on Christian ethics, puts this whole idea of development into stark relief. Welch contends that, for Dorner, this development tells us about ourselves. It takes the form of a myth, which dissects the believer and, at the same time, inspires personal piety. This is because 'Dorner', Welch writes,

interpreted the development of the conception of God from Greek and Hebrew religion as continuing dialectic between genuine personal life and unchangeable self-identity. In the *System* also the dialectical argument was prominent. The true understanding of faith emerges as the transcendence (and synthesis) of antithetically inadequate notions of the merely "historical" faith and of the purely "ideal". Here as elsewhere the final solution must arise out of the moments that have emerged in history; the inner course of history determines the sense of further progress. (Welch 1972:274.)

This emphasis on development which Briggs brought back from Germany, with its primary emphasis on history as opposed to revelation, had the subtle but significant effect on the credal statements of the Presbyterian Church, her repository of doctrine, of making them much broader and more all-inclusive. With this new developmental outlook, her doctrinal constructs were taken to be little more than the record of her own self-understanding and its progress over the centuries, a theme

71

which Briggs would continue to develop under the rubric of Biblical Theology.

As great as his debt was to Dorner in Berlin, Briggs was equally beholden to Professor Ewald of the University of Göttingen. Since he had been unable to find satisfactory instruction in Old Testament at Berlin, in his last year in Germany he decided upon Professor Ewald for his celebrated lectures in the Pentateuch. Briggs gained much from the teaching, especially in the area of methodology as Ewald applied the methods of higher criticism (Rogers 1964:30). For Briggs this was a breath of fresh air and, never believing for a moment that it would have any adverse effect on his evangelical views, he reveled in it (Rogers 1964:31). Writing to his uncle Marvin, Charles recounted with an undoubted sense of reverence and awe that, 'I cannot doubt but that what I have been blessed with a new-divine light. I feel a different man from what I was five months ago. The Bible is lit up with a new light' (quoted by Rogers 1964:31).

According to Rogers, as the year progressed, 'Briggs became increasingly enamored of the critical methodology; but he saw the primary value of this as related to the construction of a comprehensive Biblical Theology' (Rogers 1964:33). And it is in this synthesis that the fruit of his time in Germany was seen for the first time. In this Biblical Theology, as Briggs understood it, there was a fusion of the critical methodology of Ewald and Dorner's concept of theological progress or development. Briggs synthesized these two theological streams; the details of which he would continue to develop for years to come.

Charles Briggs returned home in the spring of 1869 on news of his father's ill health. The change of venue in no way dampened his ardent zeal for biblical and theological study. Building on his studies abroad, he wrote an article of a truly seminal nature for *The American Presbyterian Review* in the early months of 1870. Under the title of 'Biblical Theology with Especial Reference to the New Testament,' Briggs advanced conclusions which were to become the hallmark of his stormy career, not the least of which was his theory of the inspiration of the Scriptures. Showing his debt to Dorner, Briggs describes the relationship of the Scriptures to history, demonstrating in the process why Biblical theology is the only means for their adequate resolution. He writes:

> Biblical Theology in the course of history, while ever
> based on the Scriptures, gives biblical truth a form, a
> force, a direction and an emphasis such as the wants of

the respective periods require. The Bible is ever the ideal source, and presents to us a theology adapted to the wants of each and every age; history, however, has shown us that each age has its own peculiar tendencies, and these must receive the stamp and decision of holy Scripture. The form that scripture truth takes to itself in the various periods of history is not the same as that which is presented to us in the Scriptures, which was determined by scripture times. (Briggs 1870:296.)

Along with his discussion of the relevance of the sacred text for each successive generation of Christians, Briggs takes bold steps to make clear his burgeoning views on inspiration, views which, considering the date of the article, were already set prior to any controversy in the church. Keeping within the parameters of Biblical Theology that he stated earlier, Briggs predicted with confidence concerning inspiration that:

> Biblical Theology has entirely modified the doctrine of the nature and use of the Scriptures; in estimating the human element and individual peculiarities, it has shown that the old idea inspiration is untenable. We can no longer believe in an inspiration of the very words, letters or signs of Scripture, or that the biblical authors were merely passive instruments of the Holy Spirit, scribes writing from dictation; but inspiration admits of the self-conscious, active and assured operation of the human soul, in all its activities, according to the varied characters of the writers themselves, and the varied condition of their birth and training, their geographical position, and their place in the world's history. Biblical Theology recognizes an inspiration which gives truth in manifold forms, while one eternal spirit breathes through the Word of God.... Biblical Theology alone can solve the problem of the inspiration of the Scriptures, and show the proper relation of the divine and human elements therein. (Briggs 1870:304.)

Briggs's views, radical for their day within American Presbyterian circles, strangely enough attracted no attention. 'The title of the article was significant of the new attitude towards the Bible,' writes his lifelong friend and colleague Henry Preserved Smith, 'but the church paid no heed, and the review in which the essay was published soon ceased to appear. The reunited church was for the moment resting in the belief that controversy was over and that, doctrine being settled, it could give itself wholly to practical work' (Smith 1913:504-505).

Almost simultaneous with the publication of his burgeoning, confessionally divergent views, Briggs was offered and accepted a call to serve as pastor the First Presbyterian Church of Roselle, New Jersey, a post which the records indicate he filled with distinction; he even gained a certain notoriety for his preaching skills. In 1873, because of the failing health of Henry Boynton Smith, Briggs was called to serve part-time at Union Seminary, a position which he accepted despite the urgings of his former professor Dorner to return to Germany and finish his studies. A year later in 1874 Briggs received his first full-time appointment to the Union faculty, in spite of his distinct lack of qualifications; he had no earned degrees, never having graduated from any of the schools which he attended (Sawyer 1994:8, North 1996:169). This fact, however, did not stop the new professor from becoming a truly prolific and original author.

His first years at Union were uneventful, and he gave himself unreservedly to his growing interests, which interests always seemed to center on the use of the critical method in biblical study and Biblical Theology. The latter was the only way of approaching the Scriptures, according to Briggs, which took into proper account their inherently developmental character. In his *The Higher Criticism of the Hexateuch* (1893), Briggs illustrated his developing historicist understanding of the text and the doctrines it contained. Beginning on page 146 under the caption 'Argument from Biblical Theology,' he launched into a detailed discussion of religious and theological developments in the Old Testament period. Following closely the chronology of the biblical text, he concentrated on the doctrinal developments within the four great historical narratives; those of the Jahwist (represented by 'J'), the Elohist (represented by 'E'), the Priestly code (designated by 'P'), and the Deuteronomist (indicated by 'D')—known more recently as the Documentary Hypothesis. Looking at questions of integrity, authenticity, literary form, and credibility (Briggs 1893b:2-3) in relation to these four narratives, he followed the course of doctrinal development in the history of God's chosen people, all the while viewing the text of the Old Testament as a historical composite of Israel's collective religious experience. This together with his well-honed critical method led him to conclude, when discussing the copy of the Priestly Code discovered just prior to the reign of King Josiah, that,

> This document was a private code for the priesthood at Jerusalem. It elaborated the priestly legislation far beyond existing circumstances. The ideal in it is so prominent that many of its laws have never been realized in fact. The private priestly character of this document is the reason why it was unknown to the author of the Deuteronomic code or disregarded by him. For the author of D wrote a people's book in view of the conditions and circumstances of his times. This code was composed shortly after P, and reflects the religion and doctrines of the times of Jeremiah. When discovered in the temple, it became the basis for the reform of Josiah. But the priests' code did not become a public code until after the exile, in the times of Ezra and Nehemiah. (Briggs 1893b:133.)

Briggs saw his investigations, regardless of their apparent novelty, as an aid to the life and scholarly pursuits of Presbyterianism (Briggs [1891] 1972:4-7). Not everyone, however, agreed with this noble-sounding ideal and, although earlier writings may have been overlooked by an otherwise preoccupied church, this one was not. It was William Henry Green of Princeton who criticized what he considered the 'questionable findings' of his counterpart at Union. 'What conceivable sense is there,' rails Green, 'in saying that the historical credibility of the Pentateuch is strengthened by its being made up of four narratives dating respectively four, eight and ten centuries after the Mosaic age, instead of being a single narrative from the pen of Moses?' (Green 1893:530). With an acute sensitivity to weakness, Green links together Briggs's critical method and his historicist understanding of truth. He links them in such a way that:

> The universal affirmation of those that accept the partition hypothesis is that the history must be reconstructed; that the true course of events is not that which lies upon the face of the narrative, but it must be ascertained by eliminations and fresh combinations. And the only difference between the critics is their varying estimates of the amount of truth which can be extracted

from the mass of legendary accretions, later codifications and parenetic settings. (Green 1893:531.)

It is from this aggregate of sources that the truth, i.e. Reformed doctrine or dogma, emerged, to summarize Briggs's maturing developmental insights—truth which derived from the personal and corporate interaction of individuals with their God; truth which has been conditioned by people, time, and cultural setting; and truth which has developed over the centuries and millennia, progressing and changing with each new discovery. The truth and its interpretation, or application, seemed to rise in an almost spontaneous fashion from the various historical contexts. With differing assessments regarding the amount of truth which could be gleaned from the historical record, the Scriptures came to be regarded in the growing critical circles not so much for the "theoretical" truths which commanded assent but for "practical" truths which gave evidence of Christian character. This change of perspective that was occurring was not just a shift from the "theoretical" to the "practical". Rather, it was a redefinition of just what it meant to be a Christian, a reappraisal of the very foundation of the Presbyterian Church itself, as the events of the Fundamentalist/Modernist Controversy will undoubtedly show. What constituted the Presbyterian Church and her authority was not the questions that were on everyone's lips during Briggs's rise to public prominence, but they were at bottom the questions that ultimately needed to be answered. Answers were not, however, forthcoming, at least for some years. In the meantime, the theological evolution of Professor Briggs continued.

It must be kept in mind that throughout his career Charles Briggs always seemed to reverence the Bible as the Word of God. He believed that 'the Scriptures are human productions' and at the same time 'truly divine' (Briggs 1883a: 27). In *Biblical Study* he wrote that 'the scientific study of the Word of God should be combined with a devout use of it' (Briggs 1883a:viii). Yet, his biblical-theological method seemed to contradict these very convictions. This was true because, as Gary Johnson says, 'Briggs was more than willing to give an ear to the scientific authorities of his day and to quickly incorporate these views in his critical methodology' (Johnson 1987:13). (I say biblical-theological method because however much advocates of Biblical Theology, Professor Briggs included, try to demonstrate that their discipline is a substitute for Systematic Theology their arguments do not seem convincing. Biblical Theology is not, I submit, really theology in the proper sense at all. Biblical Theology is a method. More precisely, it is a methodological category under which is subsumed a wide variety of historical-critical methods for biblical study. A thorough substantiation of my claim is Joseph Blenkinsopp' *A Sketchbook of Biblical Theology* (Blenkinsopp 1968).) This dichotomy, overlooked repeatedly, came to the attention of the church at large with Briggs's appointment as co-editor of a new journal. This new publication was inaugurated for the purpose of bringing both sides in the Presbyterian Church together in order to benefit from a mutual exchange of ideas. A brainchild of Union Seminary President William Adams, the new review was to be edited by both parties of the reunion of 1869. In this way, it was hoped, there would not be either prejudice or monopoly by either theological perspective. President Adams communicated his proposal for the new theological organ to Professor A. A. Hodge of Princeton Seminary. While Hodge was not overly enthusiastic with respect to Adam's proposal, he did not air his sentiments (Jeschke 1966:9-10). In fact both seminaries forthrightly recognized the need for a new publication that would be conducive to a better understanding and closer cooperation. One timely impetus for the two sides to cooperate was the growth of Premillennialism in several Midwestern presbyteries. 'Largely as a consequence of the prophetic conference held in 1877', writes Channing Jeschke,

> Premillennialism had received renewed attention among Protestant conservatives. Embodying a static view of revelation and theology, supported by a literal method of biblical interpretation, several leading Midwestern Presbyterians became identified with premillennial views. Both Princeton and Union opposed the premillennial views, but the former remained silent, apparently not wishing to oppose openly those who were otherwise closely in harmony with them. (But this stance was not adopted in New York.) Briggs, on the other hand, waged a vigorous and sharp attack against this doctrine in the pages of the *New York Evangelist*. Marshalling the forces of the whole army of Christian theologians since the ancient church in array against these views, Briggs concluded: "We are not yet prepared to discard the great teachers of the Church or to put out the lights of Christian history". (Jeschke 1966:5-6.)

While the theological affinities of Professor Briggs were known to his counterparts at Princeton (Jeschke 1966:12), his articles in the *New York Evangelist* went a long way towards ameliorating any suspicions concerning his proposed association with the new journal. It has been suggested that on a personal level Briggs was forceful and bombastic, bordering on arrogant (Jeschke 1966:141 & Johnson 1987:65-69). So his articles against premillennialism gave a more favorable impression to his detractors than he could, or would, have given in person. While his credibility was greatly enhanced in the eyes of his colleagues at Princeton by his articles on premillennialism, this new-found status was to be quickly diminished by another article soon afterwards. In the very first issue of the new journal, Briggs chose to give a summary of the libel trial of Professor William Robertson Smith (1846-1894) of Aberdeen, Scotland. Briggs defended his colleague in Scotland, much to the ire of his Presbyterian brethren in Princeton (Massa 1990:57). The reason for this defense of William Robertson Smith was Briggs's own views on both higher criticism and credal Presbyterianism. As Gary Johnson says:

> Briggs' opinion of the Princeton theologians and men like his colleague as Union, W. G. T. Shedd, makes for sad reading. He obviously considered the debate over inerrancy vs. the right of Higher Criticism a fight to the death. The two could not co-exist. It should be noted that it was not the Princeton men who first drew blood in this battle. The call to arms against the invasion of Higher Criticism did indeed involve the Princetonians. But it should be remembered that Princeton directed its early attack not against Briggs, but against the likes of William Robertson Smith and the German Higher Critics. Briggs, however, took this as a personal attack against his own views. (Johnson 1987: 62-63.)

In his reporting on the Scottish trial, Briggs began his account in a rather straight forward historical fashion. 'But the blood pressures of at least half the editorial board must have soared when the last paragraph of the notice was reached,' writes Mark Massa (Massa 1990:57). Actually, the whole article would likely have caused great consternation among his conservative compatriots. Robertson Smith was called to account by the General Assembly of the Free Church of Scotland (Douglas 1992:630) for various articles that he wrote for the ninth edition of the *Encyclopedia Britannica* regarding Angels, the Bible, Canticles, and Chronicles, among others. The church court judged that 'these articles, especially the one on the Bible, gave great offense:

> (1) By their bold and fearless rejection of views long established in the Church, and regarded by most people as inseparable from orthodox views of the inspiration and authority of the Bible as the Word of God; (2) by the confident and assured statement of opinions that were strange to the British and American public as if they were unquestionable and accepted by all competent scholars; (3) by the bald statement of theories that were ordinarily associated with Foreign Rationalists in their attacks on the Christian religion, without those qualifications and explanations that would be expected from an evangelical Presbyterian, in separating himself from them. (Briggs 1880b:738.)

Professor Smith did not appear apologetic in his initial response to these charges. Rather, he seemed somewhat annoyed that the church court should have anything to say to him at all on this matter. Showing his impatience, Smith responded to the General Assembly:

> It is right that an Encyclopedia should contain a fair and impartial account of the present state of critical questions, and the account was more likely to be fair and impartial if written by a person whose criticism was not enlisted in the service of a destructive theology. I would not have undertaken the article if I had thought that a critical statement, within the limits of the plan of the Encyclopedia, would tend to cast any doubt on the Divine authority of Scripture. But I am convinced that there is nothing in what I have written to touch a faith which moves in the lines of sound Protestant doctrine, and rests on the bases indicated in the first chapter of our Confession; and I cannot be answerable for the effect of my teaching on men whose belief in the Bible moves in other lines, and rests on other foundations. (quoted by Briggs 1880b:738.)

Although all formal charges against him were dropped in 1880 (Douglas 1978:911), Robertson Smith still received a stern warning from the General Assembly in regard to his "differing opinions." There were

79

those in the assembly who felt that Smith's convictions were clearly outside the boundaries set by both the church and the confession. These, however, being in the minority, were ultimately frustrated in their desire to see the matter pursued further (Massa 1990:19-21, Beidelman 1974:20-22). While Briggs's commentary emphasized the positive side in the events surrounding the Smith trial, not everyone on this side of the Atlantic agreed with the conclusions which he drew. 'Two very important points have been made in the history of this discussion (i.e. the action of the General Assembly of the Free Church-PB),' commented Professor Briggs,

> (1). That critical views of the sacred Scriptures, which do not conflict with the Westminster Confession, should be decided by discussion, among competent scholars; and (2). That evangelical men should be extremely careful not to make loose and unguarded statements and give offence and anxiety to their brethren in the Church.... If therefore the discussion should be conducted still further, in the proper spirit, with Christian charity and mutual toleration of legitimate differences, without the sacrifice of truth or principle, the result will be that many troublesome difficulties will be removed from the study of the Scriptures.... (Briggs 1880b:745.)

While giving customary deference to the confessional stance of the church, Briggs's suggestions for an end to the Robertson Smith Case put forth scholarship as the true arbiter of confessional Presbyterianism as opposed to the church's duly elected commissioners. With one sweep of the pen he cast doubt on any judgment rendered by the ecclesiastical court in the Smith Case, and, in a sense, prejudiced any future judicial action. According to Briggs, competent scholars are to be preferred to any of the church's current representatives. In fact, his very wording insinuated that those currently serving the Presbyterian Church in a judicial capacity were not competent. Competence, however, for Briggs, seemed predicated upon the acceptance of those critical theories which themselves were under dispute. These insinuations by the professor from New York did not go unnoticed in Princeton, and he received a curt letter for his troubles (Massa 1990:57-58). Mark Massa sums up Briggs's editorializing in the Robertson Smith affair:

> With breathtaking alacrity Briggs thus appeared to dismiss, in an aside utilizing the editorial "us," the

competency of church courts to judge the veracity of the complicated new critical theories. Likewise, he had more than intimated that the "technicalities" of ecclesiastical trials hindered more than helped the honest search for theological truth, a search that only competent scholars, and not good-willed but ignorant church officers could evaluate. But most unconscionable by far was Briggs's description of Robertson Smith's theological position as "legitimate differences" that might be accepted within a broadly evangelical Presbyterian church, a description that itself constituted the theological position against which conservatives in both Scotland and America had fought for some time. (Massa 1990:57.)

Smith and Briggs were of a similar nature theologically. Actually, Smith represented a more mature and thoroughly developed viewpoint based essentially on the same historicist worldview that was taking shape in Professor Briggs. Or, as Smith himself says:

The fundamental principle of the higher criticism lies in the conception of the organic unity of all history. We must not see history only as a medley of petty dramas involving no higher springs of action than the passions and interests of individuals. History is not a stage-play, but the life and life-work of mankind continually unfolding in one great plan. And hence we have no true history where we cannot pierce through the outer shell of tradition into the life of a past age, mirrored in the living record of men who were themselves eyewitnesses and actors in the scenes they describe. Not mere facts, but the inner kernel of true life, is what the critical student delights to find in every genuine monument of antiquity; and the existence of such a kernel is to him the last criterion of historical authenticity. A tradition that violates the continuity of historical evolution and stands in no necessary relation to the conditions of the preceding and following age must be untrue; and, above all, an ancient writing is no frigid product of the school, but is instinct with true life, must be a product of that age which contained the conditions of the life it unconsciously reflects. (Smith 1912:164-165.)

Robertson Smith was concerned primarily with the evolutionary change continually taking place in both society and religion. As one of the pioneers in the field of sociology of religion, and as one who was of profound influence upon the celebrated sociologist Emil Durkheim, he spoke of development as affecting both in concert. Historical criticism was thus a tool given for the improvement of both religion and society. To Smith, religion was a product of society, and it changed and developed accordingly as a part of society. Whatever the dogmas of society and religion were, they were really little more than theories until properly validated by criticism. Yet even this is a process which must be repeated over and over in each successive generation. This truth is spoken in a time of crisis by an innovator (Beidelman 1974:40). This truth, in turn, is replaced by a more perfect development as the history of the human race continues to develop and progress. This is the view of Smith scholar and biographer T. O. Beidelman, who insists on Smith's behalf that:

> This, of course, is a view of social change consistent with Christian theology, with its concentration on the innovative prophets from Moses to Christ. It mattered little that these prophets presented their views merely as clearer, more accurate formulations of a basic truth that had to be seen as changeless from the beginning.... The social group was epitomized by custom and socially sanctioned ritual was led by a priest, often in the service of a king. The innovative, individual prophet, while speaking in terms of social values and morality, ultimately stood outside the temporary and relative frame of reference of the present social status quo; the conservative social group was contrasted with the innovative individual conscience, the priest-king with the prophet.... A prophet, while innovative or reformist, could only speak to his own time. A prophet could only convey his message in terms meaningful to his own society. Thus, while all of God's prophets presented some form of the truth, men were, as their awareness improved, prepared for ever more complex and higher forms of prophetic revelation.... Thus, while God's ultimate message was ever the same, men and society in

which men lived and from which much of men's perspectives derived were manifested in different forms and levels of development in history. A prophet could only present God's word in terms meaningful within that time and culture. Prophets could therefore innovate, but never so far as to be incredible and meaningless to the people and modes of thought of a particular time. Prophets could be "ahead" of their society and time, but never too far. They were the convenient diachronic link between different synchronic stages of society. (Beidelman 1974:40-41.)

In one respect Smith took the whole of life and made of it a theological exercise. His was a theology that was never static and, regardless of what he said at his trial, it was not a theology given to confessional systematization. It seems that, given his preoccupation with the prophetic nature of the innovator, Smith envisioned himself in that role, especially as one who was persecuted for the message of God that he brought. After all, did not Israel stone the prophets? Maybe this is why Smith felt so out of place in the church at large. He saw the confessionalism and the theologians as wanting to retain the form while allowing the message to escape (Watts 1882:148-153). 'Smith was somewhat ill-disposed towards theologians and their emphasis upon a neat (i.e. confessional-PB) theology,' writes Beidelman,

> at least if this distracted believers from fellowship and communal activities. Smith advocated a mastery of the ideas of the church, but he saw theology only as a means, ever developing and being perfected through research and scholarship, for achieving proper Christian social action. Early in his career he expressed a religious view consistent with his sociology: "the Church is not the fellowship of Christian love—which requires no unity of organization—but the fellowship of Christian Worship. The common worship of many individuals must be the expression in intelligible form of their common relation of faith towards God." (Beidelman 1974:65-66.)

Beidelman further asserts that Smith viewed any opposition to his views from within the church simply as primitive and, in many ways, retrograde (Beidelman 1974:41-42). He considered all religion, with its speech about God and truth, as a sociological phenomenon which manifested itself differently depending on time and location.

Smith received his education and much of his general theological perspective in Germany. This was also the case with the Professor from Union who defended him in the pages of *The Presbyterian Review*. Briggs's views were not developed to the degree that Smith's were, at least not yet. Briggs, however, was an indefatigable researcher and writer, and his views were becoming more pronounced. Confessionalism, which had been the hallmark of American Presbyterianism, was not consistent with the emerging Smith/Briggs understanding of the origins and nature of the faith. Was this faith timeless and changeless, consistent with it being revelation from God as the confession asserted, or was it a systemization of the praxis current in the church in any given age, as Smith's research intimated (Beidelman 1974:38-42)? Were the Scriptures 'given by inspiration of God, to be the rule of faith and life' (Westminster Assembly [1647] 1983:21) as the Confession states, or were they merely a product of the religious development of various peoples? The answers that Charles Briggs would pose to these questions in his inaugural address as the Edward Robinson Professor of Biblical Theology at Union were to have a decisive effect on both the Presbyterian Church and his own career.

2.3 Conclusion

Charles Briggs was given to asking questions. His questionings subsequently led him to Germany in search of answers. The answers he found there opened for him new methodological vistas, which, in turn, would characterize all his future theological efforts. In his questionings of the faith, and his concern for its relevancy and applicability for the modern world, Briggs could be classified as either a Centrist or a Futurist, given Murray's categories. Drawing on some of the more rationalistic elements in Germany might favor his designation as a Futurist, yet this association is not decisive. The rationalistic elements were in favor of interpreting Christianity in terms of modern philosophy, and this is exactly the line of inquiry that put Arius in the Futurist camp (see chapter 1). The historical-critical methods which Briggs brought back with him from Germany would, however, cause him eventually to prefer scientific and philosophic conclusions over those established by the Presbyterian Church in her confession. It is in this respect that Briggs most resembled Arius. In spite of this assertion I would still classify Professor Briggs as on the border between Futurist and Centrist, as least at this point in the discussion. Those at Princeton who opposed the ideas of the professor from New York were themselves Centrists it seems to me. They were, however, more clearly committed to the confession of the Presbyterian Church and its dogmatic formulations, both in letter and in spirit. These labels, however, will change as our story continues.

I would also contend that up to this point in the history that we have been considering, no substantive development of doctrine had taken place. Professor Briggs was honing and developing his methodology, and what application he did make of it was not widely circulated. It is true that the Robertson Smith case gave Briggs a good deal of exposure, but his editorial on the case was a description of a heresy trial, and not a systematic exposition of doctrine. With this said, his calling Smith's opinions "legitimate differences" did indicate quite clearly where his own doctrinal sentiments lay. While the Briggs editorial on the Smith Case may have alerted his protagonists at Princeton as to these sentiments, this did not lead, in turn, to any clarification or more precise doctrinal definition on their part. Both sides stood squarely within the Presbyterian and Reformed tradition, McGrath's "Tradition 1" (McGrath 1993:135-136).

After some initial remarks on the beginnings of Modernism/Liberalism in the modern church, I have concentrated the remainder of the discussion on the early years of Charles Augustus Briggs of Union Theological Seminary in New York. My reason for doing this is the pivotal nature of the Briggs tenure for American Presbyterianism. Ideas which Briggs would make prominent were in the air long before his arrival on the ecclesiastical scene, but it was Briggs who would ignite the revolution by his advocacy of historical-critical methods, and the conclusions which he drew from them. To this end, an overview of his intellectual pedigree was in order. Under the rubric of Biblical Theology, Briggs gained recognition of a sort for much of what constituted the theological methodology in Presbyterianism even to this day. His investigations, beginning in the field of Old Testament studies, led him to adopt the documentary hypothesis and other critical conclusions. Increasingly, Briggs began to see the Christian faith as evolving out of Hebrew and early Christian society. This view was slowly developing in Briggs even as he defended William Robertson Smith of Scotland, who was one of its primary proponents. Unlike Smith, however, Briggs never saw this evolution of the Christian faith as taking place entirely apart from divine influence. It was through his defense of Smith that Briggs began gaining some notoriety, not all of which was positive, especially among his fellow Presbyterians at Princeton. Yet, all seemed calm, at least for the moment. Then Briggs gave his inaugural address, and all that changed.

Chapter 3

Scripture and Criticism

In the latter part of January, 1891, Charles Briggs accepted the appointment to be the new Edward Robinson Professor of Biblical Theology at Union Theological Seminary in New York, and in so doing delivered one of the most celebrated and, at the same time, one of the most controversial acceptance-speeches in the history of Presbyterianism. The speech came as a complete shock to many, and the reaction to it was swift in coming. Professor Briggs was subsequently subjected to a protracted heresy trial, which in itself created further turmoil in the Presbyterian Church, all the while serving to give Briggs even greater exposure in the church at large. In his inaugural address, Professor Briggs articulated his burgeoning ideas in a clear and unmistakable fashion. These were ideas which seemed to follow naturally from the critical methodology which he ardently advocated.

The address accentuated the fact that the rift between Briggs and his more confessional colleagues at Princeton had widened considerably. Yet Princeton's response was to use the same methodology as Briggs, albeit in a more watered down form, in order to defend the 'historic' position of the Presbyterian Church. Both sides in the developing conflict were using ideas whose origins were located more in the continental Enlightenment than in either the Reformation or the Westminster Confession, where Presbyterianism had historically looked for support. It is with these themes that this chapter will be concerned.

3.1 Briggs's Inaugural Address and the Ensuing Controversy

On the evening of 20 January 1891 a mood of tense expectation pervaded the audience in the Adams Chapel at Union Theological Seminary and Professor Briggs did not fail to excite, even to electrify those present (Hatch 1969:29-35). History was being made as Charles Briggs, under the rubric of Biblical Theology (Briggs [1891] 1972:28), delivered an inaugural address that immediately catapulted him into the ecclesiastical limelight. Most of those present, however, probably would not have described their experience as electrifying. As contemporary church historian, Carl Hatch, relates: 'Adams Chapel was filled with angry silence. The thoughts of the orthodox were mirrored in the countenance of Dr. William G. T. Shedd, Professor of Systematic Theology at Union. Though he attempted to mask his feelings, Shedd's masquerade was a failure. It was obvious he could hardly contain himself' (Hatch 1969:33).

Whether it was the restrained, even polite, response to the Robertson Smith editorial from the more conservative side of the church (Massa 1990:57, Sawyer 1994:23), or whether it was the 'boisterous applause' of his students that punctuated the course of his address (Hatch 1969:33), Briggs threw caution to the wind and delivered each successive point in his address with 'greater abandon' (Hatch 1969:33). Exhibiting the concern of a lifelong churchman (Sawyer 1994:47), Briggs spoke of barriers which keep people from the Bible. The barriers about which he spoke, however, were, it seemed to many, the time-honored truths of the faith, revered by all those who up to now had called themselves Presbyterian. 'Protestant Christianity builds its faith and life on the divine authority contained in the Scriptures,' Briggs began with utter solemnity,

> and too often depreciates the Church and the Reason. Spurgeon is an example of the average modern Evangelical, who holds the Protestant position, and assails the Church and Reason in the interest of the authority of Scripture. But the average opinion of the Christian World would not assign him a higher place in the kingdom of God than Martineau or Newman.... (Briggs [1891] 1972:28.)

After several other comments by way of introduction, Briggs launched into the heart of the matter. Beginning with the simple acknowledgment of the Bible as the Church's greatest treasure, he purposed to tell things as he saw them regardless of their controversial nature or even, it seems, of their consequences to his own ecclesiastical position. With singular clarity he continued:

> The Bible is the book of God, the greatest treasure of the Church. Its ministry are messengers to preach the Word of God, and to invite men to His presence and government. It is pharisaic to obstruct their way by any

fences or stumbling-blocks whatever. It is a sin against the divine majesty to prop up divine authority, however great or extensive.... And yet this is the way men have been dealing with the Bible, shutting out the light of God, obstructing the life of God, and fencing in the authority of God. (Briggs [1891] 1972:29-30.)

This, he proceeded to expound, is manifested in at least six barriers erected artificially by man which have the effect of obscuring of the Word of God.

The first barrier that obstructs the way to the Bible is *superstition*.... Superstition is no less superstition if it takes the form of *Bibliolatory*....The second barrier, keeping men from the Bible, is the dogma of *verbal inspiration*.... No such claim is found in the Bible itself, or any of the creeds of Christendom.... The third barrier is the *authenticity of the Scriptures*. The only authenticity we are concerned about in seeking for the divine authority of the Scriptures is *divine authenticity*, and yet many theologians have insisted that we must prove that the Scriptures were written by or under the superintendence of prophets and apostles.... It may be regarded as the certain result of the science of Higher Criticism that Moses did not write the Pentateuch.... Isaiah did not write half the book that bears his name.... The fourth barrier set up by theologians to keep men away from the Bible is the dogma of the *Inerrancy of Scripture*.... I shall venture to affirm that, so far as I can see, there are errors in the Scriptures that no one has been able to explain away; and the theory that they were not in the original text is sheer assumption, upon which no mind can rest with certainty.... The Bible itself nowhere makes this claim. The creeds of the Church nowhere sanction it.... The fifth obstruction to the Bible has been thrown up in front of modern science. It is the claim that the *miracles* disturb, or violate, the laws of nature and the harmony of the universe.... Another barrier—number six—to the Bible has been the interpretation put on *Predictive Prophecy*, making it a sort of history before the time, and looking anxiously for the fulfilment of the details of Biblical prediction. Kuenan has shown that if we insist upon the fulfilment of the details of predictive prophecy of the Old Testament, many of these predictions have been reversed in history; and the great body of Messianic prediction has not only never been fulfilled, but cannot now be fulfilled, for the reason that its own time has passed forever.... (Briggs [1891] 1972:30-38.)

Leaving many in the audience stunned, along with his colleague William G. T. Shedd (Hatch 1969:33), Briggs, in a singularly bold ecclesiastical move, maybe even more so than any other part of the controversial address, proceeded to give his own prediction for the future of Christendom. He described his vision of a future world as a place of hope and beauty where every impediment to faith is removed. Let us strive, he continued, to make this new world a reality.

Let us cut down everything that is dead and harmful, every kind of dead orthodoxy, every species of effete ecclesiasticism, all merely formal morality, all those dry and brittle fences that constitute denominationalism, and are the barriers of Church Unity. Let us burn up every form of false doctrine, false religion, and false practice. Let us remove every encumbrance out of the way for a new life; the life of God is moving throughout Christendom, and the spring-time of a new age is about to come upon us. (Briggs [1891] 1972:67.)

Unlike the silence that had greeted many of his earlier efforts, when it came to Briggs's inaugural address it seemed the church was listening (Sawyer 1994:23). Two articles appeared in rapid succession; one by Dr. McPheeters in the *Presbyterian Quarterly* and another by Talbot W. Chalmers in the *Presbyterian and Reformed Review*. Both took to criticizing Professor Briggs's inaugural address in great detail. The editorial notes by Chalmers were clearer and more objective than McPheeters's work, yet neither sought to understand Briggs but only to correct and instruct. One commendable feature in Chalmers's critique was that he identified Professor Briggs's statements as part of the larger context of "Broad Churchism" (Chalmers 1891:483). This idea of an inclusive church was an area of Christian scholarship that always held a particular interest for Professor Briggs as evidenced by his book, *Church Unity* (Briggs 1909). It was only, however, after his expulsion from the Presbyterian Church that he was able to devote more of his energies to this other area of intense interest. The inaugural address was to date the broadest, most inclusive statement of his ecclesiological hopes that Briggs had dared to air in public—although, in a previous work he had indicated his desire for '…the organic union of all branches of the Presbyterian family in a broad, comprehensive, generous, catholic Presbyterianism' (Briggs 1885:xiii). Chalmers paid due deference to the Professor Briggs's 'entire sincerity and good faith,' even admitting that 'he firmly believes in the truth of the positions he has laid down and in their entire harmony with the Westminster Standards.' But, Chalmers hastened to add:

> He has yielded to the movement which seeks to relax the demands of the Christian faith, to do away with the offense of the cross and to win men by paring off points of dogma. Standing inside the Church and holding a prominent position in a seminary of high character, he has borrowed the thoughts and the language of known errorists, and made a great stir by reproducing them after a fashion of his own. They are paraded as the result of a fresh and independent study of the divine Word, from which great things are justly to be expected…. But in truth, as has been said, the Professor has discovered nothing. What he considers new truths are simply old errors. (Chalmers 1891:493.)

Chalmers then proceeded with a detailed analysis of each of the "barriers" to the faith that Briggs had treated in his speech and attempted to show in each case that the barrier is one specifically erected by Briggs. These barriers, according to Chalmers, were really nothing more than rhetoric, rather than being real obstacles to faith. Further, Chalmers considered these barriers erected by Professor Briggs as themselves prohibitions to biblical and thus saving knowledge. Believing that all the barriers detailed by Professor Briggs had their common origin in his view of the Scriptures and their authority in the church, Chalmers dissected Briggs's view of the Bible. Chalmers proceeded to concentrate his criticism on barriers three and four that Briggs outlined in his inaugural. Concerning the third barrier: *the authenticity of Scripture*, Chalmers declared that:

> It is Prof. Briggs who constructs a *chevaux-de-frise* around the Bible, and not the traditional Church view.

The latter leaves things so plain that the wayfaring men, yea fools, shall not err therein but the former requires men to approach the catapult, if not a siege train. A third "barrier" is found in the *authenticity of the Scriptures*. All the evidence on this point which has been carefully sifted and established by the toil of scholars in the past centuries is scornfully scouted as "floating traditions," and the arguments founded on it is held to be reasoning in a circle. But to what purpose is such empty rhetoric? According to the usual methods men are invited to determine the authenticity of the sacred writings just as they that of any other ancient writings. No fence is erected around them, but the acknowledged principles of historical criticism are applied, and the result is satisfactory. Having ascertained that these writings are what they profess to be... faith rests upon the testimony of Him whom they disclose. But this does not satisfy Dr. Briggs. He says that the "Higher Criticism has forced its way into the Bible itself and brought us face to face with the holy contents, so that we may see and know whether they are divine or not;" or, as he elsewhere declares, it is by *divina fides* that we know the Bible to be the Word of God. But what a mighty barrier he thus erects across the path of sinful man! The only way for him to find out the truth about the Bible is to believe with a true faith what it says. And the author of this wretched sophism charges other folks with reasoning in a circle! The mystical, unsound and revolutionary character of Dr. Briggs' theory has been abundantly shown.... It is not enough to remark that in his effort to "remove obstructions that have barred the way of literary men from the Bible," he has put an impassable obstacle in their way, and shifted the authenticity of Scripture from its natural, reasonable and adequate basis to a vague mysticism, as unreal and flighty as any Phrygian Montanism. He tells us, moreover, that it is "the certain result of the Higher Criticism that a Moses did not write the Pentateuch," nor did Isaiah "half of the book that bears his name," nor Solomon the Son of Songs; and David wrote only a few of the Psalms. This is a fair specimen of the confident, not to say arrogant, tone that pervades the Address. Extremely questionable conclusions, resting upon tenuous arguments, and controverted by scholars as able as those who put them forth, are gravely announced as "certain." (Chalmers 1891:486-487.)

After scathing criticism of Briggs's third barrier, Chalmers turns to the fourth barrier: *the inerrancy of the Scriptures*:

The fourth "barrier" is Inerrancy. Dr. Briggs says that this claim drives men from the Bible, whereas, in fact, where it repels one it attracts a hundred. Men like something on which they can depend, whereas to tell them that "there are errors in Scripture that no one has been able to explain away," undermines confidence. How are they to distinguish the truth from the error? Under the pretext of demolishing a barrier, Dr. Briggs has constructed one of very serious character. He puts a dangerous weapon into the hands of the adversaries of the Gospel. And without any reason. ...It is not easy to see how any old-fashioned believer can accept his theory for a moment. He would limit inspiration "to the essential contents of the Bible, to its religion, faith and morals," while all else is remitted to the category of "circumstantials." Has the Professor ever heard the maxim, *Falsus in uno, falsus in omnibus*? Is it any more difficult to guard from error in historical or geographical details than it is in doctrines? And if it once be admitted that there are errors in the Bible, is it not open to any inquirer when confronted with a distinct Scripture utterance to insist that such utterance is one of the mistakes of the sacred penmen? No doubt Prof. Briggs would vehemently and sincerely deny the justice of any such course, but it is none the less certain that it would be taken, and that the faith of many in the divine Word would be utterly dissipated. It should be added here that Dr. Briggs distinctly affirmed to the directors of the Seminary his belief that "the Bible is inerrant in all matters concerning faith and practice, and in everything in which it is a revelation from God or a vehicle of divine truth, and that there are no errors which disturb its infallibility in these matters, or in its records of the historic events and institutions with which they are inseparably connected." Still the Address remains, and to all appearance is not retracted. (Chalmers 1891:486-487.)

While the Chalmers's critique is cogent and sincere, and in many ways equitable, from a confessionalist perspective, it does not attempt an in-depth study of the concerns and questions that had led up to the Briggs inaugural address; rather, it treats the address as if it were an isolated event. Chalmers was primarily concerned to point out the error of Briggs's ways without dealing in any substantive way with any of his concerns or methods. He believed that '...the author of the Address is not content with indirectly degrading the Bible by lowering its claims to an equality with the voice of reason and the Church, but proceeds directly to assail the Book and its authority' (Chalmers 1891 :484). Yet, in focusing on the theme of Biblical theology, Chalmers came close to the heart of the matter—Briggs's method. Unfortunately, however, he did not pursue this theme at any length. In touching upon the issue, however, he did criticize some of Briggs's conclusions. He writes, for example:

> Part III of the Address is devoted to Biblical Theology, and begins with a very clever synopsis of the theophanies and institutions of the Old Testament. In treating of God we are told that Israel learned only by degrees that God was the God of all the earth, whereas this truth runs through the narrative from beginning to end, nor is anything more sophistical than the argumentation by which Kuenen and others seek to show that ethical monotheism did not become dominant in Israel until the eighth century B.C. (sic). ...In treating the Doctrine of Man, it is said that "Jew and Christian alike exaggerate the original innocency." What a monstrous assertion! We are told in Genesis that God created man in His own image, and then that he "saw everything that He had made, and behold, it was very good." Can it be possible to exaggerate innocence so described? But the trouble with the Professor is that this view "conflicts with ethical and religious philosophy." Suppose it does; are we to surrender the plain statements of Scripture at the demand of philosophy? And is this the Biblical Theology which Union Seminary proposes to teach? In the pages

that follow there is a very careless use of language. "Redemption," it is said, "comprehends the whole nature of man, his whole life and the entire race." ...But the language of the Address, being without limitation or qualification, seems to us well adapted to mislead. Under the next head we are told, as if it were a novelty, that redemption "comprehends the whole process of grace." We have yet to see any accredited system of theology among the Reformed that hold a different view. This is not the case with the next point the Professor makes, the extension of the process of redemption to the middle state. It is asserted with unspeakable hardiness that "progressive sanctification after death is the doctrine of the Bible and the Church" (p. 54). We assert, on the contrary, that there is not a word in all Scripture in favor of this view, but much against it. And it is directly in the face of the Confession of Faith (xxxii. 1), which says that at death the souls of the righteous are "made perfect in holiness." ...In the concluding article of this part, Dr. Briggs teaches election, but an election of love (does anybody teach an election of hate?); and distinctly affirms that some will be unredeemed and lost, but assigns as one of the causes of this fact, their "descending into such depths of demoniacal depravity in the middle state,"— from which it would seem that their case is not decided in this world, but, in part at least, depends upon what they do between death and judgment, which is so near the doctrine of a second probation (which the Professor distinctly disavows) that the words should not have been written. Indeed, this is a just complaint against the whole inaugural, that it skirts the dividing line between truth and error so nearly, that often it is difficult to see just where the author stands and how his words are to be understood. (Chalmers 1891:490-491.)

Chalmers was gracious in his conclusion that 'No one who has any personal acquaintance with the author of this Inaugural Address will for one moment doubt his entire sincerity and good faith' (Chalmers

1891:493). He was also tempered in his evaluation that Briggs wrote in a vague sort of way that '...skirts the dividing line between truth and error' (Chalmers 1891:491). While Chalmers was generally positive in his overall assessment, he saw this 'vague sort of writing' as a perennial problem with Briggs's work. Others, however, were not so generous in their appraisal. Gary Johnson, who wrote a dissertation on Briggs in the late 1980s, believed that the only creed by which Charles Briggs would be bound was Higher Criticism, all else was show. Thus, '...his professed allegiance to the Westminster Confession turns out to reveal something of a lack of personal integrity.' (Johnson 1987:51). Elsewhere, commenting on what he saw as glaring contradictions in Briggs's writings, Gary Johnson has argued that

> An examination of his writings demonstrates that at times Briggs displayed a lack of personal integrity. He reveals that his committment to the methodology of Higher Criticism allowed him to <u>assume</u> that he was right and that time would eventually prove him right. He would claim fidelity to the historic Reformed position and yet feel free to turn it on its head to make it fit his purposes. He likewise could differ sharply with some of the major tenets of Reformation theology and at the same time blast the Princetonians and W. G. T. Shedd for espousing a theology that he claimed to be alien to Reformed thought. He could claim that he was loyal to the Westminster confession of Faith and write (before his trial and while still a Presbyterian), "Another great barrier to reunion of Christendom is subscription to elaborate creeds. This is the great sin of the Lutheran and Reformed Churches." (Johnson 1987:75-76.)

Johnson concluded his observations by saying that 'For Briggs, then, to pay lip-service to the Confession and then to seek to adjust the Confession to his own views (or dismiss portions which could not be made to square with his position) was simply dishonest' (Johnson 1987:78). Gary North, moreover, was even more blunt in his criticism of Briggs. He simply said that, whenever it was convenient, Briggs lied (North 1996:231-232, 237-238).

It seems that the criticisms of both Johnson and North in this matter are not entirely without substance. In his 1889 book *Whither? A Theological Question for the Times*, for example, Briggs stated concerning sanctification that 'Sanctification is a work that is carried on by God in a gradual process until perfect holiness has been attained by man' (Briggs 1889:147). He proceeded to argue that the Confession '...does not say that man is made perfect at the moment of death. The progress in sanctification goes on after death in the middle state, until it is perfected there, and man is prepared by the process of grace for the final judgment' (Briggs 1889:147). In the wake of the Inaugural Address where similar ideas were espoused (Briggs [1891] 1972:53-54) and, as Max Rogers says, 'as the situation continued to deteriorate...' (Rogers 1966:102), Union's Board of Directors put a series of eight questions to the now controversial Professor in order to ward off any more serious ecclesiastical repercussions (Prentiss 1899:543-544). One of the questions of Union's Board was: 'Is your theory of progressive sanctification such that it will permit you to say that you believe that when a man dies in the faith he enters the middle state regenerated, justified and sinless? Answer. Yes.' (Prentiss 1899:544). This answer to Union's Board came within a year of the publication of the third edition of his book *Whither?* (North 1996:231), in which he contradicted his answer to the Board.

In view of the growing response to Professor Briggs's Inaugural Address and the inadequacy of the series of questions published by the Board to quell that response, the faculty issued a statement in which they admitted fully that the positions held were not novel for Professor Briggs, but were in fact his mature thought.

> With the conviction that Christian courtesy, modesty and mutual respect for difference of opinion should characterize theological controversy, we distinctly recognize and deprecate the dogmatic and irritating character of certain of Dr. Briggs' utterances in his Inaugural and in others of his writings: while, on the other hand, we do not recognize, even in these, any warrant for persistent misrepresentations of his views, and for the style and temper in which he has in many cases been assailed. 1. *The views propounded by Dr. Briggs in his Inaugural are not new.* They have all been stated by him in one or another of his published works, in articles in the Presbyterian Review, during his ten years' editorship, and in more recent contributions to other periodicals. ...The present excitement is, as we believe, due, largely, to the

tone of the Inaugural Address, to certain unguarded expressions, and to an impression that the transfer of the author to the Chair of Biblical Theology would be subject to the veto of the General Assembly. 2. *The Address contains, in our judgment, nothing which can be fairly construed into heresy or departure from the Westminster Confession, to which Dr. Briggs honestly subscribed at his recent inauguration.* ...Dr. Briggs declares that, conjointly with the Bible, the *Church* and the *Reason* are *sources* of authority in religion. He uses the term "reason" as embracing the conscience and the religious feeling. We object to the term "sources," since there is but one source of divine authority—God himself. We prefer to say that the Bible, the Church, and the Reason are *media* and *vehicles* through which we recognize and receive the divine authority. This is the generally-accepted Protestant position. Every Church in Christendom admits that the church is a medium of divine authority. ...But Dr. Briggs does not, with the Romanist, exalt the Church above the Bible and the Reason. He does not, with the Rationalist, place the Reason above the Bible and the Church. Neither does he, as has been often charged, *co-ordinate* the three sources. His position is the Protestant and Presbyterian position, assumed in his subscription to the declaration of the Confession, that the Scriptures are "the only infallible rule of faith and practice," and asserted in his address in the words: Protestant Christianity builds its faith and life on the divine authority contained in the Scriptures." That Protestant Christianity too often depreciates the Church and the Reason is an entirely distinct statement, involving a question of fact; and the statement and its discussion in no way affect Dr. Briggs' endorsement of the Protestant doctrine of the supreme authority of Scripture. ...*(c). The consistency of Dr. Briggs' position as to the supreme authority and divine quality of Holy Scripture, is in no way affected by his views of the nature of Inspiration.*

His mature thought also included a repudiation of the verbal inspiration of the Scriptures:

While asserting the plenary inspiration of Scripture, he denies that inspiration involves *absolute inerrancy*—*literal, verbal accuracy, and perfect correspondence of minor details.* In this view there is nothing original or new. It is the view of Calvin, and of an overwhelming majority of Protestant divines in Europe and America. It was propounded at least eight years ago by Dr. Briggs in his "Biblical Study." Inspiration, in the sense of literary inerrancy, is nowhere claimed for Scripture by Scripture itself. It is contradicted by the contents of Scripture in the form in which we have it. It involves, logically, a minute, specific divine superintendence of each detail of the entire process of transmission—copying, translating, printing—and the prevention of all errors. It confronts those who maintain it not only with discrepancies of statement in the present text, but with the innumerable textual variations in the Hebrew and the Septuagint. To meet these facts with the assertion of the inerrancy of the original autographs, is to beg the whole question in dispute, to lay down a purely arbitrary, *a priori* hypothesis, and to introduce into the discussion an entirely irrelevant factor, seeing that the errors and discrepancies remain and the original autographs cannot be recovered. To make the inspiration of Scripture turn upon verbal inerrancy is to commit the Church to an utterly untenable position, and to place her apologists at the mercy of cavilers who are only too glad to evade broader and deeper issues and to shift the discussion to the region of mere verbal details, where they are sure to have the best argument. Dr. Briggs holds and teaches the doctrine of the divine inspiration, infallibility, and authority of the Holy Scriptures in all matters of Christian faith and duty, which is all that any evangelical divine is bound to maintain on that subject. The Westminster and other Confessions of Faith clearly and strongly assert the *fact* of divine inspiration, but wisely abstain from defining the *mode* and *degrees* of divine inspiration. The former is a matter of *faith*, the latter of *human theory*, on which there must be liberty if there is to be any progress. To impose upon a Christian teacher any particular theory of inspiration not sanctioned by the Bible itself is tyranny.

Progressive sanctification after death became an especially troublesome topic:

> (d). Dr. Briggs is further charged with a departure from the Westminster Eschatology in teaching *progressive sanctification after death*. While we are not to be understood as accepting or endorsing Dr. Briggs' conclusions on this point, it is sufficient to say that he is here in an open field, where, having expressly repudiated the doctrines of future probation, universal restoration, and the Romanist purgatory, he is certainly entitled to the largest liberty in an attempt to elucidate a subject so little understood, and on which the standards are open to differences of interpretation. ...After years of familiar acquaintance with Dr. Briggs and his teaching, we are moved to utter our emphatic protest against the spirit and language with which, in so many cases, he has been assailed. ...We know Dr. Briggs to be an earnest Christian, a devout student of the Bible, an indefatigable teacher and worker, and one who holds the standards of the Church with an intelligence based on an exhaustive study of their history and literature. The numerous testimonies of his students during the seventeen years prove that he inspires them with a deep reverence and enthusiasm for the Bible. ...It is in the interest of God's truth to set forth Scripture as it is, and not to expose its friends and teachers to humiliation and defeat by claiming for it that it cannot be substantiated. In the words of Ullman, "Not fixedness nor revolution, but evolution and reform, is the motto of our times." We maintain that human conceptions of the Bible and of its inspired teachings are subject to revision. (Prentiss 1899:545-550.)

Not everyone, however, was reassured as to the orthodoxy of Professor Briggs by the faculty's statement. A notable example was Briggs's own colleague at Union, William G. T. Shedd, who, in response to what he saw happening to doctrinal purity in the aftermath of the Briggs case, wrote *Calvinism: Pure and Mixed, A defense of the Westminster Standards* (Shedd 1893). The last chapter entitled "Denominational Honesty and Honor," which Gary Johnson believed was written expressly with Briggs in mind (Johnson 1987:79), summed up Shedd's thinking on the whole matter. He wrote:

But heresy is not so great a sin as dishonesty. There may be honest heresy, but not honest dishonesty. A heretic who acknowledges that he is such, is a better man than he who pretends to be orthodox while subscribing to a creed which he dislikes, and which he saps under pretense of improving it and adapting it to the times. The honest heretic leaves the Church with which he no longer agrees; but the insincere subscriber remains within it in order to carry out his plan of demoralization. (Shedd 1893:158.)

It seems that any calm or truly objective discussion of the issues involved in Professor Briggs's inaugural address had ended with the last words of the address, since charges of heresy followed almost immediately. Instigated by the Reverend George Birch of Bethany Church in Manhattan, '...the Presbytery of New York had appointed an investigatory committee "to consider the Inaugural Address and its relation to the Confession of Faith"' (Massa 1990:93). Meeting throughout the first part of 1891, the deliberations of the investigatory committee finally came to an end on May 11, 1891 recommending '...to the New York Presbytery that it enter at once into judicial proceedings against Briggs...' (Massa 1990:94). The charge against Briggs was: '...holding three positions in conflict with the Westminster Confession: (1) that reason was a source of divine authority that "savingly enlightened men"; (2) that the process of sanctification was not complete at death, but extended into the "Middle State"; and (3) that there were proven errors in the original text of the Scriptures' (Massa 1990:94).

The report of the investigative committee and its recommendations were forwarded to the up and coming General Assembly slated to convene in Detroit, Michigan. Francis L. Patton of Princeton, as chairman of the Committee on Theological Seminaries, exhorted the General Assembly, based on the voluminous correspondence which his committee continued to receive, to veto Professor Briggs's appointment to the Edward Robinson Chair of Biblical Theology at Union Seminary (Massa 1990:95). Union Seminary had, in a previous statement issued by the majority of the faculty, already dismissed any such action as outside the authority of the General Assembly (Prentiss 1899:546). Notwithstanding, Patton's recommendation to veto the Briggs appointment was adopted by the General Assembly (Massa 1990:95). In a bold move, Union Seminary responded to the actions of the General Assembly by taking its stand on the side of Professor Briggs. As Mark Massa tells us:

> ... the Union faction viewed the war as far from over, even if the confessionalists had won that particular battle. Less than a week after the assembly's meeting, Union's Board of Directors issued a public statement that announced its intention to abide by its decision to transfer Briggs to the new chair. The assembly's veto of Briggs's transfer, Union's Board declared, constituted a flagrant intrusion of partisan politics into the running of a legally autonomous, constitutionally governed institution. (Massa 1990:96.)

Briggs's response was of a twofold nature. He manifestly denied the charges against him, all the while affirming his commitment to the accepted standards of the Presbyterian Church (Massa 1990:97-98). He also questioned the propriety of the charges against him, informing the court '...that the charges tendered against him were invalid according to the Book of Discipline' (Massa 1990:98), since they were framed more as vague, general accusations and did not cite specific instances of Confessional violation (Massa 1990:98). With the help of Princeton University Professor Henry Van Dyke, and much to the chagrin of his confessionalist detractors (Massa 1990:98), the charges against Professor Briggs were dropped. But as it turned out, the victory was short-lived.

On November 13, 1891 the committee headed by George Birch refiled the charges against Briggs, not, however, with the Presbytery which had just dismissed them, but with the General Assembly straightway (Massa 1990:99). Defending this latest action was Briggs's colleague at Union, and growing antagonist, William G. T. Shedd. His rationale was that the question of Charles Briggs '...brings before the General Assembly a question more serious and important in results than any that has ever been presented to the Assembly, the question, namely, whether a type of theology utterly antagonistic to the traditional theology of the denomination shall be solemnly condemned by its highest tribunal, or whether it shall be endorsed by it directly in words, or indirectly by inaction and tolerance' (quoted by Loetscher 1954:56). Meeting in the city of Portland, Oregon, the General Assembly of 1892 eventually decided to hear the particulars of the Briggs case, despite protests regarding legality from Briggs and others (Massa 1990:101). The decisions of the Assembly, known as the Portland Deliverance, stated that it 'would remind all under its care that it is a fundamental doctrine of this church that the Old and New Testaments are the inspired and infallible Word of God. Our church holds that the inspired Word, as it comes from God, is without error, and the assertion to the contrary cannot but shake the confidence of the people' (quoted by Massa 1990:103). This decision made the inerrancy of Holy Scripture the *cause célèbre* of the Briggs case, and, by implication, 'The theories of "verbal inerrancy" and the "original autographs," offered by Hodge and Warfield a decade before, were now raised form the level of adiaphora (the level at which theologians could honestly differ about theories) to canon of orthodoxy' (Massa 1990:103). An immediate consequence of the issuance of the Portland Deliverance was a curt, public statement from The Board of Directors of Union Seminary. It said in effect that '...the agreement between the Union Theological Seminary and the General Assembly of the Presbyterian Church should be, and hereby is, terminated (quoted by Massa 1990:104).

On the 25th of May 1893, after much wrangling from both sides in the dispute, the General Assembly reached a decision concerning Briggs. It concluded that:

> ...Charles A. Briggs has uttered, taught and propagated views, doctrines and teachings as set forth in the said charges contrary to the essential doctrine of Holy Scripture and the Standards, and in violation of his ordination vow.... Wherefore this General Assembly does hereby suspend Charles A. Briggs, the said appellee, from the office of minister in the Presbyterian Church in the United States of America, until such time as he shall give satisfactory evidence of repentance to the General Assembly of the violation by him of the said ordination vow. (quoted by Massa 1990:108-109.)

The decision rendered by the General Assembly in the matter of Charles A. Briggs revealed a profound difference of opinion that had been developing in the Presbyterian Church regarding the nature of the Scriptures, and the proper method in dealing with them. Briggs did not believe that the Scriptures which the church now possesses are free from errors (Johnson 1987 deals with this matter throughout). Consistent with this view of the nature of Holy Writ, Briggs advocated the higher-critical approach to its study. However, the more conservative wing of the Presbyterian Church, with its scholarly center at Princeton Seminary, saw the perspective on the Bible advocated by Professor Briggs as heretical. The Princetonians considered their view of both the nature of the Bible and the proper approach to it as diametrically opposed to what was taught at Union. While this type of thinking accounts for much of the confrontational attitude that pervaded the Briggs trial, and the Fundamentalist/Modernist Controversy in general, it was not entirely warranted. Those who claimed the higher moral and theological ground were, at times, in a rather dubious position.

3.2 Princeton's Response

Princeton, in condemning the legacy of Professor Briggs, failed at times to consider its own intellectual and theological pedigree. This pedigree, as I indicated in the last chapter, derived from what George Marsden described as a 'component of the classic Enlightenment' (Marsden 1991:129). More specifically it was a '...dedication to the general philosophical basis that had undergirded the empirically based rationality so confidently proclaimed by most eighteenth-century thinkers' (Marsden 1991:129). Theodore Dwight Boseman, in his book on *Protestants in an Age of Science*, called this dedication the 'beatification of Bacon' (Boseman 1977:72). Considered by a growing body of historians as "common sense realism" or "Scottish common sense" (Marsden 1991, Noll 1985, Boseman 1977, Ahlstrom 1955), the philosophy enshrined at Princeton exhibited a commitment to science that would rival that of Briggs himself. Gary Johnson, in his comparison of the ideas and methods in circulation at both Union and Princeton during the Briggs era, has noted with great interest that 'Briggs cites with approval two of the most noted defenders of the "Scottish Common Sense Realism," Sir William Hamilton and (can it be?) James McCosh' (Johnson 1987:72). Johnson quickly adds by way of question and answer: "Did Briggs himself advocate the "plague of Princeton," the Common Sense Realism? He most certainly did not' (Johnson 1987:72), as if to protect Princeton as much as possible from any taint by Briggs. Yet the "Common Sense" at Princeton served to unite empiricism and induction in a scientific approach to the Scriptures, a legacy from their Puritan forebears (Marsden 1991:130). Princeton's approach to the Scriptures, however, was not something new in response to Briggs; it was part of the fabric of the school from the days of Archibald Alexander (1772-1851) and Charles Hodge (1797-1878) (Loetscher 1983).

In a general discussion of the inductive method as it applies to the natural sciences, the grandfather of Princeton theology, Charles Hodge, laid down certain principles which he in turn applied to the study of the Scriptures. First were the assumptions held by the man of science as he approached his subject: 'he assumes the trustworthiness of his sense perceptions, ...he must also assume the trustworthiness of his mental operation, ...he must also rely on the certainty of those truths which are not learned from experience, but which are given in the constitution of our nature.... From facts thus ascertained and classified, he deduces the laws by which they are determined.' Having dealt with qualities in a general sense, Hodge proceeded to bring the Scriptures into the domain of scientific study. 'The Bible,' he continued, 'is to the theologian what nature is to the man of science. It is a storehouse of facts; and his method of ascertaining what the Bible teaches, is the same as that which the natural philosopher adopts to ascertain what nature teaches' (Hodge 1979:9-10).

While Hodge exhibited a very "rational" scientific approach to the Word of God, his assessment regarding textual irregularities was decidedly different from those who would follow in his footsteps at Princeton Seminary in later years. In the course of his magnum opus, the *Systematic Theology*, he dealt with the text of Scripture scrupulously, continually observing those canons of the scientific method which he previously discussed. Considering the guidance of the Biblical writers by the Spirit of God, he confessed that 'it is enough to impress any mind with awe, when it contemplates the Sacred Scriptures filled with the highest truths, speaking with authority in the name of God, and so miraculously free from the soiling of human fingers.' Even with such a high view of the Scriptures, Hodge was not remiss to add:

> The errors in matters of fact which skeptics search out bear no proportion to the whole. No sane man would deny that the Parthenon was built of marble, even if here and there a speck of sandstone should be detected in its structure. Not less unreasonable is it to deny the inspiration of such a book as the Bible, because one sacred writer says that on a given occasion twenty-four thousand, and another says that twenty-three thousand, men were slain. Surely a Christian may be allowed to tread such objections under his feet. Admitting that the

Scriptures do contain, in a few instances, discrepancies which with our present means of knowledge, we are unable satisfactorily to explain, they furnish no rational ground for denying their infallibility. "The Scripture cannot be broken." (John 10:35). This is the whole doctrine of plenary inspiration, taught by the lips of Christ himself.... Yet here and there isolated cases of monstrosity appear. It is irrational, because we cannot account for such cases, to deny that the universe is a product of intelligence. So the Christian need not renounce his faith in the plenary inspiration of the Bible, although there may be some things about it in its present state which he cannot account for. (Hodge 1979:170.)

These carefully considered conclusions were "developed" further within the Princeton circle over the next eleven years. This transformation, moreover, came to occupy center stage in the church in conjunction with the new journal, *The Presbyterian Review*, co-edited by both Charles Briggs and the eldest son of Charles Hodge, Archibald Alexander Hodge (1823-1886). The younger Hodge did not succeed his father to the chair of systematic theology, an honor which went to the Kentuckian, Benjamin B. Warfield (1851-1921). Warfield's influence on Princeton during his tenure was enormous. His learning is said to have been so prodigious that he could well have occupied almost any department on the theological faculty with equal ability (Letis 1984:98-99). But unlike his theological forbears, he sought a scientific certainty for the theological disciplines that far outstripped that of his predecessors. He sought what could only be described as a mathematical certainty for the historic doctrines of the faith. With a Scottish Common Sense craving for the factual, Warfield strove for a doctrinal position that was based on an absolutely certain foundation (Letis 1991 discusses this entire matter in detail). To this end, he co-authored with A. A. Hodge a truly original article on the inspiration of the Holy Scriptures for the new *Presbyterian Review*. The claims made for the Scriptures in this article were both innovative and, I would argue, beyond the realm of proof. Concerning the Sacred Record, Hodge and Warfield wrote that '...The mere fact of Inspiration ... or the superintendence by God of the writer in the entire process of their writing, which accounts for nothing whatever but the absolute infallibility of the record in which the revelation, once generated, appears in the original autograph.' The result of this "inspiration" was '...an infallible record of that revelation absolutely errorless, by means of Inspiration' (Hodge & Warfield 1881:226-227).

During the Briggs trial these claims, advocated in the Hodge/Warfield article, became the single most important test of Presbyterian orthodoxy, as evinced by statements in the Portland Deliverance (quoted by Massa 1990:103), and the response of Union Seminary to its adoption by the 1902 General Assembly—Union terminated any association with the General Assembly (Massa 1990:104). It was obvious that those in the Assembly who adopted these novelties believed sincerely that they were exceptional explanations of time honored truth; otherwise such ideas probably would not have gained the widespread support that they did. Thus, they seem to have been accepted by many as authentic "developments," or more accurately, "restatements" of the truths binding on all Presbyterians. I contend, however, that they were, in fact, new developments in line with the prevailing philosophy of Princeton, Scottish Common Sense (Letis 1991 argues this point and points to Warfield as the catalyst).

It had been the belief at Princeton since its founding that the Holy Scriptures were infallible, but this was also true at Union Seminary. Hodge and Warfield, specifically Warfield however, wanted a more mathematically precise rendition of the doctrine of inspiration. 'We do not assert,' they stated with confidence, 'that the common text, but only that the original autographic text was inspired. No "error" can be asserted, therefore, which cannot be proved to have been aboriginal in the text.... A proved error in Scripture contradicts not only our doctrine, but the Scripture claims and, therefore, its inspiration in making those claims' (Hodge & Warfield 1881:245). Mark Noll relates that criticism regarding this novel view was swift in coming. British evangelicals said that 'American evangelicals have given pride of place in their thinking about Scripture to "verbal inspiration" at the expense of "plenary inspiration." Or to put it another way, they have tended to speak as if the Bible's saving truthfulness rested on its factual truthfulness, instead of assuming—with both the reformers and Protestant dogmaticians until the eighteenth century—the reverse' (Noll 1985:230). While Noll relates what happened, in a rather off-handed manner, he bypasses altogether its meaning and importance. Theodore Letis, however, who has made a special study of the events that transpired in connection with the publication of the Hodge/Warfield article, has unraveled much of its original significance and explained the consequences that followed.

According to Letis, Warfield spent a year in Germany studying at the University of Leipzig prior to assuming full-time teaching duties at Princeton. Undertaken at the urging of Caspar Wistar Hodge—younger son of Charles Hodge—and with a letter of introduction from Union Seminary's Philip Schaff, Warfield was determined to absorb the very latest in biblical criticism that the continent had to offer. His was not a desire to emulate but to counteract. He considered the German higher criticism, as a product of the Enlightenment, to be a destructive force in the arena of theology. To know their arguments, however, was a prerequisite to answering them. Warfield practiced, on his return to the U.S. and in defense of the faith, what come to be known as "lower criticism." At the time, the difference between "higher criticism" and "lower criticism" was seen as the difference between night and day. Thus, for Warfield, the higher criticism advocated by Professor Briggs was the enemy of the Word of God, undermining its integrity, but lower criticism could be used in the service of the church. Lower criticism was a gift of God given for the restoring of the original text of Scripture and, thus, the strengthening of the church of Christ (Letis 1984:81-89). There was nothing arbitrary or destructive about that, so he reasoned. While Warfield's motives may have been irreproachable, his conclusions and their consequences were a watershed in Princeton's history.

The change that took place in Warfield after his return from Germany, and in the church as a result, can be better understood by distinguishing between the "autographa" and the "apographa." The autographa were understood as the original documents of Scripture given by God to humanity (Letis 1990:17-18). They were the pieces of parchment or papyrus that the writers of Scripture either composed themselves or, as in the case of the Apostle Paul, were present at their composition. The apographa, on the other hand, were not the originals but copies or transcripts of the originals (Letis 1990:17-18). Warfield's doctrine of inspiration took into account only the autographa, the originals (Hodge & Warfield 1881, Letis 1984:100, Warfield [1893]1983:268-274). Here was the sole domain in which the inspiration of God occurred. Only those originals that were written directly by the Scripture writers were inspired, and thus inerrant and worthy of the confidence of the church (Hodge & Warfield 1881, Letis 1984:100, Warfield [1893]1983:268-274), but the autographa are lost. The originals of Scripture have not to date been found. The mass of Biblical manuscripts that are extant, i.e., the apographa, abound with variant, or alternate, readings in places too numerous to mention (Warfield [1893] 1983:268-274)—the majority of variant readings are found in the New Testament. Yet, it was upon the autographa alone that Warfield based his doctrine of inspiration (Letis 1984:100, Hodge & Warfield 1881). Not discouraged by obvious problems involved, Warfield assured his readers that:

> If, then, we undertake the textual criticism of the New Testament under a sense of duty, we may bring it to a conclusion under the inspiration of hope. The autographic text of the New Testament is distinctly within the reach of criticism in so immensely the greater part of the volume, that we cannot despair of restoring to ourselves and the Church of God, His Book, word for word, as He gave it by inspiration to men. (Warfield 1887:14-15.)

The method by which Warfield wanted God's Word to be restored to the church was textual criticism, which he defined '...as the careful, critical examination of a text, with a view to discovering its condition, in order that we may test its correctness on the one hand, and, on the other, amend its errors' (Warfield 1887:4). Having given both a critical and expert evaluation of the Scriptures as to their condition, as his definition required, Warfield concluded that 'the reply will necessarily vary according to the standard of comparison which we assume. If we take an ordinarily well-printed modern book as a standard, the New Testament, in its common current text, will appear sorely corrupt' (Warfield 1887:11). Thus, according to Warfield, the Scriptures as we now possess them are essentially corrupt after centuries of transmission. Presumably this corruption was the proliferation of variant readings which inundated the Sacred Text over the centuries (Warfield [1893]1983:272). Most Biblical scholars would agree that most, if not all, of these variants have had little to no effect on the message of Scripture. The Bible which is in current circulation is trustworthy and would remain substantially the same whether the originals were ever found or not. (As evidence of this assertion check the various editions of the Nestle-Aland *Novum Testamentum Graece* and see if the any of the different variant reading chosen in any of the successive editions in any way substantially changes the Biblical message. Also see Clark 1986.).

Warfield, however, could not abide such a view. As already quoted, he asserted that a proved error in Scripture contradicts our doctrine of inspiration as well as the claims to inspiration made by the Scriptures themselves (Hodge & Warfield 1881:245). And what is a variant but an error? Stevens Buckminster of Harvard understood this to be the case. As an opponent of verbal inspiration, he persuaded Harvard officials in 1809 to publish a critical edition of the New Testament because he believed the variant readings of a critical text to be '...a most powerful weapon to be used against the supporters of verbal inspiration' (quoted by Letis 1991:1). If a given text allows for two readings, regardless of similarity, one must be the correct reading and the other an error. By Warfield's own admission, one '...error in Scripture contradicts not only our doctrine, but the Scripture claims and, therefore, its inspiration in making those claims' (Hodge & Warfield 1881: 245). But this argument was relevant to the Bible only as it was currently in the possession of the church, which Bible for all intents and purposes, according to Warfield, was hopelessly corrupt. The inerrant, infallible, and trustworthy Bible that his doctrine of inspiration touted was not one that was in the possession of the church, or ever had been for that matter. Warfield's inerrant Bible existed exclusively in his mind. It was mainly the subject of speculation for the text critical methodology which he introduced to Princeton and upon which he pinned so much hope (Letis 1984:102-103).

Responses to Warfield have come from many different quarters. Henry Preserved Smith, a colleague and posthumous biographer of Charles Briggs for example, objected that,

> Warfield in an article in the *Presbyterian Review* stated the doctrine [inerrancy] is not concerned with the accuracy of our present Bible, but interests itself in affirming a perfection of the original autographs which has in some cases at least been lost in transmission.... None the less does the new theory depart widely from the confessional doctrine. That the Word of God as we now have it in Scripture is infallible... this is the Affirmation of the Confession. Its interest is in the present Bible for present purposes, and those purposes are practical purposes. That an inerrant autograph once existed is a speculative assertion, interested in establishing a supposed perfection which no longer exists, and which may conceivably (and even probably) never be recovered. (quoted by Letis 1990:35.)

Scottish church historian and a contemporary of Warfield, Thomas Lindsay, was even more caustic than Smith. He wrote:

> But when all is said they are bound to admit [Warfield and his advocates] that the attribute of formal inerrancy does not belong to the Scriptures which we now have, but to what they call... original autographs of Scripture.... It follows that the Scriptures as we now have them are neither infallible nor inspired in their use of these words. This is not an inference drawn from their writings by a hostile critic. It is frankly and courageously said by themselves, "We do not assert that the common text, but only that the original autographic text was inspired." The statement is deliberately made by Dr. Hodge and Dr. Warfield. This is a very grave assertion, and it is one which cannot fail, if seriously believed and thoroughly acted upon, to lead to sad conclusions both in the theological doctrine of Scripture and in the practical work of the Church.... Where are we to get our errorless Scripture? In the *ipsissima verba* of the original autographs? Who are to recover these for us? I suppose the band of experts in textual criticism who are year by year giving us the materials for a more perfect text. Are they to be created by-and-by when their labours are ended into an authority doing for Protestants what the "Church" does for Roman Catholics? Are they to guarantee for us the inspired and infallible Word of God, or are we to say that the unknown autographs are unknowable, and that we can never get to this Scripture (today this is the consensus-PB), which is the only Scripture inspired and infallible in the strictly formal sense of those words as used by the Princeton School? I have great respect for historical and Biblical critics, and have done my share in a humble way to obtain a recognition of their work, but I for one shall never consent to erect the scholars whom I esteem into an authority for that text of Scripture which is alone inspired and infallible. That, however, is what this formalist theory is driving us to if we submit to it. I maintain, with all the Reformers, and with all the Reformed Creeds, that the Scriptures, as we now have

111

them, are the inspired and infallible Word of God, and that all textual criticism, while it is to be welcomed in so far as it brings our present text nearer the *ipsissima verba* of the original autographs, will not make the Scriptures one whit more inspired or more infallible in the true Scriptural and religious meanings of those words than they are now. (quoted by Letis 1990:35-36.)

When Warfield, in an article in the *Sunday School Times* on 2 December 1882, discounted the long ending of the Gospel of Mark, stating that it was not part of God's Word. Letis recounts that in response:

Professor N. M. Wheeler, of Lawrence University, challenged him on this point. Insisting that Warfield's view of the matter implied that "we must ask the critics every morning what is (sic) the latest conclusions in order to know what is the Scripture inspired of God," Wheeler sensed the near relationship between what Warfield was doing and what was being proposed on the higher critical plain. (Letis 1991:7.)

Even Charles Briggs, echoing much the same sentiments, added:

It is admitted that there are errors in the present text of Scripture, but it is claimed that there could have been no errors in the original documents. But how do we know this? We do not have the originals and can never get at them. Biblical criticism brings us closer to the originals, but does not remove the errors. It is in accordance with sound logic and scientific methods to form our conception of the original documents from the best documents we have. The presumption, therefore, in regard to errors in the best texts, is that they were also in the original documents. It is sheer assumption to claim that the original documents were inerrant. No one can be persuaded to believe in the inerrancy of Scripture, except by *a priori* consideration from the elaboration of the doctrine of verbal inspiration....This statement of these recent divines (Warfield et al.) is contrary to the facts of the case, for—(1). The historic faith of the Church is to be found in the official symbolical books and nowhere else. None of these symbols state that the "*ipsissima verba*

112

of the original autographs are without error." (2). It is well known that the great Reformers recognized errors in the scriptures and did not hold to the inerrancy of the original autographs. Are these Princeton divines entitled to pronounce Luther and Calvin heterodox, and to define the faith of the universal Church? (3). The Westminster divines did not teach the inerrancy of the original autographs. (Briggs 1889:68-69.)

What then are the implications of such a problem in the Warfield position? Was Briggs, in fact, the authentic descendent of the Reformers after all? He certainly clearly saw the novelty of the view that Warfield was foisting on the church and the havoc that it would wreack. He addressed this novelty in his inaugural address as one of the barriers to men coming to the Bible, but Briggs's criticism went unheeded. He was tried for heresy for his views and expelled from the ministry of the Presbyterian Church USA.

At Princeton, Warfield was lauded far and near as the great champion of Reformed orthodoxy. His novel ideas were to become the standard of Reformed confessionalism. Yet, as Theodore Letis points out, '...he (Warfield) marks a distinct departure from the earlier Princetonian tradition of Archibald Alexander and Charles Hodge by introducing German N.T. criticism at Princeton' (Letis 1990:17). Although, at the time, "lower criticism," as opposed to what was seen as the destructive German "higher criticism" practiced by Professor Briggs at Union, was considered to be neutral, maybe even beneficial for a proper study of God's Word (Letis 1984:86-89). Eldon Jay Epp of Harvard, in his article "The Eclectic Method in New Testament Criticism: Solution or Symposium" (Epp 1976), demonstrates that the "lower" and "higher" criticisms are really not separate and distinct, but actually varying degrees of the same discipline. Letis, building on the work of Harry Boer, concurs.

> Eventually, it became a commonplace among Reformed academics that it was dishonest and unworkable to construct a wall between lower criticism and higher criticism. As Harry Boer observes: "In view of the history of higher and lower criticism in the past one hundred years there is a profound irony in the relationship in which these two disciplines are regarded in

the Church. Whereas higher criticism has a bad name in large parts of the Church, lower criticism has an eminently favorable name. Both kinds of criticism are governed by methods that ...have an identical basic rational, scientific approach to their specific task.... The two forms of criticism are so inter-related and basic in the study of the Bible that it is impossible to use the one properly without acknowledging the legitimacy and necessity of the other. (Letis 1984:106.)

Thus, the difference between the conclusions of Briggs and Warfield were rather a difference *in degree and not in kind* (Letis 1984:103). This is why Letis classified Warfield's volume on text criticism as '...the first handbook on New Testament text-critical method authored by an American from the Enlightenment point of view' (Letis 1984:87). This is also why, when Warfield tried to reconcile his eclectic method with the providence of God, he ended up defending a "restoration" of the text as opposed to its "preservation" by God (Letis 1984:89). In the course of discussing God's providential care of His Word, in his *Critical Reviews*, Warfield, employing a neat turn of phrase, admitted that

> ...just because we believe in God's *continuous* care over the purity of His Word, we are able to look upon the labors of the great critics of the nineteenth century—a Tregelles, a Tischendorf, a Westcott, a Hort—as well as those of a Gregory and a Basil and a Chrysostom, as instruments of Providence in preserving the Scriptures pure for the use of God's people. (Warfield [1932] 1981:36.)

This, it would seem, is contrary to the Westminster Confession, which states in Chapter 1:VIII: '[Scripture]...being immediately inspired by God, and by his singular care and providence kept pure in all ages, are therefore authentical...(The Westminster Assembly [1647] 1983:23). Warfield believed in a corrupt Bible; he said so. He also believed in a Bible that was to be perfected only by the methods of criticism, not one that has been kept pure throughout the ages (Letis 1984:97-99).

3.3 Conclusion

What significance, then, does this dispute over Scripture and biblical criticism have for the question of Presbyterian doctrinal development? Briggs's use and defense of higher criticism challenged various and important ideas held within traditional Presbyterianism. His approach was one that emphasized the *historical process* rather than either Scripture or the creeds per se. In this sense, he was not particularly interested in preserving and developing the received tradition along the lines of further definition and clarity. Massa has aptly described Briggs's concerns in the following way:

> Amid the welter of conflicting journalistic coverage, it was generally overlooked at the time (the time of Briggs's inaugural address) by the press that Briggs himself published an article that purported to explain the real import of his address and the furor it set off. Briggs argued in "The Theological Crisis" that he had sought to elucidate a religious and cultural crisis that was essentially neither biblical not creedal, but far more troubling. This crisis involved the recognition that traditional ways of conceiving the universe were no longer viable, and that an entirely new theological world was called for: "We stand on the heights of the last of the great movements of Christendom.... It must be evident to every thinking man that the traditional dogma has been battling against philosophy and science, history and every form of human learning.... There can be little doubt but that the traditional dogma is doomed. Shall it be allowed to drag down into perdition with it the Bible and the Creeds?" Briggs asserted that the most important theological questions of the day were "beyond the range of orthodoxy itself," a state of intellectual affairs brought about by a new understanding of historical evolution and relativity. "Progress in doctrine and life is a necessary experience of a living church," and such progress never ceased until the church had attained its goal in the "knowledge of all the truth, in a holiness reflecting the purity and excellence of Jesus." Their age [the age of Briggs] was a "period of transition" because modern evangelical scholars offered, over against "American dogmatic systems," a critical new *historical* theology, or rather a theology both critical and historical in a new way. The modern basis for proceeding in theology, Briggs announced, was no longer "dogmatic speculation" based

on any of the older sources—Scripture, creed, or theological system. Rather, modern theology must proceed on the basis of that "given" upon which all modern scholarship proceeded, the facts of the historical process itself.... (Massa 1990:91.)

Charles Briggs, rather than further *clarifying* the historic dogmatic statements of Presbyterianism, chose instead to *redefine* the historic affirmations of the faith as enshrined in the symbols of the Presbyterian Church. He wanted a contemporary faith; one that, as he said, evolved out of the history of the church. It was to this end, I would suggest, that his methodological developments under the caption of Biblical Theology were aimed. In all this, Charles Briggs showed himself to be a Modernist. Despite the subtitle of Max Rogers thesis (Conservative Heretic (Rogers 1964)) and despite the later developments in Modernism—which were admittedly much more radical than Briggs (Cauthen 1962:147-209)—, Briggs wanted a faith that was both relevant and consistent with modern thought, and, as I have attempted to show, he was willing to reshape the affirmations of the faith in order to achieve his desired end.

Even as Arius in the fourth century of the Christian era wanted to reinterpret '...the Christian faith in terms of contemporary philosophies' (Murray 1964:54), so Charles Briggs argued that a doctrine could only be framed '...in accordance with the dominant philosophical and theological principles of the times' (Briggs [1900] 1970:111). His attitude towards the Scriptures and his use of biblical criticism were expressions of this fundamental position. Gary Johnson points to several instances where Briggs insisted that higher-criticism, science, even psychology, should have a hand in redefining the historic tenets of the faith (Johnson 1987:13, 19, 31, & 33). In this regard, then, Professor Briggs can be classified as a Futurist: one for whom the affirmations of the faith are open-ended; never permanently settled but constantly open to change.

If Briggs be classified as a Futurist for whom doctrine was open-ended, I believe that Benjamin B. Warfield of Princeton, at least in his restructuring of the doctrine of the inerrancy of Scripture, should be classified as an Archaist. He insisted on the necessity of an inerrant Bible, one, moreover, which could not have a single error; otherwise, the authority of the whole of Scripture would be nullified. This position was not far removed from the insistence of Eusebius of Caesarea on the necessity of maintaining the "sacred words" of Scripture; the abandonment of these sacred words would mean the end of the faith.

116

Eusebius and Warfield were, of course, dealing with their own particular, historically-conditioned problems, but were doing so along very similar lines of thought. Warfield's insistence that the doctrine of inerrancy could not admit any deviation from the "sacred words" of the autographs, like the position of Eusebius, exposes him to the charge of an open-ended view of doctrine. The church does not possess the autographs upon which Warfield pinned his entire theory. Without these autographs, which Warfield contended were indispensable to his doctrine of Scripture, the church ultimately is left in a nebulous state of never having the sacred words upon which her existence depends and of always having to defend the legitimacy of Scripture against the possibility of a single error.

With doubts about the Scriptures being planted by both Futurists such as Briggs and Archaists such as Warfield, it was not long before the confessional identity and exclusivity of the Presbyterian Church were called into question. Futurists like Briggs wanted a church that was relevant and sympathetic to modern thought. Archaists like Warfield wanted to maintain the "sacred words" of the historical biblical documents as a bulwark against new questions and new problems. It seems that, for better or worse, Briggs's inaugural address and subsequent trial stimulated a rethinking of some important doctrinal issues, especially the doctrine of the inerrancy of Scripture as promoted by Princeton and opposed by Union. This rethinking became a prelude to doctrinal redefinition, that is, to proposed confessional revisions. This redefinition, while promoted by Futurists and opposed by Archaists, was, however, really carried through by the Centrists in the church. In the next chapter we will look at how this was done.

Chapter 4

Theological Revision and Ecclesiastical Reunion

In the last chapter we discussed the emergence of both Archaism and Futurism within American Presbyterian circles. In this chapter we will concern ourselves more with the emergence of the Centrist position. While this terminology is certainly not without its problems, I would suggest that a kind of Presbyterian Centrism did, in fact, emerge within the context of attempts at theological and confessional revision. By this I mean, in contradistinction from Archaism and Futurism, those in the church who sought only to further define and clarify the existing statement of faith, ameliorating in the process, what they saw, as some of the confession's "harsher statements" This amalgamation, which I refer to as Centrist, was rather less well defined than either the prevailing Archaism or Futurism. In fact, it is best seen in retrospect after the all the wrangling over confessional revision had ceased. It is to this development, then, that we must turn our attention.

In 1900, 'The General Assembly was petitioned by over three dozen presbyteries to begin consideration of [confessional] revision' (North 1996:351). Charles Briggs, for one, recognized that the confessional revision was, to a certain extent, a grass roots movement (Briggs 1890b:45). He characterized this movement as one '...without leadership, and it has puzzled the leaders of the church to keep abreast of it' (Briggs 1890b:45). The impetus to revise started well before Briggs's inaugural address and the trouble that ensued. I believe that a crucial push towards confessional revision had already occurred in 1881. In fact, the events which took place at that time might even have had an effect on Professor Briggs's inaugural address. (This is a suggestion that will probably not meet with the approval of more conservative Presbyterian chroniclers.)

In this chapter we will be looking at two separate moves towards theological reinterpretation and confessional revision within the Presbyterian Church USA—those of 1881 and 1903. Then, we will look at the reunion of the Presbyterian Church USA and the Cumberland

Presbyterian Church and its significance for the history of Presbyterian theology.

4.1   1881: A Conservative Revision

The first confessional "revision" began with a scholarly, academic reinterpretation of the confessional understanding of Scripture. As I indicated in the previous chapter, in 1881 two of Princeton Seminary's leading theologians, Benjamin Breckenridge Warfield and Archibald Alexander Hodge, penned a seminal article entitled "Inspiration," published in the *Presbyterian Review*. We must now consider the significance of this article in terms of the push towards theological reinterpretation and confessional revision.

The idea for this article came from the younger Hodge who '...invited Warfield to write the essay with him, with Hodge writing the first half dealing with the doctrinal aspects, "to be followed by a discussion statement illustration [sic] proof of the truth as to 1st the effect of the prevalent new criticism...."' (Letis 1984:98). Hodge wanted Warfield, in the course of the article, to address 'the state of actual facts (as to the New Testament) in regard to the asserted inaccuracies —or contradictions' (quoted by Letis 1984:98). The product that Warfield delivered was somewhat different than what A. A. Hodge had expressly requested. Taking a decidedly new track in dealing with the inspiration of the Biblical text, Warfield wrote that 'We do not assert the common text, but only that the original autographic text was inspired. No "error" can be asserted, which cannot be proved to have been aboriginal in the text' (Hodge & Warfield 1881:245). As I have already pointed out, Warfield regarded only the original autographs as inspired and held that a single proven error anywhere in the text of Scripture would completely negate the doctrine of inspiration of Scripture altogether, and, to follow Warfield's leading, presumably the church as well. He wrote: 'A proved error in Scripture contradicts not only our doctrine, but the Scripture claims and, therefore, its inspiration in making those claims' (Hodge & Warfield 1881:245). In the previous chapter I suggested that this view of inspiration was a novel one, especially within the Presbyterian Church. Nor was the certainty that Warfield sought for in his doctrine of Scripture even prevalent in the Princeton Seminary environment.

Archibald Alexander (1772-1851), founding professor at Princeton recognized at least 60,000 textual variants in the New Testament (Letis 1984:72, Loetscher 1983:228). According to Theodore Letis, he

'...probably did not think the autographs were inerrant.' (Letis 1984:72). Lefferts Loetscher relates that

> When Dr. Alexander turned to lecture on the text of the New Testament, he conceded, as he had done in the case of the Old Testament, "that it is even possible that some of the aut9*ographs, if we had them, might not be altogether free from such errors as arise from the slip of the pen, as the Apostles and ["had"] amanuensis [-es] who were not inspired." Thus here, as in treating the Old Testament, Alexander avoided asserting the literal "inerrancy" of the original autographs of the New Testament. ...Alexander suggested that interlinear correction by the author himself of such a pen slip would be impossible to distinguish from an emendation by a later scribe. He sought deftly to turn this concession to advantage by arguing that "the loss of the autographs therefore need not be considered of so much importance as we know that they were copied with the utmost care." (Loetscher 1983:228.)

Charles Hodge, arguably the most famous and influential of the Princeton school, took essentially the same approach as Alexander when dealing with the inspiration of Scripture. He did not hold to an inerrant autographa, as those who followed in his footsteps. Ernest Sandeen has pointed out that 'Hodge was firm enough in enunciating the infallibility of the Bible, but ...his own faith in the inspiration of the Bible did not depend upon inerrancy. As a result, in his discussion of the possibility of errors in the Scriptures, Hodge was relaxed and quite calm' (Sandeen 1962:315). Hodge himself wrote:

> The errors in matters of fact which skeptics search out bear no proportion to the whole. No sane man would deny that the Parthenon was built of marble, even if here and there a speck of sandstone should be detected in the structure. Not less unreasonable is it to deny the inspiration of such a book as the Bible, because one sacred writer says that on a given occasion twenty-four thousand, and another says that twenty-three thousand, men were slain. Surely a Christian may be allowed to tread such objections under his feet. ...So the Christian need not renounce his faith in the

plenary inspiration of the Bible, although there may some things about it in its present state which he cannot account for. (Hodge 1979:170.)

Charles Hodge's sentiments also appear to have been the sentiments of his son A. A. Hodge, co-author with Warfield of the famous article on inspiration. In a letter to Benjamin Warfield dated 14 November 1880, A. A. Hodge does not even hint at the idea that the autographs of Scripture might be inerrant. He postulates instead:

> But the question remains was this book [the Bible] with its (1) human (2) oriental & (3) Hebrew characteristics <u>intended to stand the test of microscopic criticism as to its accuracy in matters of indifferent detail</u>? It appears that my father [Charles Hodge] was speaking of the possibility of infinitesimal inaccuracies of no importance relative to the end designed, in <u>Systematic Theology</u> Vol. I, p. 170. I say so too—very heartily. But the question remains what degree of minute accuracy do the facts prove that God designed to effect? That is for you critics and exegetes to determine. (quoted by Letis 1984:76-77.)

According to Theodore Letis, Warfield, in line with his own "Enlightenment" ideas, shifted the emphasis of the Presbyterian doctrine of the inspiration of Scripture (Letis 1984:88). He says that 'Since his (Warfield's) common-sense philosophy allowed him to adopt the "scientific" method of text criticism, he reasoned that this method must be God's means of restoring the true text. He shifted from the notion of providential <u>preservation</u> to one of providential <u>restoration</u>....' (Letis 1984:89). This distinction advocated by Warfield was a result of his positing inerrancy in the autographa alone. He believed that the text of Scripture in hand was full of errors; hence it was only the autographs that were actually inspired and inerrant to the smallest detail (Hodge & Warfield 1881). This theory was, in reality, a mental reconfiguration of the confessional statements on inspiration.

The Westminster Confession, in contrast, says that the Scriptures '...being immediately inspired by God, and by his singular care and providence kept pure in all ages, are therefore authentical...' (Leith 1982:196). No where is the word "inerrant" mentioned in the confessional statement. Neither is any distinction made between the inspired autographs of the Scriptures and the Bible in current circulation. If anything the Confession precludes those conclusions advocated by Hodge and Warfield. A. A. Hodge in a commentary on the Westminster Confession of Faith first published in 1869, in his pre-Warfield days, stipulated 'That the original sacred text has come down to us in a state of essential purity. ...The differences are found to be unimportant, and essential integrity of our text is established' (Hodge [1869] 1983:41). Nowhere in any of these older statements is there any mention of the original autographs of the Scriptures. In commenting on the Scriptures in general, words like "purity," "pure," and "inspired" are used throughout. Inerrancy did not even become an issue until the Hodge/Warfield article of 1881. I would suggest, therefore, that the Hodge/Warfield article altered the sense and interpretation of the Westminster Confession on the doctrine of Scripture. Thus, the Hodge/Warfield article of 1881 might be considered a confessional reinterpretation on an academic theological level, rather than on an ecclesial level.

In order to introduce their changes to the doctrine of inspiration, Hodge and Warfield begin their famous article by stating that 'The word inspiration, as applied to the Holy Scriptures, has gradually acquired a specific technical meaning, independent of its etymology' (Hodge & Warfield 1881:225). The "specific and technical meaning" referred to is their theory of the inerrancy of the autographa of Scripture, which the remainder of the article describes in some detail. More recently, Randall Balmer has tried to defend the Hodge/Warfield statement that "inspiration" had indeed acquired the "specific technical meaning" that they claimed (Balmer 1982). In so doing, Balmer has quoted a vast assortment of works that predate the Hodge/Warfield article on inspiration. He quotes Baptists (Balmer 1982:358-359), Methodists, Lutherans (Balmer 1982:359), and Congregationalists (Balmer 1982:355-358) in the course of his thorough inquiry. In almost every instance the source quoted by Balmer speaks of only the autographs of Scripture as directly inspired by God. For instance, Enoch Pond of Bangor Seminary in Maine wrote that 'It should be understood ...that when speaking of the inspiration of sacred writings, we refer only to the original copies' (quoted by Balmer 1982:356). The one thing, however, that none of those quoted by Balmer say is that those "original copies" were inerrant. Additionally, Balmer does not refer, in his extensive deliberations, to any Presbyterians. So even if the ideas of Hodge and Warfield existed in other communions, they still had to be adopted in Presbyterian circles for the confession to be affected. While Balmer does not prove the entry of these concepts into Presbyterianism, he does give an interesting account of their provenance in general.

Historian Ernest Sandeen does not share the conclusions of Randall Balmer that the Hodge/Warfield article was just clarifying the meaning of the Westminster Confession on the doctrine of inspiration. Sandeen considered the ideas on inspiration set forth in the Hodge/Warfield article to be "new refinements" and "a new emphasis" (Sandeen 1970:128). Speaking specifically about the theory of the "inerrant autographa" that the Hodge/Warfield article was promoting, Sandeen writes:

> The collaborative article of A. A. Hodge and B. B. Warfield in the *Princeton Review* (1881) elevated the concept to an especially prominent place in the Princeton doctrine of inspiration. That this concept of the original autographs had been recently added to their apologetic was never mentioned by Warfield and Hodge. Their silence might seem to imply that they did not view the new refinement as significant. But what might seem to be a casual change was in fact a significant retreat. (Sandeen 1970:128.)

Further, Sandeen believed the motivation of Hodge and Warfield in writing the famous article to be nothing less than: 'A minority of Evangelicals rushed to the defense of the Bible convinced that their faith could not stand if the infallibility of the Bible was undermined' (Sandeen 1970:107). Interestingly, Sandeen characterized the efforts of Hodge and Warfield as "Fundamentalist," (and I might add, "Archaist") in perspective (Sandeen 1970:107).

Another person who saw the Hodge/Warfield article as advocating a view of inspiration that was alien to historic Presbyterianism was none other than Charles Briggs. While he may have shown himself a Futurist in the majority of what he said in his inaugural address, he still managed to define the problem of inspiration created in the wake of the Hodge/Warfield article with particular clarity. In fact, Lefferts Loetscher sees the connection between ideas in the Hodge/Warfield article and Briggs's inaugural address as one of cause and effect (Loetscher 1978:130). In the course of speaking of those "barriers to the faith" which he decried as man-made, Briggs said:

It has been taught in recent years, and is still taught by some theologians, that one proved error destroys the authority of Scripture. I shall venture to affirm that, so far as I can see, there are errors in the Scriptures that no one has been able to explain away; and the theory that they were not in the original text is sheer assumption, upon which no mind can rest with certainty. If such errors destroy the authority of the Bible, it is already destroyed for historians. Men cannot shut their eyes to truth and fact. But on what authority do these theologians drive men from the Bible by this theory of inerrancy? The Bible itself nowhere makes this claim. The creeds of the Church nowhere sanction it. (Briggs [1891] 1972:35.)

Briggs also recognized that the redefinition of the doctrine of inspiration by Hodge and Warfield was essentially a confessional change (Massa 1990:105). During his trial Briggs stated his objections to this confessional revision thus:

He alleged that the prosecution's inclusion of "verbal inspiration" and "inerrancy" under the rubric of Westminster doctrine, clearly taking its lead from the recent deliverance (The Portland Deliverance), was so obvious an anticonfessional use of that symbol as to constitute itself serious grounds for judicial proceedings. The late assembly, he declared, had overstepped constitutional limits in defining doctrine outside of an official heresy trial. The confession clearly affirms that "by God's singular care and providence, the Scriptures have been kept pure in all ages"; thus, adherence to those standards "no less than to common sense" demanded that Presbyterians affirm that the *present* text of Scripture was as pure (and as uncorrupted) as the original text. Jerome, Augustine, Luther, and Calvin had freely admitted to errors in Scripture; this admission in no way constituted a compromise of biblical authority. (Massa 1990:105.)

Briggs maintained that this doctrinal revision would cost the Presbyterian Church members: 'It will cost us (Presbyterianism) ten thousand and hundreds of thousands unless the true Westminster doctrine is speedily put in its place' (Briggs 1889:73). While Professor Briggs was usually a Futurist in his deliberations on the doctrines of historic Presbyterianism, in his analysis and recommendations regarding the redefinition of the inspiration of Scripture by Hodge and Warfield, Briggs seemed rather to occupy a Centrist position. Briggs believed that the ideas of Hodge and Warfield were a novelty and a danger to the plain and historic meaning of the confession. This change in understanding of the meaning of the Confession was a change in one of Presbyterianism's historic affirmations of the faith, carrying with it a charge of Futurism against Warfield and Hodge. Briggs spoke about the revision, and he also wrote about it, but to no avail. It was thus to Briggs's dismay that the General Assembly of 1892, in the course of remanding his heresy case back to the presbytery of New York, issued what came to be known as the Portland Deliverance. This statement gave the official sanction of the Presbyterian Church to the understanding of inspiration advocated by Hodge and Warfield (Loetscher 1978:130 & Massa 1990:103). The Portland Deliverance, then, raised the theological opinions of Hodge and Warfield to a much higher ecclesiastical level. That this declaration was indeed a confessional reinterpretation and revision can be seen in the action of Union Seminary, which, in protest, immediately terminated its relationship with the General Assembly of the Presbyterian Church (Massa 1990:104). The scholarly reinterpretation of an existing article of the Westminster Confession of Faith by Warfield and Hodge in 1881 became, in effect, an ecclesial, confessional revision in 1892 when the General Assembly gave its official stamp of approval to the Portland Deliverance.

Inasmuch as the Hodge/Warfield article sought to preserve the "sacred words" of the faith that its authors believed were in danger of being lost, it was Archaist in character. In addition, it was also Futurist in scope as well, inasmuch as it proposed not a new articulation of the church's confession in light of new problems and questions, but a new and different doctrine. This situation brought out a Centrist response in the person of Charles Briggs, whose main concern was to see that the plain meaning of the confession was retained, even in the face of strong opposition. Archaism and Futurism were instrumental in the unofficial revision of 1881, and the response was voiced by Centrists. In contrast, in 1903 a revision is proposed by Centrists and, as we shall see, Archaism tried mightily to stifle it.

One might argue that the confessional revision engendered by the Hodge/Warfield position was simply a new stage in the development of the doctrine of Scripture, since it sought to clarify a point of doctrine already in the confession. I would suggest, however, that this was not the case. The article of Hodge and Warfield did not clarify a point of doctrine already held in the Presbyterian Church; it changed its meaning entirely. In fact, it changed substantially the article of the Westminster Confession dealing with the church's understanding of Scripture. Moreover, the theory of the inerrancy of the original autographs of the Scriptures is impossible to prove since none of the autographs of Scripture are extant. If the tenets of the Confession of Faith are based upon Scripture, as throughout they purport to be, then the Hodge/Warfield revision is at most an unproven theological opinion, not doctrinal development. One might even argue, as does Letis, that the origin of this reinterpretation of the Confession's position on Scripture is a very modern, even a "Modernistic" one, inasmuch as it was based on an Enlightenment methodology which Warfield's Common-Sense philosophy caused him to embrace. In this sense, Warfield's position on the nature of biblical inerrancy warped the Confession itself in order to fit his own needs in the face of questions raised by the new biblical criticism (Letis 1984:90).

4.2 The Revision of 1903

Lefferts Loetscher of Princeton, in writing of the popular (Centrist) movement to revise the Westminster Confession of Faith, said that '...the General Assembly of 1889 received memorials from fifteen presbyteries asking that the Westminster Confession be revised' (Loetscher 1978:130). In addition to the popular (what I would call Centrist) call for revision, John Hart, also of Princeton, credits Charles Briggs with initiating '...an effort to revise the Westminster Confession of Faith in 1889' (Hart 1978:17). In the same year, Briggs's colleague and Professor of Church History at Union Seminary, Philip Schaff, penned a reasoned plea for confessional revision entitled *Creed Revision in the Presbyterian Churches* (Schaff 1890). At the outset Schaff argued that: 'This truth and duty (to revise the confession) have taken deeper hold on the mind and heart of the living Church than ever before, and must overrule the particularism and exclusivism of the Augustinian and Calvinistic system, with its doctrines of reprobation, preterition, and wholesale damnation of the non-Christian world' (Schaff 1890:v). Those who fail to move ahead, who fail to accept this progress, he added, '...will be left behind and outgrown' (Schaff 1890:1).

127

As the move to revise the confession was gaining momentum, 'conservatives' (or, those whom one might call Archaists) not in favor of a revision under any circumstances began to worry (Massa 1990:83-84). These 'conservatives' began to look for a way to defeat the revisionist impulse. As Mark Massa relates, Charles Briggs gave them their desired opportunity:

> The meteoric advance of the revision issue ...thus appeared to most of the Old School faction to be a direct result of Briggs's critical efforts; indeed, those evangelical conservatives who had always proudly worn the sobriquet of "confessionalists" viewed the revision campaign under his direction as the last theological straw. It was now time for them to mount a massive campaign against Briggs and his "cause" before the next meeting of the General Assembly. Little did they dream ...that their campaign against Briggs and his critical methods would be most successfully pressed by Briggs himself. For on the evening of November 11, 1890, the Board of Directors of Union Seminary formally accepted the large donation offered by their chairman, Charles Butler, to establish a new chair at the seminary, to be named after Union's first scripture professor, Edward Robinson. The Board of Directors likewise accepted Butler's request that Charles Briggs, himself a student of Robinson's, be named the chair's first incumbent, and voted (in what they thought would be a routine administrative action) to transfer Briggs from the Davenport (prior to the vote, Briggs was Davenport Professor of Hebrew and Cognate Languages-PB) to the newly created Robinson Chair. Thus did the Board of Directors of the resolutely progressive Union Seminary create the means for defeating the most successful (and most feared) campaign for the cause of historical criticism in America. (Massa 1990:84.)

Thus it is from January 1891, the date of the Briggs inaugural address, that Mark Massa dates the beginning of the division in Presbyterianism's evangelical mainstream into "Modernists" or "Liberals" and "Fundamentalists"—about whom I will have more to say later. (Following Mark Massa, I am using these terms in a conventional sense, but I do not mean anything derogatory by their use.) It was the Briggs inaugural that caused the conservatives, or Fundamentalists, to

128

mobilize. Under the leadership of Princeton's William Henry Green, the next General Assembly '...buried the creedal revision question remaining from the previous assembly (considered the most volatile issue on the agenda)....' (Massa 1990:95). The question of creed revision remained '...tabled during the progress of his (Briggs's) trial' (Hart 1978:18).

While the Centrists in the Presbyterian Church, as we shall see, wanted the revision of the Confession in order to retain what was best in the Presbyterian tradition, while, at the same time, correcting some of the more problematic or objectionable areas (Hart 1978:18), the agenda of both Liberals or the Fundamentalists was something other than this. One can see, for example, the more radical character of the Liberal agenda as expressed by one of its spokesman, W. W. Fenn of Harvard in 1913. Fenn readily acknowledged Liberalism's experiential nature and its consequent conflict with credalism in general. Further, he viewed all the historical creeds of the church to be a kind of crystallization of the experience then current among believers, rather than a crystallization of any divine revelation. He writes:

> So far it has been too often an endeavor to adapt old phrases and usages to fit the religious life of today, whereas the urgent need is to aid that religious life in creating its own forms of expression. The motive for this attempt is clear and from one point of view praiseworthy. Language which has been employed for many generations to express the deeper life of man becomes saturated with religious feeling and hence sacred, with the sacredness of the experience which it relates, and moving, through its rich and powerful inheritance of association. To give up the verbal form seems like renouncing the reality which originally fashioned it. (Fenn 1913:519.)

Similarly, Shailer Mathews, whose book *The Faith of Modernism* (1924) was a Liberal response to J. G. Machen's *Christianity and Liberalism* ([1923] 1946) (Dennison 1992:1), argued for a far less doctrinally-controlled form of Christianity than was commonly found within confessional Presbyterianism.

> The position of Protestant dogmatists is to all intents and purposes the same as that of Pius X. All over the world they are asking ministers and teachers to answer "yes" or "no" to questionnaires concerning the belief in

the literal inerrancy of the Scripture; the deity and virgin birth of Jesus; the substitutionary atonement offered by Christ to God; the biblical miracles; the physical resurrection, the ascension, and the physical return of Jesus from heaven. The acceptance of all these supernatural elements, they hold, is essential to real Christianity; they are the "fundamentals" without which religion is not Christianity. ...But a man is not a Modernist because he disbelieves orthodox theology. Modernism is hardly less different from Confessionalism than it is from Unitarianism. Both Confessionalism and Unitarianism are on the same plane of theological rationalism. Modernism is concerned with the historical method of discovering the permanent values of Christianity, and the religious rather than the theological test of religion. It is not aiming at a system of theology but at organizing life on a Christian basis. ...It (Modernism) is not a denomination or a theology. It is the use of the methods of modern science to find, state and use the permanent and central values of inherited orthodoxy in meeting the needs of a modern world. The needs themselves point the way to formulas. Modernists endeavor to reach beliefs and their application in the same way that chemists or historians reach and apply their conclusions. They do not vote in conventions and do not enforce beliefs by discipline. Modernism has no confession. Its theological affirmations are the formulation of results of investigation both of human needs and the Christian religion. The Dogmatist starts with doctrines, the Modernist with the religion that gave rise to doctrines. The Dogmatist relies on conformity through group authority; the Modernist upon inductive method and action in accord with group loyalty. (Mathews 1924:21-23.)

Kenneth Cauthen's work on Liberalism's impact on America (Cauthen 1962) does not portray Liberalism as being quite as a-theological as Mathews's depiction of it. Liberalism's source of theology, however, differed greatly from that of historic Presbyterianism. In his analysis of Mathews, Cauthen writes that:

> He (Shailer Mathews) affirmed that religion arises in experience and is given theological expression in

categories which are derived from the prevailing social patterns. Theology is transcendentalized politics. The background of theology is social experience, not metaphysics. Thus, the theologian is more like a social analyst than a metaphysician. The present-day task of theology ...is to discover by a study of history the functional significance of the previously employed socio-theological patterns and to set forth the modern equivalent in twentieth-century language. (Cauthen 1962:35.)

As these remarks demonstrate, Liberalism, or at least certain strains within it, began moving in an a-theological, even non-theological, direction; away from the traditional sources of Reformed theology, that is, the Scriptures and the Confession. The emphasis, rather, was placed on the collective experience of the people of God through the centuries (Cauthen 1962:35). In this sense, Karl Barth's description is quite apt that: '... theology becomes "the science of religious experience as it takes place in the Church"' (quoted by Cauthen 1962:44-45). Moreover, Liberalism's understanding that 'the background of theology is social experience, not metaphysics' (Cauthen 1962:35) forced it to adopt a historicist view of the origin of Christian truth. Its striving to interpret this 'experience' '...in terms of the methods and categories of early twentieth-century science and philosophy' (Cauthen 1962:30) put it in a decidedly Futurist category, where changing the historic affirmations of the faith were increasingly viewed as a quest for relevance.

On the opposite end of the theological spectrum were those who came to be known as Fundamentalists. Included within this classification were those of a more Centrist nature who adhered to the church's confession, i.e. confessionalists. Indeed, as the years progressed, Centrists were increasingly classed as Fundamentalists until the majority of both groups departed from the Presbyterian Church USA in Machen's day. These Fundamentalists, however, were not necessarily the ignorant, maniacal lot that Norman Furniss, in his history of Fundamentalism, has portrayed them (Furniss 1954). Instead, as Kenneth Cauthen observes, they were concerned and honest Christians who '... were much less inclined to revise traditional beliefs in the face of modern ways of thinking' (Cauthen 1962:31). Cauthen argues that:

131

Fundamentalism as a theological movement is a distinctly twentieth-century phenomenon. It represents the reaction of the older orthodoxy against the new theology. These men defended what they believed to be the true faith against the onslaughts of science, Biblical criticism, and the liberal reinterpretation of Christianity. They believed that Christianity did not need to come to terms with modern thought, since there was to be found in the Bible an infallible source of religious truth. Those conclusions of science, philosophy, or liberal theology which contradicted what they believed to be the plain and literal teaching of the Bible were immediately rejected. An explicit, thoroughgoing supernaturalism was reaffirmed, along with a stern insistence on the miraculous nature of revelation. (Cauthen 1962:31.)

The Fundamentalists were, however, at least to my mind, Archaists, and their Archaism showed itself primarily in reaction to the Liberal (Futurist) desire for confessional revision. As much as the Liberals in the Presbyterian Church wanted to revise the confession, the Fundamentalists resisted any change that was not of their own doing. The Futurists, to be relevant, were ready to change the affirmations of the faith as their historicist view of the origins of the faith dictated. Archaists (Fundamentalists), who viewed 'Christianity as a gift of God (that) came into the world from outside' (Machen 1976:20), saw any revision proposed by either the Liberals, or those of the more amorphous "Center,"—I say amorphous Center because at this time there was no well defined Center—as a repudiation of the historic stance of the church. Machen, from what many have considered the Fundamentalist perspective, addressed this very issue of revision.

Why should there not be still further doctrinal advance? If the church advanced in doctrine up to the time of the Westminster Standards, why should it now not proceed still further on its upward march? Well, there is no essential reason why it should not do so. However, before it attempts to do so, it is very important for it to understand precisely what Christian doctrine is. It should understand very clearly that Christian doctrine is just a setting forth of what the Bible teaches. At the foundation of Christian doctrine is the acceptance of the full truthfulness of the Bible as the Word of God. That is often forgotten by those who today undertake to write confessional statements. Let us give expression to our Christian experience, they say, in forms better suited to the times in which we are living than are the older creeds of the church. So they sit down and concoct various forms of words, which they represent as being on a plane with the great creeds of Christendom. When they do that, they are simply forgetting what the creeds of Christendom are. The creeds of Christendom are not expressions of Christian experience. They are summary statements of what God has told us in His Word. Far from the subject matter of the creeds being derived from Christian experience, it is Christian experience which is based upon the truth contained in the creeds; and the truth contained in the creeds is derived from the Bible, which is the Word of God. Groups of people that undertake to write a creed without taking the subject matter of their creed from the inspired Word of God, are not at all taking an additional step on the pathway on which the great Christian creeds moved; rather, they are moving in an exactly opposite direction. What they are doing has nothing whatever to do with that grand progress of Christian doctrine.... Far from continuing the advance of Christian doctrine, they are starting something entirely different, and that something different, we may add, is doomed to failure from the start. The first prerequisite, then, for any advance in Christian doctrine is that those who would engage in it should believe in the full truthfulness of the Bible and should endeavor to make their doctrine simply a presentation of what the Bible teaches. (Machen 1973:150.)

Though often classified as a Fundamentalist, Machen was rather part of that amorphous confessional Center. In contrast to the Liberals, he reminded the church that experience was not a suitable source for doctrine, since this inevitably leads to changing the historic affirmations of the faith. He contended that the Scriptures were the historic source for the truths that historic Presbyterianism held dear. In response to Archaism's insistence on "sacred words," Machen put forth a Centrist theory of doctrinal development, which consisted of better definition and

133

a further clarification of the time honored doctrines of the Confession (Machen 1973:149-157).

But where, one might ask, did Professor Briggs fit in the continuum between Archaist and Futurist? After all, in the scholarly reinterpretation of 1881, he occupied, as I have argued, the Centrist position, urging the traditional meaning of the confession over against a "Fundamentalist" innovation. According to the historian John Hart, Briggs was a prime mover in the more popular drive for revision culminating in the revision of 1903 (Hart 1978:17). Was he a Centrist in this revision cause also? Actually, the Centrist faction in the revision of 1903 was not nearly as well defined as it was in the revision of 1881 since the Centrists were not the only ones to call for revision. This was part of the Futurist platform as well. The Centrist, though, was the more popular call for revision which represented a rather broad cross section of the denomination as a whole. Then there was the endorsement by certain Presbyterian theologians, spearheaded by professors like Charles Briggs and Philip Schaff of Union Seminary. Philip Schaff recounts both the impetus and the rationale of the revision movement as a whole:

> The General Assembly of 1889 has opened a new chapter in the history of American theology. This chapter involves some of the profoundest problems that have exercised the human mind since the days of St. Paul, and have never yet been satisfactory solved. The Presbyterian Creed Revision movement is inspired by the central truth of God's saving love *to all men* (John iii. 16), and the corresponding duty of preaching the gospel *to every creature*, in obedience to Christ's last command (Mark xvi. 15; Matthew xxvii. 19, 20). This truth and duty have taken a deeper hold on the mind and heart of the living Church than ever before, and must overrule the particularism and exclusivism of the Augustinian and Calvinistic system, with its doctrines of reprobation, preterition, and the wholesale damnation of the non-Christian world. The movement cannot be traced to any individual, nor to any theological school or party; nor has it any leader. Like the Kingdom of God, it has come "without observation." It has broken out suddenly, though not without long, silent preparation, and is spreading with astonishing rapidity over the Presbyterian Churches in Europe and America, among laymen as well as ministers. The participation of

intelligent elders in the discussion is a striking feature which distinguishes it from earlier theological controversies. The discussion has been conducted so far with admirable Christian temper. May its further progress give an example to the world that theologians can engage in a tournament of thought as courteous and honorable gentlemen, "with malice towards none, with charity for all." In battling against each other, they also battle for the common end—the promotion of truth which both have at heart, with all good men, as the supreme object of their desire. I was unexpectedly, though not unwillingly, drawn into this discussion. I take my stand on the side of revision of the Westminster Creed, in accordance with the advanced stage of theology and Christianity.... (Schaff 1890:v-vi.)

Schaff believed that revision would consist of '...sundry improvements in minor details without detriment to the substance' (Schaff 1890:1). Charles Briggs, however, did not share Schaff's more moderate (Centrist) vision for the revision of the confession. What Briggs wanted was a revision of a more radical sort. As a rational for his more radical vision, Briggs believed that 'an advance in the study of the Bible (was) the nerve of the revision movement' (Briggs 1890b:46). Since it has already been shown that Briggs's whole life was devoted to disseminating the views of the higher-critical method, I do not think it unreasonable to assume that this was what he meant by "an advance in the study of the Bible." Mark Massa also sees the connection, for Briggs, between confessional revision and the furtherance of his higher critical views. In making this connection, Massa demonstrates that in his desire for revision Briggs was not a Centrist but a Futurist. 'For Briggs saw in the creedal revision issue,' writes Massa, 'the most immediate, practical opportunity to present the needed scientific theology in a form accessible to church-going Christians, while reconstructing the entire Reformed doctrinal system along more critical, modern lines' (Massa 1990:78).

In order to distance himself from the prevailing standards of the Church, Briggs proposed a dichotomy between what he called "orthodoxism"—Presbyterianism under the prevailing confessional standards—and "orthodoxy"—Presbyterianism as he envisioned it after the necessary confessional changes. He wrote concerning the prevailing orthodoxy:

> Orthodoxism assumes to know the truth and is unwilling to learn; it is haughty and arrogant, assuming the divine prerogatives of infallibility and inerrancy; it hates all truth that is unfamiliar to it, and persecutes it to the uttermost. ...(Orthodoxism) refuses to accept the discoveries of science or the truths of philosophy or the facts of history... on the pretense that it conflicts with (the) orthodoxy of the standards of (the) church, prefer(ing) the traditions of man to the truth of God.... (Briggs 1889 :7, 9.)

In an article in the *Andover Review*, Briggs made his more radical intentions for confessional revision perfectly clear. He wrote that 'Such a revision can be made only in the form of a new creed, that will be born of the life, experience, and worship of our age' (Briggs 1890b:60).

In light of these statements from Briggs, I think two observations are in order. 1) The changes to the confession proposed by Briggs were sweeping as opposed to the more moderate ones sought by his colleague at Union, Philip Schaff. In fact, Briggs wanted an entirely new confessional statement, as opposed to Schaff, who preferred to update and clarify the existing document. This in itself did not put Briggs in a Futurist category, but the scope of his proposed confessional changes did. Briggs wanted a statement of faith that was more amenable with the findings of modern science, philosophy, history, and psychology. He wanted a creed, as he said, '...born of the life, experience, and worship of our age' (Briggs 1890b:60), which would inevitably change the confessional affirmations of historic Presbyterianism. In his desire to alter radically Presbyterianism's confessional statement Briggs was a Futurist. 2) I would suggest that, in his aim to base his new confessional statement on the life and experience of the age, Briggs was also a historicist. His theology thus would not come from the same sources as that of traditional Presbyterianism—Scripture and the Confession, rather it would come from the contemporary collective experience of believers. In this assessment I am giving Briggs the benefit of the doubt by assuming that when he referred "our age" he meant Christian believers. The benefit of the doubt, however, was not accorded to him by all. There were more than a few who believed that 'Dr. Briggs has undertaken to write the Presbyterian Church out of existence' (Massa 1990:80). This seems to be a fairly clear indication that what others saw in Professor Briggs's work, with respect to confessional revision, is what I have elsewhere labeled "Futurism."

A committee to study the idea of revision in detail was appointed by the General Assembly of 1901, with Dr. Henry van Dyke, an English Professor at Princeton University, as its chairman (Hart 1978:18). Henry van Dyke was well acquainted with Professor Briggs; having defended him before the prosecuting committee in the first year of his heresy trial (Massa 1990:98). In a pamphlet dating from 1893, Van Dyke indicated what areas of the Westminster Confession he would have liked to see amended. Standing mid-way between Philip Schaff who wanted clarification of existing doctrine and Charles Briggs who wanted a new confession, Van Dyke

> ...was deeply offended, personally and theologically, about statements in the Westminster Confession of Faith relating to eternal damnation and the implication that 'elect infants' meant some infants would be sent to Hell. As early as 1893, in a privately printed pamphlet entitled Is This Calvinism or Christianity? He emphatically repudiated this doctrine as unscriptural and unchristian. It was, he wrote, 'a horrible doctrine', and he took his place with those who were advocating a revision or declaratory qualification of the doctrine. At the end of the pamphlet, he wrote: 'I intend to keep right on disbelieving and ignoring that doctrine, and if necessary denying it, by teaching that there are no infants in Hell, and no self-imposed limits on God's love.... Is that Calvinism? I do not know. I do not care. It is Christianity. (Kerr 1988:297.)

The revision committee, chaired by Van Dyke, made its recommendations to the General Assembly of 1902, recommendations which were eventually adopted by the General Assembly (see appendix I for the sections of the Confession revised in 1903). Lefferts Loetscher recounts the changes proposed by the committee:

> Making use of the discretion granted it, the committee employed three methods of revision—by declaratory statement, by textual modifications, and by supplementary statement. A Declaratory Statement

explained that "Chapter III, of God's Eternal Decree," was to be interpreted in harmony with the belief that God loves all mankind; and that Chapter X, Section 3, which speaks of "elect infants" "is not to be regarded as teaching that any who die in infancy are lost. We believe that all dying in infancy are included in the election of grace." The committee proposed three textual modifications. In Chapter XVI, 7, which discusses the good deeds of unregenerate men, the committee recommended slight verbal alterations, especially to change the statement that these deeds are "sinful" to read "they come short of what God requires." The committee suggested omitting from Chapter XXII , 3, the statement that it is sinful to refuse a legal oath, and dropped from Chapter XXV, 6, the accusation that "the Pope of Rome" is "antichrist." The third type of revision, supplementary statement, was used to add two new chapters to the Confession entitled, respectively, "Of the Holy Spirit" and "Of the love of God and Missions. (Loetscher 1954:87.)

The significance of these changes to the Confession, especially the addition of two new chapters, was to make the Confession more personal. By the removal of several harsh statements and the addition of the new chapters, the meaning of the Confession was not changed. Rather, its meaning was further clarified. The changes emphasized the love of God for humanity, even with respect to election, not viewing the two as mutually exclusive. Not willing to consign any of those who die in infancy to perdition, one amendment stipulated that these infants are also "included in the election of grace." Another amendment recast the wording for all the deeds of man as not entirely "sinful,' but rather as "coming short of what God requires," thereby removing the more fatalistic associations. The revision also dropped the section designating as "sinful" a refusal to take a "lawful" oath, as well as the section calling the Pope of Rome "the Antichrist." The two additional chapters, "Of the Holy Spirit" and "Of the Love of God and Missions," were simply new categories set up to clarify, under separate headings, what the Confession said elsewhere.

Benjamin Warfield of Princeton resisted the confessional revision every step of the way (Loetscher 1954:89). Oddly enough though, as Loetscher relates, 'his (Warfield's) criticisms of the revision overtures were directed against their diction rather than their theology. "there are few accurately conceived or justly expressed sentences in them," he said, "Why should a great Church adopt such a body of loosely expressed sentences as part of its profession of faith'" (Loetscher 1954:89). Contrary to the objections of Warfield, and others, the vote at the 1903 General Assembly favored the revision. While not concurring with the changes adopted in 1903, Warfield tacitly admitted that the meaning of the Confession was not altered in the revision process. In fact, in a rather disapproving sort of way, he even conceded that doctrinal development actually took place:

> It would not be true to say that either the Declaratory Statement or the whole mass of revision accomplished in 1903 in any way or to any degree modifies our doctrinal system: though it may possibly be true that some elements of truth not always recognized as provided for in our doctrinal system are emphasized in it. (Warfield 1904b:298.)

Voicing a more positive note, and exhibiting a more Centrist perspective on the whole matter of revision, Philadelphia's *Public Ledger*

> ...hastened to pay its editorial tribute to the Church's action. Viewing the spreading belief in divine immanence as well as current tendencies to simplify theology as forces operating against Calvinism, the *Ledger* marveled at the vitality of Presbyterianism which without altering the basic doctrines of its Confession was able "to render it instantly so much more congenial to the modern mind." (Loetscher 1954:89.)

The Liberal faction in the Presbyterian Church, taking a more Futurist view of the changes adopted, believed that 'while relieving some pressure, these limited amendments failed to give the church a really contemporary expression of its faith' (Loetscher 1978:131). They saw this deficiency as eventually leading to a situation in which ministerial subscription was more politicized, being '...broadly interpreted by ordaining presbyteries' (Loetscher 1978:131), and in which the church would ultimately be deprived of '...an agreed-upon norm of its real present faith' (Loetscher 1978:131).

In the revision of 1903 the popular, Centrist, thrust for better definition and clarification of the existing confessional statement won the day. The Archaists simply resisted any change as unhealthy in itself. The Futurists, on the other hand, wanted to write an entirely new confessional statement; one that was more in line with the "spirit of the age." In the deliberations that surrounded the revision, it seemed that Benjamin Warfield of Princeton Seminary led the opposition. Charles Briggs, by wanting to substitute a confessional statement that was more in line with modern philosophy and science in place of the Westminster Confession, revealed a decidedly Futurist disposition in the matter. Centrism was amply represented by Philip Schaff and Henry Van Dyke, whose concern for clarification, and thus development, of the existing faith overshadowed more radical opinions on both the right and the left.

That the revision accomplished was of a Centrist inclination is evident from the objections from the opposition. The most that Warfield could say by way of opposition was that the diction of it all was superfluous. After the changes were adopted, he declared that the changes amounted to nothing as far as the original meaning of the confession was concerned. Hence, according to Warfield, the changes made to the confession amounted to nothing. This was essentially the same position as that of the Futurists. The Futurists saw the changes as mere token changes, with nothing of substance being accomplished. The motivation in saying this was their desire for an entirely new confessional statement, one which, probably, given some of their statements, would have bore little, if any, resemblance to the traditional symbol of Presbyterianism, that is, the Westminster Confession of Faith. Given these criticisms from the opposition on both sides, I think it reasonable to say that the Centrist cause triumphed in the revision of 1903.

Was there development of doctrine in the revision of 1903? I think that the answer to this question is a definite "yes," and that the proof for this position is again seen in the words of the opposition. Development is not a break with the past, it is continuity with it. The development in 1903 took the form of further defining and clarifying objectionable and obscure doctrinal statements in the existing Confession and amplifying areas, by means of two new chapters, which the Confession only touched upon elsewhere in the course of discussing other topics. Even Warfield himself was quoted as saying of those sections revised in 1903: '...that some elements of truth not always recognized as provided for in our doctrinal system are emphasized in it (the revision)' (Warfield 1904b:298). The revision consisted of removing or amending some of the harsher, more objectionable, statements of the Confession such as: those who die in infancy are now considered as being included in the "election of grace;" no longer is the Pope of Rome described as the Antichrist; no longer looking are all the deeds of humanity viewed as "sinful" but rather as a "falling short of what God requires;" and the section on "lawful oaths" was removed altogether. The addition of the two new chapters, Of the Holy Spirit and Of the Love of God and Missions, drew together under separate headings what the Confession only said elsewhere in the course of expounding other doctrines. The result of the changes enacted in 1903 were of a simple sort: God was said to have more concern for mankind in general, as opposed to just a select core group, and statements belittling humanity were toned down a bit, giving humanity more dignity in the unfathomable designs of God's Providence. In the end, God was brought a little closer to man, and man to God.

The Archaists were against development altogether since, generally, they were against revision of any sort. They seemed to be suggesting, moreover, that the revision was a failure since it really did not change anything in the existing statement of faith. Yet, the stated goal of the revision was not to change the existing affirmations of the faith, but to clarify and simplify those affirmations. The goal of the revision must, therefore, have been accomplished or the Archaists would have complained bitterly—which they did not do—of material changes to the historic affirmations of the faith as originally set forth in the Westminster Confession. The Futurist platform to change the confession altogether would have resulted in a radical change in the historic affirmation of the Reformed faith; this is especially so given the sources proposed for the new tenets of the faith, such as contemporary experience, life, and worship—McGrath's Tradition 2 (McGrath 1993:135-136). Thus, neither the staid Anarchism nor the innovative Futurism advocated a program for the development of doctrine. Only the Centrist position, with its focus on the revision of the existing confessional statements—McGrath's Tradition 1 (McGrath 1993:135-136)—, qualified as a genuine of development of doctrine.

Contemporary Presbyterian historian Bradley Longfield said that: 'though doctrinal revision can always be a matter of debate, it seems clear that the confessional revision of 1903 hardly made the Presbyterian Church an Arminian body' (Longfield 1991:24). Longfield surmised, as did Warfield, that things in Presbyterianism remained essentially the same. Many people in the Cumberland Presbyterian Church, however, did not entirely agree. They saw the 1903 revision as making the Presbyterian Church USA significantly more acceptable to them. It is to this positive evaluation and subsequent reunion of the two Presbyterian bodies that we must now turn our attention.

4.3 Reunion

Many in the Presbyterian Church USA thought that the confessional revision, as enacted in 1903, gave much greater clarity to the standards of the faith. The first group, however, to take action on the basis of the changes resulting from the revision was the Cumberland Presbyterian Church; a body regarded by some in the Presbyterian Church USA as decidedly non-Reformed in their theology. Almost as soon as the revision was enacted, representatives of both churches began discussing, unofficially at first, the possibilities of a merger of the two churches (Hart 1978:19) In fact, according to John Hart, 'At the General Assembly of 1904 (Presbyterian Church USA), various delegates (Including J. Ross Stevenson, a professor at McCormick Seminary and soon to become president of Princeton Seminary) stated that a union "ought to exist" with the Cumberland Presbyterian Church' (Hart 1978:19). In 1906, two thirds of the presbyteries of the Presbyterian Church USA voted to make the proposed merger a reality. John Hart has argued that 'The union with the Cumberland Church brought the first phase of the Fundamentalist-Modernist controversy within Presbyterianism to an end. During this period, the Church had indicated its ambivalence about the future; at the same time, the strength of the new theology had become apparent' (Hart 1978:19). I take his reference to "the new theology" as a reference to the rising tide of Liberalism, which I also refer to as Futurism, in the Presbyterian Church. Lefferts Loetscher was also persuaded that theological problems would eventually arise from the Cumberland merger. He wrote that,

> The union with the Cumberland Church had unmistakable theological implications. The Presbyterian General Assembly had officially declared that there was sufficient theological agreement to warrant union with a Church which some had previously regarded as non-Calvinistic. ...The action involved an official broadening of the Church's attitude towards certain doctrines [According to the Archaists, those doctrines which had traditionally flowed from the concept of the sovereignty

142

of God were at issue-PB]. In the coming years, too, many of the former Cumberland men supported the party favoring broader theological policies. (Loetscher 1954:96-97.)

Benjamin Warfield, showing both a distrust and a certain dislike for his Cumberland brethren, commented that 'it is distressingly easy for signatories of differing traditions to attach differing interpretations to documents they sign in common' (Warfield 1904b:302). He was correct, though, when he pointed out, urging a certain caution, that '...our Cumberland brethren do not come to us out of the sky, as it were, with no past behind them, with no present accompanying them—with only a future lying before them and us' (Warfield 1904b:304). The history of the Cumberland Church was, for many of the Old School mind, a sordid history indeed.

The Cumberland Church takes its name from the county in Kentucky in which it was born. It was a child of the revivals, which according to William Warren Sweet of the University of Chicago were '...often called the second Great Awakening....' (Sweet [1944]1965:119) produced by the coordinated efforts of the Presbyterian Church of the Middle States and New England Congregationalism (Sweet [1944]1965:119-134). In 1801 the "Plan of Union" between the Congregationalists and the Presbyterian Church in the USA was initiated for the express purpose of evangelizing the frontier of the expanding states (Marsden 1970:10-12). Kentucky became just another place where these combined efforts were manifested in a very memorable, and visible, way. The spectacle of revival is captured vividly by William Warren Sweet:

> The camp meeting likewise originated among western Presbyterians, and the most spectacular one ever held, that at Cane Ridge, Kentucky, in August 1801, was organized under their leadership. The first great Presbyterian frontier revivalist in the West was James McGready, and it was as a result of the drawing power of his revivalistic preaching that the camp meeting movement was inaugurated. ...The great Cane Ridge camp meeting in Bourbon County in August 1801, is the dividing point in western Presbyterianism. Barton W. Stone was the Presbyterian minister most responsible for

143

this spectacular gathering. It was a general camp meeting and people of all denominations attended. The numerous contemporary accounts all agree in the vast multitudes on the ground and the awe-inspiring effects produced. ...The "falling exercise" was generally considered a clear manifestation of the power of God working on the hearts of people. The other exercises agitated hundreds, as jerking, rolling, dancing, and barking, were looked upon as dubious, to say the least. Throughout it all—the meeting lasted for several days—there was constant noise and confusion. Many who attended were dissolute and irreligious characters, and they outnumbered by far those who came with religious intent. There was much drinking of raw whiskey plentifully supplied by hucksters from wagons on the outskirts of the campgrounds. To those accustomed to quietness, dignity, and order in worship such confusion was, of course, most distasteful and many looked upon it as a travesty on religion. (Sweet [1944]1965:122-124.)

This New England revivalism, which began for all practical purposes with Jonathan Edwards in Massachusetts (Sweet [1944]1965:30-31), and which manifested itself in the "camp meeting" in western Kentucky (Sweet [1944]1965:124), became part of the very fabric of the Cumberland Presbyterian Church. The chief characteristic of revival and the "camp meeting," as they gained momentum throughout this section of the country was the singular emphasis on experience (Sweet [1944]1965:119-128, Loetscher 1978:78-79). In this respect, the Cumberland Church was no exception. The revival had, moreover, always complained against Calvinism and '...its tyranny over religious experience' (Hatch 1989:171). Even though the revivalism of Kentucky originated in the Presbyterian Church, a church whose symbols are traditionally Reformed, '...the kind of revivalism which swept the frontier was Arminian in emphasis' (Sweet [1944]1965:128). Timothy Smith, author of *Revivalism and Social Reform*, writes that '...revivalism and Arminianism went hand in hand' (Smith [1957]1976:27). Smith goes on to say that, by 1855, Cumberland Presbyterians '...had long since declared for free will and a universal election of grace' (Smith [1957]1976:28). If the human will is bound, they contended, evangelism, the revival, is futile. For the preaching of the Gospel to be of any use to the sinner, he or she must be able respond to it in a positive way. Calvinism's insistence

144

on God's sovereign choice in human conversion, outlined in chapter 3 of the Westminster Confession (Leith 1982:198-199) was simply unacceptable from a purely practical point of view. Correlatively, the older idea of original sin as imputed guilt was also replaced with the idea of the 'diseased condition of the moral nature' (Smith [1957]1976:28).

In New England, the ideas of the revival, when systematized, became known as the New Divinity. According to Allen Guelzo, '...the New Divinity was the first indigenous American theology' (Guelzo 1989:137). In assigning the New Divinity a class of its own on the theological spectrum Guelzo is undoubtedly correct, but to give it the distinction of being the first indigenous American theology may represent somewhat of an overstatement. In considering Edwards the origin of this new thought, Guelzo, however, rightly identified the theological basis of revival. As he points out,

> A little reflection, however, will show that the New Divinity doctrine represented hardly more than an elaboration on the foundation Edwards himself had laid. First, by abandoning the imputation of Adam's sin as the grounds of natural depravity, Edwards had already undercut any similar imputed connection between Christ and the elect. Second, and far more important, the New Divinity balked at the idea of a limited atonement because it seemed to conflict with Edwards's notion of the natural ability of all sinners to repent. Limited atonement implied that, for some, repentance was doomed to be a natural inability. As Bellamy saw it, the chief virtue of an unlimited atonement was precisely this: "it is attributed to sinners themselves that they perish at last—even to their own voluntary conduct." It is true that nothing in Edwards's published works openly embraces a governmental or unlimited atonement. But in his private notebooks—the bulk of which remain unpublished—he inclined sharply towards such ideas.... (Thus) the New Divinity was an Edwardsean movement.... Above all, the New Divinity was a prescription for Edwardsean revival.... (Guelzo 1986:161-163.)

It was this Edwardsean revival, occurring outside of the confines of New England, which gave birth to the Cumberland Presbyterian Church.

Presbyterians residing in Kentucky, Tennessee, and adjoining areas, themselves the results of the revival, constituted themselves as a separate entity on 10 February 1810, in protest over actions initiated by the Presbyterian Church. 'About the year 1799 or 1800,' related Finis Ewing, one of the founders of the new movement, 'God revived religion in a remarkable manner in the western country, through the instrumentality of some Presbyterian preachers; consequently, many new congregations were soon formed and organized. But to continue to supply them all, by the then licensed and ordained ministers was impracticable' (Ewing [1814] 1826:486). Since Presbyterianism had always insisted on a ministry thoroughly trained in the classics and sciences as well as in theology, no significant increase in pulpit supply was forthcoming. Responding to a growing need for clergy to minister to the increasing numbers, the preachers who were at the forefront of the growing revival decided to choose from amongst the laity, encouraging them to prepare themselves for the work of the ministry. A bold move, this proposal did not meet with the favor of those in authority in the established church. Nothing, however, was done in haste. The men from Kentucky and Tennessee were not admitted to the Gospel ministry solely on the basis of the needs of the moment. They were made to study for a period, two years or more, periodically writing reports on assigned topics, in addition to themes of their own individual interest. From the view of the classical standards required, they were, however, still woefully deficient. Not one of the three young men chosen by the preachers conducting the revival had any knowledge of the biblical languages, Hebrew and Greek, or Latin (Ewing [1814] 1826:485-489).

From the perspective of historic Presbyterianism, and the ministerial qualifications set down by the Westminster Assembly, this arrangement arrived at by the proponents of revival in Kentucky was unacceptable. The *Directory for the Public Worship of God*, in a subsection entitled "Of the Preaching of the Word," reads: 'It is presupposed, (according to the rules for ordination,) that the minister of Christ is in some good measure gifted for so weighty a service, by his skill in the original languages, and in the arts and sciences...' (Westminster Assembly [1645] 1983:379). Another of the historic standards of the Westminster Assembly, *The Form of Church-Government*, defined these ministerial qualifications further under the sub-head of rules for examinations. It stipulated that: 'He (the ministerial candidate) shall be examined touching his skill in the original tongues, and his trial to be made by reading the Hebrew and Greek Testaments, and rendering some portion of some into Latin; and if he be defective in them, enquiry shall be made more strictly after his other learning, and whether he hath skill in logick and philosophy' (Westminster Assembly [1645] 1983:413). The latter document made provision in extraordinary circumstances for actions outside the established order imposed by the Assembly, with the stipulation that, when good order was established, the matter dealt with extraordinarily may be reviewed (Westminster Assembly [1645] 1983:412).

Evidently, the needs of the Kentucky synod did not, in the minds of some, meet the requirements of the Westminster Assembly for extraordinary measures to be undertaken. Disagreement over this point led those in Kentucky who were closer to the situation, and who considered themselves in a better position to evaluate it than others at great distance, to take those steps which they considered proper. At the meeting of the presbytery in 1809 three candidates were received into the ministry of the Word in the Presbyterian Church; they were: Alexander Anderson, Finis Ewing and Samuel King. As Ewing himself relates:

> These men, although two of them had no knowledge of the dead languages; yet from their discourses, extempore, as well as written, and from the petitions of hundreds of serious Christians, praying that they might be licensed; the Presbytery thought they could not be out of their duty in promoting them to the work of the ministry; in which opinion they were afterwards fully confirmed. (Ewing [1814] 1826:486.)

Even though the presbytery was earnest in its intentions, several protests were immediately filed with the denomination complaining of irregularities within the presbytery. This action divided the licensing presbytery who, by majority vote, reconstituted themselves as the Cumberland Presbytery. This action occurred, according to Finis Ewing, because of those in the presbytery who were unfriendly to revival (Ewing [1814] 1826:486). The Presbyterian Church tried to mediate this growing rift. A commission appointed by the presbytery of jurisdiction summarily ordered those of the newly constituted Cumberland Presbytery to gather and to give an account of their actions, an order that the Cumberland Presbytery complied with eagerly (Ewing [1814] 1826:486). The charges issued were essentially two: 'First, Licensing men to preach who had not been examined on the languages. Second, That those men who were licensed, both learned and less learned, had been only required to adopt the confession of faith partially, that is, as far as they believed it to agree with God's word' (Ewing [1814] 1826:486). On the first point the Cumberland Presbytery invoked the *Westminster Directory* and its provision for extraordinary cases. Additionally, they appealed to the New Testament, inquiring of the commission whether there was any precept upon which they based their charges of ordaining 'unlearned' men. Is it not possible, they questioned, whether '...God could not as easily call a *Presbyterian* not classically learned, to preach the Gospel, as he could such of any other denomination' (Ewing [1814] 1826:486)?

The second point, relating to the doctrines of the Confession, seemed to be another matter entirely. 'With respect to the doctrines,' Ewing says, 'the presbytery believed their candidates had departed from no *essential* doctrine taught in the confession of faith; and therefore ought to have been indulged in their conscientious scruples about tenets not *essential* or important' (Ewing [1814] 1826:486). The wider church did not see eye to eye with the newly constituted Cumberland Presbytery in this matter. In fact, the commissioners ordered those whose ordination was under consideration to be surrendered for further examination and evaluation by the larger body. In this the Cumberland Presbytery refused to accede, seeing this demand as an unwarranted encroachment upon the prerogatives and privileges granted by the Westminster Assembly to presbyteries (Ewing [1814] 1826:486-487).

Having seen no success in dealing with the Cumberland Presbytery as a whole, the Presbyterian commissioners then ordered the young candidates to submit individually and of their own accord. The candidates, siding with their presbytery, summarily refused; whereupon the commissioners pronounced a sort of Protestant interdict on the entire Cumberland Presbytery. This judgment prohibited all within the Cumberland Presbytery from preaching or from administering of the sacraments until a resolution could be reached. For a while afterwards, it seemed that the General Assembly of the Presbyterian Church might have been willing to admit the impropriety of these rather harsh measures. This impression gave many in the Cumberland Presbytery hope for a speedy resolution to the ongoing dispute. They petitioned, argued, and prayed for almost four years that the matter be dealt with finally, but it was not to be. In which case the three Cumberland ministers, Samuel M'Adow, Finis Ewing and Samuel King, after becoming convinced that the Presbyterian Church saw itself as justified in its illegal acts, decided to chart their own course as the Cumberland

Presbyterian Church (Ewing [1814] 1826: 486-489). Cumberland historian Hubert Morrow relates the details of their decision:

> When Samuel M'Adow, Samuel King and Finis Ewing reorganized Cumberland Presbytery in 1810, they reaffirmed their loyalty to the Westminster Confession. At the same time they asserted the right to scruple with respect to any doctrine contained in the Confession that was not fully in keeping with Scripture. This right to scruple was established by a New Jersey minister, Jonathan Dickinson, as the key condition to the compromise in 1729 that ended the Subscription Controversy in American Presbyterianism. The Subscription Controversy was over a proposal to make the Westminster Confession the doctrinal standard of American Presbyterianism. Dickinson said he would subscribe to the Westminster Confession provided there was agreement that he or any other person were given the right to scruple about points of doctrine that were judged to be non-essential. The right was important, Dickinson said, because "...subscription to any human composure as the Test of our Orthodoxy, is to make it the standard of our Faith; and Hereby to give it the Honor only due to the Word of God." The particular doctrines about which M'Adow, King and Ewing had scruples were predestination and the limited atonement. These doctrines do not fit into the category of non-essential, but the authority of a document of "human composure" in relation to Scripture was at issue. (Morrow 1994:17.)

In the declaration by which the Cumberland Presbytery was reconstituted as the Cumberland Presbyterian Church, the three young ministers stated the objects of their scruples point by point. It reads in part:

> They dissent from the Confession—in, 1st, That there are no *eternal* reprobates.—2nd, That Christ died not for a *part only*, but for *all* mankind.—3rd, That all infants, dying in infancy are saved through Christ, and sanctification of the Spirit.—4th, That the Spirit of God operates on the *world*, or as co-extensively as Christ has

made the atonement, in such a manner as to leave all men inexcusable.

As to the doctrines of predestination and election, they think, (with many eminent and modest divines who have written of the subject,) they are mysterious, and they are not well pleased with the application that rigid Calvinists, or Arminians make of them. They think the truth, or *that*, as well as many other points in divinity, lies between the opposite extremes. They are confident however, that those doctrines should not, on the one hand be so construed as to make any thing the creature has done, or *can* do, at all meritorious in his salvation; or to lay any ground to say "well done I;" or to take the least degree of the honour of our justification and perseverance from God's unmerited grace, and Christ's pure righteousness. On the other hand, they are equally confident those doctrines should not be so construed as to make God the author of sin, directly or indirectly; either of Adam's sin, or any subsequent sin of his fallen race; or to contradict the express and repeated declarations of God's word, on the extent of the atonement and operations of the Spirit; or to contradict the sincerity of God's expostulations with sinners, and make his oath to have no meaning, when he swears he has no pleasure in their death; or to resolve the whole character of the Deity into his sovereignty, without due regard to all other of his adorable attributes. Finally, they think those doctrines ought to be thought and spoken of in a consistency with God's moral government, which always has for its object the happiness of his intelligent creatures, when it consists with his justice and honour of the divine throne. (quoted by Ewing [1814] 1826:488.)

When the young ministers declared that they stood in the company of a long line of eminent divines in regard to their particular theological emphases, they spoke the truth. Although the Presbyterian Church USA refused to hear their case because of a prejudice against revival theology (Sweet [1944]1965:112-140), it is significant that none of the founders of the Cumberland Presbyterian Church were ever accused of heresy, which further served to validate the Cumberland's claim to a place in Presbyterianism. Their theology, not accepted in its entirety by those churches which considered themselves Reformed, nonetheless, still hearkens back to the Reformation; that is to say, they were also part of that great movement in covenant theology. One stream of covenant theology has been known as Calvinism. The other stream has been known as Arminianism.

Calvinism has taught that God and man were related solely in terms of a covenant. A covenant which God both established and maintained out of His good pleasure with those whom He had chosen from all eternity. This relationship is essentially one-sided; it is ultimately governed by God's eternal decree, which again is based on nothing other than God's good pleasure. Reformed theologians have made much of the distinction between those vessels created for honor and those vessels created for dishonor. All of which was due entirely to the sovereign discretion of the creator. As Calvin himself wrote:

> Again I ask: whence does it happen that Adam's fall irremediably involved so many peoples, together with their infant offspring, in eternal death unless because it so pleased God? Here their tongues, otherwise so loquacious, must become mute. The decree is dreadful indeed, I confess. Yet no one can deny that God foreknew what end man was to have before he created him, and consequently foreknew because he so ordained by his decree. If anyone inveighs against God's foreknowledge at this point, he stumbles rashly and heedlessly. What reason is there to accuse the Heavenly Judge because he was not ignorant of what was to happen? If there is any just or manifest complaint, it applies to predestination. And it ought not to seem absurd for me to say that God not only foresaw the fall of the first man, and in him the ruin of his descendants, but also meted it out in accordance with his own decision. (Calvin 1960:955-956.)

Arminius, who had studied for a time in Calvin's Geneva, and others militated against this view of Calvin's, especially as it was given a more rigorous slant by Theodore Beza, Calvin's successor. They maintained that Calvinism makes God the author of sin, a charge which the Scriptures repudiate. Then there were the reprobate: a whole class of people who were condemned by God to eternal suffering before they were ever born or had had the opportunity to do either good or evil. As Carl Bangs, biographer of Arminius, explains:

> There is, then, a determinate class of people born reprobate. Of these, some are cut off as infants, but others are allowed to come to maturity, to whom is reserved "a more sharp judgment." But how are such mature reprobates to regard themselves? Well, they are in ignorance about it, because one difference between election and reprobation is that the former is revealed to the individual (but not to anyone else) by the Spirit of God, while reprobation "is ever hidden from man, except it be disclosed by God, contrary to the common course of things." A person whose election is doubted by himself and by others, even for manifestly good cause, should nevertheless not give up hope, "for who can tell, if God has determined to show mercy at the last hour of death to him who has spent all his life past lewdly and wickedly." (Bangs 1971:69-70.)

All this choosing on the part of the all-powerful God was understood as taking place within the context of a covenant. It was done relationally, but one in which humanity had absolutely no say, as God had dictated the terms and then fulfilled those terms in whomsoever He wished. These ideas were abhorrent to the covenant theologians of the seventeenth century who followed Arminius. For them, God's covenant was not without conditions aimed at humanity. The part given humanity was the whole object of the redemption tendered by the suffering of Christ. All had been children of God; and, likewise, all had gone astray. But God, they maintained, had sought man out because of His great love, and determined then and there to make provision for the whole host of his shortcomings, all of which were an affront to the holiness of the God of the universe. Arminius gave humanity a place of importance in the plan of God. He gave humanity a responsibility towards God which had been downplayed by the prevailing Calvinism. These digressions from the Calvinistic concept of the unconditional covenant were nevertheless seen by Arminius's followers and theological heirs as developments within the covenant scheme. Speaking specifically of seventeenth-century "federal theology," Richard Muller describes succinctly the Remonstrant (Arminian) advance. 'Arminius's concept of the covenant,' he argues, has all the characteristics of a suzerainty treaty into which God enters unilaterally but which, once unilaterally decreed, has a bilateral function. Human responsibility before and relation with God arises under conditions set forth by God. Much of the development of Reformed covenant theology can in fact be described in terms of the incorporation of themes of divine sovereignty and human responsibility, of unilateral or monopleuric covenant and bilateral or duopleuric covenant into the federal language of theology. (Muller 1991:242-243.)

This renewed insistence on human responsibility tended to give covenant theology a more practical bent, inclining it away from its earlier focus on causality alone. A greater balance was being struck between the theoretical and the practical sides of humanity's covenantal relationship with God. Showing this development, Muller argues that

...the identification of theology as a practical, teleologically conceived discipline was typical of Reformed covenant theology in the seventeenth century.... Following Arminius, Remonstrant theology in the seventeenth century stood firm against a speculative, deductive approach to doctrine and consistently argued that theology, considered as a practical discipline, directed Christians towards both the proximate goal of moral goodness in this life and the ultimate (and ultimately related) goal of union with God, the highest good, in the next. (Muller 1991:68.)

As seventeenth-century Calvinism became increasingly intricate in its theological formulations, the laity clamored for "life." They wanted a relationship with God that could be experienced; a relationship that could be felt and rejoiced in; a relationship that met the needs of everyday Christians in everyday circumstances. In Europe "scholastic" Calvinism was being eclipsed by the growing appeal of a Dane, Søren Kierkegaard, as he methodically exposed the evils of a dead orthodoxy. A new era, one inspired by the more personal theology of Friedrich Schleiermacher, was about to dawn.

In America, while there was not an exact correspondence with events on the continent, similar sentiments were beginning to make their presence felt. The covenant theology of Calvin, as mediated through the more moderate Puritans, had become part of American culture. The drift from the unconditional covenant to one of a more conditional nature was already under way in Puritan New England. Testimony to this was the half-way covenant, a Puritan accommodation to divergent views in their own midst regarding the position of children in the covenant. Years later it was among the remnants of the Puritans that the Great Awakening began, bringing with it a revival theology geared to produce a visible emotional response. Human responsibility fast became the centerpiece of the New England theology, especially as it manifested itself in New Jersey and in the revivals in Tennessee and Kentucky. Hubert Morrow links the human responsibility of Arminianism with the New England revival theology in the course of discussing the preaching content of the latter. In America, he argues,

> ...(the development) that reinforced Arminianism in Reformed Theology was an intense interest in the conversion experience and the style of preaching which accompanied that interest. It was a style of preaching that made the most of the Covenant of Law, for it made a calculated appeal to the fear of eternal punishment and the hope of eternal happiness. In accordance with the Covenant of Law, it assumed that persons were by nature inclined to respond to appeals to their self-interest, what William Ames called "mercenary motives." The threat of punishment being regarded as the stronger of the two motives, the sermon always began with what Gilbert Tennant called the "terrors of the law." This was the part of the sermon that put the sinner in the hands of an angry God. When what was called "law work" was done thoroughly and a sufficient sense of doom was created in both the reason and the sensibility, the time was right for an appeal for a decision to the will. This was the point where the sermon focused on the satisfaction of God's justice through the substitutionary death of Jesus Christ and the merit of his perfect obedience of the law. Hearers were told that God was giving them a second chance in the Covenant of Grace. They could escape the penalty of an angry, vengeful God by claiming the benefits of the

Covenant of Grace. The doctrine of the Fall notwithstanding, this style of preaching assumed that there was still a sufficient capacity of reason to understand the differences in the destinies that were set before them, and sufficient freedom of the will to enable persons to choose the benefits of the Covenant of Grace. This kind of preaching was widespread in the liberal and New Side wing of the Presbyterian Church in America in the eighteenth century, and was particularly evident in the movement called the Great Awakening. (Morrow 1994:13-14.)

While the fathers of the Cumberland Presbyterian Church might well have considered their rendition of the Westminster Confession to be a proper balance between the extremes of both Calvinism and Arminianism, their singular emphasis on the freedom of the will with reference to humanity put them squarely on the Arminian side of covenant theology. It is in this sense that both the "new side" Presbyterians and the Cumberland Presbyterians were considered Liberal. In the days before it meant a glorification of culture over against supernatural religion, Liberal, with its cognate liberty, meant freedom. It meant intellectual and spiritual freedom from the "bondage of the will" advocated by a strict Calvinism. In Calvinism, with its sovereign God who predestines all that comes to pass, human freedom is at best a moot point. But these sons of the revival wanted more. They wanted a faith in which a person was responsible for his or her own acts, and where the human will was free to accept or to reject the gracious offer of eternal life put forth by a gracious God. They wanted a covenant with God in which a man was not just a "stock" or a "block", a meaningless piece of flotsam whose eternal destiny was sealed. They wanted a God whose love for his creation was real, and not conditioned by some decision originating in another world, or bound up with a "secret counsel." 'For this reason,' says Morrow, evaluating their motivation, 'the Cumberland Presbyterian revisers eliminated from the Westminster Confession all those references to the "secret counsel" of God' (Morrow 1965:122). Above all, they wanted a God whom they could call fair, whose ways were known and administered predictably for all men. Robert Donnel said of the Cumberland Church that she wanted to be free and responsible. He wrote that 'She was born in this land of liberty, and is properly called an American Church, if not the only one.... In a country of equal rights, it is the privilege of everyone to think freely, investigate fairly, and explain in the most simple, plain and candid manner' (quoted by Morrow 1994:20).

In October, 1813, the newly organized Cumberland Presbyterian Church undertook by a committee of four to prepare a confessional revision, a relative catechism and a book of discipline. Having stated in their organizing charter their aversion to the idea of "fatality" that, they believed, pervaded the Confession, they began their work with chapter 3 of the Westminster Confession: "Of God's Eternal Decrees," Instead of the traditional eight sections outlining in detail the decrees of God regarding creation, the work of Christ and "the doctrine of this high mystery of predestination," the Cumberland revision retained only two of the original sections of chapter 3, with only one sentence of the original left intact in section one. The Westminster Confession reads in chapter 1, section1:

> God, from all eternity, did, by his most wise and holy counsel of his own free will, freely and unchangeably ordain whatsoever comes to pass: yet so, as thereby neither is God the author of sin, nor is violence offered to the will of the creatures; nor is liberty or contingency of second clauses taken away, but rather established. (Westminster Assembly [1647] 1983:28.)

The revision acknowledged the holy and wise counsel of God in all things but refused to follow the Westminster Confession in its teaching of God's ordaining (fatalistic) powers. Since the revisers believed that any further elaboration did indeed make God the author of sin, they end by simply acknowledging the glory of God as the logical end of all His workings. The revision says: 'God did, by the most wise and holy counsel of his own will, determine to act or bring to pass, what should be for his own glory' (Cumberland Presbyterian Church 1815:8). They departed entirely from the Westminster Confession's denial that the decrees of God are in any way based on a foreknowledge of the natural outcome of events. The Cumberland revisers used chapter 3, section 2 to negate those concepts of the decrees of God which were inconsistent with their thinking and to lay the foundation of a positive statement of the relationship of God's decrees to humanity. They assert emphatically that 'God has not decreed anything respecting his creature man contrary to his revealed will or written word; which declares his sovereignty over all his creatures, the ample provision he hath made for their salvation, his determination to punish the finally impenitent, with everlasting destruction, and to save the true believer with an everlasting salvation' (Cumberland Presbyterian Church 1815:8). The authors hasten to add, by way of a footnote, their reasons for the revisions which they have adopted in this section. They wanted to demonstrate their understanding of the decrees of God as they relate to predestination, something which the Westminster Confession expounds in detail. They wrote:

> We think it best under the head of the Decrees, to write what we know to be incontrovertible from the plain word of God, than to darken counsel with words without knowledge. We have elsewhere acknowledged the doctrine of predestination to be a high mystery. We are therefore free to acknowledge that in our judgment it is easier to fix the limits, which man should not transcend, on either hand, than to give an intelligent elucidation of the subject. (Cumberland Presbyterian Church 1815:8-9.)

The revision removed any references to the predestination of God. In its stead, God's love for all men became the controlling factor in the shaping of all men's destinies, both Christian and non-Christian alike. This fact was made abundantly plain by their handling of the question of the salvation of infants in chapter 10, section 3. With results that were distinctly similar to the 1903 revision in the Presbyterian Church USA, the Cumberland Presbyterian Church revamped the Westminster Confession in light of its new understanding of God's predestination as outlined in their revision of section 3. The Westminster Confession in chapter 10, section 3 states: 'Elect infants, dying in infancy, are regenerated and saved by Christ through the Spirit, who worketh when, and where, and how he pleaseth. So also are all other elect persons, who are incapable of being outwardly called by the ministry of the word' (Westminster Assembly [1647] 1983:55). Rather than changing the entire section, only the first word was singled out for revision. Instead of reading 'elect infants,' it was changed to 'all infants.' Here one finds more in common with the English Methodist, Richard Watson, than with any of the Reformed theologians of the period. Starting from the belief that God is no respecter of persons, Watson wrote that:

> For, as it will be acknowledged, that some children, dying in infancy, are saved, it must follow, from this principle and axiom in the divine government, that all infants are saved: For the case of all infants, as to

innocence or guilt, sin or righteousness, being the same, and God, as a Judge, being "no respecter of persons," but regarding only the merits of the case, he cannot make this awful distinction as to them, that one part shall be eternally saved and the other eternally lost. That doctrine, therefore, which implies the perdition of infants cannot be congruous to the Scriptures of truth; but is utterly abhorrent to them. (Watson 1832:73.)

Later he stated that, 'we gladly admit, in opposition to the Calvinistic Baptists, that all children, dying before actual sin committed, are admitted into heaven through the merits of Christ...' (Watson 1832:418).

The work of Christ as the Son of God and the application of that work to humanity was one of the original doctrines about which Ewing, M'Adow, and King chose to exercise their right to scruple. Their conclusions were illustrated dramatically in the Confessional revision. Chapter 8 of the Westminster Confession, subtitled "Of Christ the Mediator," states in section 5 that

The Lord Jesus, by his perfect obedience and sacrifice of himself, which he through the eternal Spirit once offered up unto God, hath fully satisfied the justice of his Father; and purchased not only reconciliation, but an everlasting inheritance in the kingdom of heaven, for all those whom the Father hath given unto him. (Westminster Assembly [1647] 1983:49.)

The Cumberland revision, to remove any stain of the doctrine of election, changed the last seven words. Wanting to stress the freedom of the will, "whom the Father hath given unto him" became "who come to the Father by him" (Cumberland Presbyterian Church 1815:21). The biggest change to this part of the Confession, impacting directly the Reformed doctrine of the limited atonement, was exercised on section 8. The Westminster Confession says at this point that,

To all those for whom Christ hath purchased redemption, he doth certainly and effectually apply and communicate the same; making intercession for them; and revealing unto them, in and by the word, the mysteries of salvation; effectually persuading them by his Spirit to believe and obey; and governing their hearts by his almighty power and wisdom, in such manner and ways as are most consonant to his wonderful and unsearchable dispensation. (Westminster Assembly [1647] 1983:50-51.)

In the revision, the first half of section 8 was changed in order to remove anything of a limiting sort which might be construed as an obstacle to the offer of salvation to all men occasioned by Christ's mediatorial work:

> As Jesus Christ, by the grace of God, has tasted death for every man; and now makes intercession for transgressors; by virtue of which, the holy Spirit is given, to convince of sin, and enable the creature to believe and obey, governing the hearts of believers by his word and Spirit; overcoming all their enemies, by his mighty power and wisdom, in such manner and in ways as are most consonant to his wonderful and unsearchable dispensation. (Cumberland Presbyterian Church 1815:21-22.)

Here again the Cumberland revision agrees with the sentiments of Richard Watson, who devoted the first hundred pages of volume three of his *Theological Institutes* (1832) to the question of limited atonement. Watson was flatly against the idea that Christ did not die for all, but during the course of his thorough and systematic argument he made a telling statement. Wishing, as he says, to quote only the most pertinent works, he has chosen in his rebuttal 'to refer to a Mr. Scott rather than to the older divines of the same school, because it is often said that Calvinism is now modified and improved' (Watson 1832:19). The improvements, to which Watson referred, were the changes the concept of the covenant underwent after it left the first generation of Reformers. With the rise of Puritanism in Britain, the theological forebears of American Presbyterianism, covenant theology took to itself in some quarters the idea of the conditional covenant. Arminian in origin, the proponents of the conditional covenant saw anything unconditional, whether an unconditional covenant or unconditional election, as an invitation to licentiousness (Watson 1832:50). This shift to a conditional understanding was continually opposed by those who insisted that the covenant was unconditional. (See RT Kendall 1979 for a detailed discussion of this transformation of the Reformed view of the covenant.) Philip Schaff, speaking before the whole presbytery of the state of New York in 1889 during debates on the revision of the Westminster

Confession, showed that there was a also a growing desire for a more conditional view of the covenant relationship between God and humanity present in the Presbyterian Church in the USA prior to the 1903 revision. Schaff declared that,

> A growing number of ministers, elders, and students are calling for relief from bondage to certain doctrines which the theology of the age has outgrown, which are no more taught in the pulpit and would not be tolerated in the pews.... I know of no Presbyterian minister in these United States who preaches the decree of reprobation or preterition, the irresponsibility of the sinner for not accepting the gospel, the limitation of the atonement to a small circle of the elect, and the eternal damnation of non-elect infants dying in infancy, and the damnation of the non-Christian world—heathen, Jews, and Mohammedans—who still constitute by far the greatest part of mankind. And yet these doctrines are supposed to be taught expressly or implicitly in the Westminster standards. If not, let us disown them publicly and officially beyond the power of contradiction. What cannot be preached in the pulpit ought not to be taught in a Confession of Faith, either expressly or by fair logical inference. On the other hand, what is taught in the Confession ought to be preached in the pulpit. The great and most serious objection to the Westminster Confession is the overstatement of divine sovereignty, at the expense, if not the exclusion, of human responsibility, and the overstatement of the doctrine of particular or partial election, to the exclusion of the general love of God to all his creatures. The last is nowhere mentioned. It is a Confession for the exclusive benefit of the elect. To this small inside circle all is bright and hopeful; but outside of it all is dark as midnight. It is the product of the most polemical and most intolerant age of Christendom. (Schaff 1890:13-14.)

It took thirteen years from the time of Schaff's speech in 1889 to the revision of 1903 in the Presbyterian Church USA. Yet, even with this growing desire for more substantial change, the changes adopted 1903 embodied simple clarification and better definition of the existing affirmations of historic Calvinism, thoroughly consistent with the

160

Westminster Confession and bearing little resemblance to the more Arminian revision made by the Cumberland Church almost a hundred years earlier. Nevertheless, Morrow insists that the impetus for the Cumberland revision of 1815 was '...not a new development in American Presbyterianism. Rather, it was a continuation of the theology of the liberal, New Side Wing of the Presbyterian Church' (Morrow 1994:21).

The Cumberland Church, however, became the scene of yet another confessional revision in 1883. The legal relationship with God that was part of the covenant of law, so amply set forth in the Cumberland revision of 1815, began to lose support within the church. Stanford Burney, Professor of Theology at Cumberland University in the 1880s, set out, as Morrow writes, to do 'for Cumberland theology what Bushnell had done for New England theology' (Morrow 1994:23). As the doctrine of fatherhood of God came into vogue throughout America, Burney taught that God's relationship to humanity was personal as opposed to legal. All vestiges of the covenant of law had to be replaced. Any idea of a penal substitutionary atonement was no longer relevant (Morrow 1994:24). A direct result of Burney's efforts was that the law, in Cumberland Presbyterian circles, was no longer viewed as covenantal in nature. Thus, in a new revision by the Cumberland Church in 1883, the confession was amended to read: 'The moral law is the rule of duty growing immediately out of the relations of rational creatures to their creator and to each other' (Cumberland Presbyterian Church [1884] 1985:33). Burney's theology is considered liberal by Morrow who interprets his view of the covenant as 'the great law of universal love' (Morrow 1994:26). The new revision by the Cumberland Church saw only one covenant as regulatory in the relationship between God and humanity: the covenant of grace. Its universalism was unmistakable. In this respect the Cumberland revision of 1883 tended to be both a much broader interpretation of covenant theology and more liberal. Morrow sees it as more liberal because '...it did liberate Cumberland Presbyterian theology from the structure of covenant theology' (Morrow 1994:26). Morrow continues to relate that 'the irony of the situation was that just at the time when the inner logic of covenant theology had made the doctrines of predestination and the limited atonement unacceptable, the whole system itself was facing collapse' (Morrow 1994:21). And collapse it did; the revision of 1883, with its sole emphasis of the covenant of grace, attests to the demise of traditional Reformed covenant theology within Cumberland Presbyterianism (Morrow 1994:25).

In 1906, after several years of deliberations, a large portion of the Cumberland Presbyterian Church merged with the Presbyterian Church USA. If the Presbyterian revision of 1903 bore only a superficial similarity to the changes that the Cumberland Presbyterian Church adopted at its inception in 1814, then the confessional revision which took place in the Cumberland Church in 1883 was even further removed from the confessional stance of the Presbyterian Church USA at the time of the merger between the two bodies in 1906. Hence, at the time of the merger in 1906 there was no doctrinal unanimity between these two churches.

4.4 Conclusion

I have argued that the revision of 1903 in the Presbyterian Church USA was a Centrist enterprise. By this I mean that the revision was concerned with further defining, clarifying, simplifying, and in certain instances, reemphasizing the doctrines of historic Presbyterianism; it did not attempt to change the historic affirmations of the faith. This, however, was not true for the Cumberland revision of 1814, since it altered the Calvinism of the Westminster Confession at many significant points. The Cumberland fathers were more radical in their changes to the Westminster Confession, but these changes were, as I have attempted to demonstrate, still within the context of Reformed covenant theology, albeit, in the Arminian end of the spectrum. This is not true of the Cumberland revision of 1883, which, in my estimation, yielded Futurist results. By this I mean that the changes enacted in 1883 were not clarifications of existing doctrine, but distinct changes to the affirmations of the faith. After the revision of 1883, there was no longer any hint of Reformed covenant theology evident in the new statement of faith. It was on the basis of this latter revision that reunion was enacted with the Presbyterian Church USA, a church whose confessional status was nearer to their Cumberland brethren in 1814 than in 1883.

It appears, then, that the merger of 1906 was of an uneven nature. Many of those in the Presbyterian Church USA who saw the merger as a natural outgrowth of the confessional revision of 1903 were of a Centrist mind. However, those with whom the merger was concluded—the Cumberland Presbyterians—were more of a Futurist mind-set. Those Cumberland Presbyterians who were party to the merger in 1906 accepted the "much less liberal creed" of the Presbyterian Church USA because, as Cumberland Presbyterian scholar, John Ames, wrote: '...they assumed that the creed was a "system of Doctrine" and that fairly wide tolerance was guaranteed in interpreting details of that system.... former Cumberland Presbyterians were conspicuous in their advocacy of "loose Subscription" and a wide latitude in interpretation' (Ames 1974:15). To many of those involved in the 1906 merger "liberal" meant something far different from what it did to either the founders of the Cumberland Church or their "new side" forebears of the Presbyterian Church USA. It was not just the freedom of the will that was the question now, but the whole of covenant theology. Big changes were in store for the united church. Ninety thousand new members and almost fifteen hundred clergy took part in the reunion of 1906, and, according to John Ames, these represented the more liberal element in the Cumberland Church (Ames 1974:15). While the Presbyterian Church USA in 1906 was essentially of a Centrist mind, I would suggest that this influx of Futurism from the Cumberland Church helped to shift the balance in the Presbyterian Church USA from Centrist to Futurist. As Ames points out elsewhere, Benjamin Warfield of Princeton saw this coming. He writes that 'Warfield knew that the official doctrinal statements of the two denominations were, if not "precise contradictions" at least far from identical' (Ames 1974:15). The question then remained as to how this ecclesiastical reunion was to shape the theological position of the new re-united Presbyterian Church.

Chapter 5

Futurism and Archaism

The reunion of the Presbyterian Church USA and the Cumberland Presbyterian Church in 1906 brought a shift in theological equilibrium to the new united church. Those entrants from the Cumberland Church, as John Ames said were '...conspicuous in their advocacy of "loose subscription" and a wide latitude in interpretation' (Ames 1974:15) with respect to the traditional credal statements of the Presbyterian Church. As I pointed out in the last chapter, in accord with their revision of 1814 and even more so in the revision of 1883, the Cumberland Church had moved away from the historic tenets of the faith that still, in 1906, characterized the Presbyterian Church as a whole. Thus the entrance of such a large number of adherents—about ninety thousand (Ames 1974:17)—had the effect of shifting the center of opinion in the new united church in favor of the Cumberland faction. Warfield saw the significance of this large influx of ministers and laity with a substantially different confessional standard. He wrote that liberty of belief in the Presbyterian Church meant that,

> ...every genuine form of Calvinism has an equal right of existence under the Confession. The Realist can accept it with as good a conscience as the Federalist [Federal Theology: A type of Reformed theology viewing Adam as the federal head of all mankind and Jesus Christ as the federal head of the new creation and building a covenant theology on this basis (Deist 1990:94)]; the Amyraldian with as good a conscience as the Cocceian. But beyond the limits of generic Calvinism the right of adoption ceases. Our vow of ordination is not a solemn farce: and the terms of our adoption of the Confession are not so phrased as to enable us to seem to adopt it while not adopting it at all. (Warfield 1904b:315.)

This shift in opinion, which Warfield saw from the start, took place gradually over a period of years. It was rather a deliberate, but quiet transformation. It was also a definite drift towards Futurism and away from the Centrism that had previously characterized much of the Presbyterian Church USA. This drift became painfully evident to many in 1924 with the drafting of the *Auburn Affirmation*, which took five of the essential affirmations of the faith outlined in the Confession, namely: the infallibility of the Bible, the virgin birth of Christ, Christ's substitutionary atonement on the cross, Christ's bodily resurrection, and miracles (Rian [1940] 1992:20), and declared that, in reality, they are '...non-essential to the system of doctrine taught in the holy Scriptures and are merely theories of those facts and doctrines' (Hart 1978:31). This Affirmation, according to John Ames, was signed by almost twelve hundred Presbyterian clergy, '...not less than 106 (of which were) former Cumberland Presbyterians' (Ames 1974:15).

All the major works on this period of Presbyterian history attest to this intellectual and spiritual shift, although each views it from a different perspective. William Weston's (1997) view, for example, is that as long as the Liberal faction (those whom I have called Futurists) in the Presbyterian Church wanted to push their agenda in a forceful manner they lost support from the Center, as in the case of Charles Briggs. However, when they began to plead for tolerance, they were not only accorded tolerance but also the coveted support of the Center. When the more conservative element in turn tried to oust the Liberals on ideological grounds, the Liberals now had the support they needed to turn popular opinion against the more conservative agenda. Gary North has written a huge monograph that purports to be '...a study of how the liberals captured one Presbyterian denomination: the main one' (North 1996:x), and, in just over one thousand pages, he chronicles the entire account in great detail. Ki-Hong Kim, in his 1983 thesis on the Presbyterian Controversy, said that 'The aim of the extreme conservatives, including Princeton and Machen was to maintain a doctrinally pure church. From this doctrinal concern derived all the major characteristics of the extreme conservative ecclesiology' (Kim 1983:208). Kim further attests to a Liberal/Modernist victory in the struggle for control of the denomination. He writes:

> The conflict within the Presbyterian Church of the USA in the early twentieth century was ended with the withdrawal of the extreme conservatives, who were called fundamentalists. The Church has enjoyed a period of theological peace since the separation, but for the protesters it was an unacceptable peace by compromise in a seriously ill Church. In 1967, when the Church formally

166

adopted a neo-orthodox creed based upon Christ and his reconciliation, they declared that "it was the death of a church." (Kim 1983:209.)

In the following pages I would like to focus on some of the particulars of this shift from Centrism to Futurism, and the Fundamentalist reaction. I will then zero in, if you will, on two prominent Presbyterians: Harry Ward and Norman Thomas. These two men were in the vanguard of those who probed the fringes of Futurism, all the while exerting a significant influence on the church at large.

5.1 The Rise of Futurism

The years that followed the Cumberland merger of 1906 were sedate by comparison, at least from an institutional perspective. Yet, there was a quiet transformation taking place just beneath the surface; a transformation about which no one was writing. It was as if the former contestants were all tired and wished that any new changes would simply vanish. All were going about their daily routines as if nothing was happening. Even the *Princeton Theological Review*, official organ of Princeton Seminary, published articles on ancient history and Old Testament studies, nothing with a sense of urgency. Only one article seemed to hone in on the changes that were quietly taking place. In the July 1906 issue William Brenton Greene wrote on "Broad Churchism and the Christian Life," in which he sharply criticized the growing '...indifference to Truth' (Greene 1906:306) within the new united church. He went on to say that the broad church mind was not only quite prevalent, but also on the increase. Although he did not discuss the different strains he saw in this broad church movement, he identified their goals with astonishing clarity. Aside from a general indifference to the historic truths of the Reformed faith, he saw their subordination of doctrine as an attempt not to divide the visible body of Christ. 'It (those indifferent) would not discuss the differences between creeds,' Greene wrote;

> perhaps they are real, but they are unimportant when a lost world waits for salvation. It would do away with doctrinal preaching: this may have been useful once, but that was before the days of slum work and of foreign missions. It would put theology under a ban: this is not to be disrespectful to Paul; it is only to go back to Christ

167

Himself and to the ethical Gospel which He preached as well as lived. Surely, when such is its declared aim, we may not question that Broad Churchism means right. It would be loyal to our Lord. It would bring in His kingdom. (Greene 1906:308.)

Greene was describing, I would suggest, not one, but two separate and distinct strains of doctrinal indifference. Although these two strains come from the same soil and always appear to be in opposition, the resemblance they bear to each other is striking. These two strains, Fundamentalism and Liberalism, were not new in the Presbyterian Church. Their inauguration was not a planned denominational event; each grew spontaneously out of separate and complex circumstances and in response to perceived needs. Yet each, in its own way, grew apart from the doctrinal heritage of Presbyterianism, bringing, in turn, the accusation of Professor Greene of doctrinal indifference. Throughout the period of confessional revision and the reunion with the Cumberland Church, Liberalism and Fundamentalism were not so clearly defined. Instead, they were diffuse movements within the boundaries of the church, and only after the institutional struggles had abated did their much broader intentions become more widely understood.

The Liberalism of the Cumberland Church, at least in its formative years, was a yearning for freedom from what they considered the fatalism of certain doctrines of the Westminster Confession. Their revision of 1814 did away with the difficulties, and, at the same time, changed their view of the covenant between God and man from one that was unconditional—one established and maintained by God alone—to one that was conditional—one in which humanity is partly responsibility for its maintenance. The 'revision of 1883,' as it was called, was in reality an entirely new confession for the Cumberland Church, one which eliminated '...the conceptions and images of Federalism and (introduced) into it the conceptions and images of the new Liberalism' (Morrow 1965:275). According to John Ames, the new confession of 1883 accomplished these changes in three ways:

> It continued the tendency of Cumberland theology, reflected in the 1814 confession, to greatly modify (sic) the reformed doctrine of the sovereignty of God; it taught an anthropological theology which made man himself the source of his own religious activities, teaching almost complete human autonomy; and it totally

abandoned the federal system of theology with its emphasis on God's election, on an imputation theory of original sin, and on the penal substitution theory of the atonement. (Ames 1971:32.)

Cumberland Liberalism, though still Christian in focus and firmly connected to a confessionally Reformed Church, was, after 1883, no longer within the fold of historic covenant theology. The Liberalism of Charles Briggs and many of his colleagues at Union Seminary, while of one mind with the Cumberlands in their desire for freedom, had a different objective in view. Briggs considered the confessional Calvinism of the Presbyterian Church as stifling to both critical inquiry and Christian unity (Woolley 1957:41). For Briggs, truth was part of the very fabric of the church, not a captive to the printed page (Briggs 1890b:45, Sawyer 1994:47-48). The church, as the truth she contained, was not immutable and static, but alive and vibrant, changing to meet each new challenge of the modern scientific world. True to his presuppositions, Briggs held that in each circumstance the truth was to change and accommodate itself to the changing cultural climate, not vice versa. The historical process was fast replacing the Scriptures as the source for the church's doctrine (that is, a kind of theological historicism) and as the rationale for her existence and mission in the world. Thus, freedom was beginning to mean a freedom from the perceived excesses of a credal faith (Briggs 1890b:65-66). This may be one reason for the almost total lack of any book-length treatments of systematic theology from a Liberal perspective. One of the last was *The Christian Doctrine of God,* written by Briggs's longtime friend and supporter William Newton Clarke in 1894 for The International Theological Library (Clarke 1909); a series begun by Briggs and Stewart Salmond of the Free Church College, Aberdeen, and designed to fuse the new learning with historic Christianity in a series of volumes covering a wide range of historical and theological topics.

The growth of Liberal theology in the Presbyterian Church paralleled closely the teaching career of Charles Briggs. During the course of these years of conflict, opinions regarding the very essence of the faith began to change dramatically. This fact presented itself again and again throughout the Briggs affair. British higher critic J. A. Cassels summed up what he saw happening in one sentence when he claimed '...that supernaturalism hurt religion by overwhelming its proper ethical content' (quoted by Noll 1991:70).

169

Liberalism, as a product of the new side (New School) of the Presbyterian Church, initially held to a conditional view of God's covenant with the human race. This view, which elevated the freedom of the human will over against the older Calvinism, adopted a more fervent preaching style more adept at reaching the multitudes of the lost. This style, known as the revival, was geared to appeal to the whole person, the emotions as well as the mind, and to evoke a decision on the part of the hearers. The "camp meeting"—preaching to large groups in the open air or in barns—went hand in hand with the more revivalistic preaching of the day. In addition to its strictly individualistic purpose of seeking an immediate decision for Christ from its hearers, the kingdom of God and its coming were used as a motivational tool in its call for a greater commitment in Christian witness and holiness of life. This conception of the church was also post-millennial in its view of the future, and for Liberalism this translated into a kingdom of God built in the here and now by a combination of God's efforts and man's. Hence, a Christian America was not something that belonged to the future but something to be sought in the present. But was this kingdom really God's kingdom, or, instead, was it just a product of man's dreams? Regardless of which it turned out to be, many found this dream highly appealing. As Robert Handy says:

> The doctrine was much emphasized by the liberal elements which were then emerging within evangelicalism. Early evangelical liberals were influenced by the currents of Ritschlian thought then so conspicuous in Germany, where many of them had studied. They found congenial the Ritschlian tendency to link religion and civilization as bearers of ideals and values which overcome the downward pull in humanity, thus advancing the kingdom. Liberals were to put a progressively interpreted concept of the kingdom of God central in their theology, but characteristically the doctrine was stated in terms broad enough to include those of various theological positions. (Handy 1984:87.)

The quest for the kingdom of God had been a perennial one in American history since colonial times (Bloch 1985:187-201), and theology had, in the past, always played a major role in any discussion surrounding this national quest for God's kingdom. With the onslaught of the "camp meeting" mentality, however, replete with attendant emotional excess, it seemed that judgments based more on traditional and confessional principles were increasingly becoming a thing of the past. The crusade became the order of the day (Woolley 1957:43). Enemies were not people, places, and things but rather personal preferences which had to be corrected at all costs, both for the good of society and the salvation of the individual (Gusfield 1963:2). Moral crusades against poverty, alcohol, and bad working conditions became to many the substance of religion (Gusfield 1963:44-45, Abzug 1994:101-103 & Woolley 1957:43). Joseph Gusfield discusses the moral crusade, which increased in popularity among Baptists and Methodists as well as Presbyterians (Gusfield 1963:44), under the rubric of "perfectionism":

Religion and individual perfectionism went hand in hand. To be saved was evidenced through a change in habits. The man of spiritual conviction could be known by his style of living. If frontier life emphasized the roughness, liberty, and dissoluteness of a society without settled institutions, then there was all the more reason to stress the need for moral rigidity and an enthusiastic response to perfectionist standards. The organizers and directors of the major benevolent societies... believed that moral and religious reform would make the convert a less radical voter and a more trustworthy credit risk. The assumption was quite clear. Sanctified men make better borrowers, better workers, better citizens. The corollary of this was not a glorification of the humble poor, obediently carrying out the dictates of the lordly. Rather, the corollary was the doctrine of self-improvement through the Lord. In the thick of Methodist development, John Wesley had been concerned with this consequence of the religious movement. As men became more industrious, sober, thrifty, methodical, and responsible they also improved their income through work. Pure religion might decay, "for the Methodists in every place grow diligent and frugal; consequently they increase in goods." (Gusfield 1963:45.)

How did one withstand the onslaught of this type of "God's" kingdom in America? The name alone seemed to sanctify any and all efforts associated with it. Theodore Dwight Weld, as an example of these efforts, was especially graphic in his work as a preacher for temperance reform.

Weld saw himself as appealing to the reason rather than to the passion of his audience, but he believed that part of such an argument was to hold up "to their view facts in all their blood." So he dramatized them. He imagined the 150,000 paupers passing "along in all their rags."

171

If that did not impress the audience, he asked them to imagine "if your last bed was going under the hammer, and your wives and children were already on their way to join this motley group." Then came the 1,500 insane—"now behold that maniac laugh"—and 16,000 criminals "dungeoned by the use of intoxicating drink." The parade ended with a finale of 300,000 drunkards—"see them spewing and hear their dreadful oaths." And soon after "pile up 30,000 bodies of dead men, in all their blood." That was the cost of intemperance. (Abzug 1994:96.)

Temperance tracts were full of speculation about various dates for the arrival of the kingdom of God (Abzug 1994:97), but '...moral reform as a political and social issue' (Gusfield 1963:2) always seemed to be at issue. Out of this murky combination of emotional excess, hopes and expectations for the dawning of the golden age of the kingdom of God, and the onslaught of the modern industrial state, it was difficult at times to distinguish the budding Fundamentalist from his Liberal counterpart. Both Liberals and Fundamentalists at times looked like purveyors of the social gospel in an age of unprecedented migration to cities. While a portion of this number were the wayward sons and daughters of heartland America, the lion's share of these numbers were new arrivals to the shores of the American dream. With little or no money, no family connections, and little English, they poured in, each looking for his own millennial kingdom, albeit on a reduced scale. These same multitudes became the objects of evangelism for men interested in both their soul and their allegiance.

Popular city preachers, in an effort to become even more popular and reach the maximum number of people in the process, adopted the ways of the frontier revivalist. As the rancher had to round up the cattle for branding periodically, so the preacher had to round up the sons and daughters of both the churched and the unchurched alike and get them branded with the mark of God's Spirit. But how can one speak of the love of God to men and women who had nothing to eat, who were clad in rags, and whose children played in the filth of the city streets? In response to the various needs posed by the "new" urban dweller, a multitude of para-church organizations came into existence. The churches themselves seemed to redefine what it meant to be a church. Is a church a place of worship, a soup kitchen, a recreation hall, and a social hall all rolled into one? Some thought this was an opportune time to apply a distinctly American way of doing things to a spiritual entity almost two thousand years old. The results were in many ways unusual, even amusing, such as the seven story church/hotel in New York City complete with conference rooms, recreational facilities, and a full hotel staff (Lundén 1988:80-82).

Some of the early social gospel preachers, Henry Ward Beecher, Phillips Brooks, and Russel Conwell were Reformed Liberals theologically in their denial of predestination and God's sovereignty, but they had not yet substituted an 'exploration of personhood' (Meyer [1965]1988a:178) for traditional spirituality. Phillips Brooks was an individual in the breech, a preacher in the time of transition. He urged his congregation to 'Believe in yourself ... and reverence your own human nature; it is the only salvation from vice and every false belief...' (quoted by Marsden 1991:19). For lack of a better word, Winthrop Hudson calls the more mature Liberalism of the social gospel the "New Theology." He writes:

> The New Theology was essentially a culture religion with a single fundamental theological idea—the doctrine of the Incarnation, interpreted in terms of divine immanence and a superficial understanding of the notion of evolution. By means of this doctrine, Christ was identified with what was conceived to be the finest cultural ideals, and the noblest cultural institutions, and the best scientific and philosophical thinking. The most significant feature of the New Theology, therefore, was its lack of normative content. It was compatible with every conceivable social attitude, and whatever stream of secular thought one might wish to support and consecrate, with whatever system of values might seem good in the light of one's own personal predilection. (Hudson [1953] 1963:161.)

The new theology, of which Hudson speaks, was not uniform even among its adherents; rather, it was a spectrum with various shades of religious sentiments. Some, as in the case of the Cumberland Presbyterians, wanted freedom from what they saw as the 'fatalism' of certain doctrines in the Calvinistic covenantal system. Others wanted freedom in a different sense entirely. Since the critical approach to theology, they argued, so prominent in recent years, had shown the Bible to be an unreliable book in matters of fact, Christians were left trying to salvage the best ethical teaching it had to offer and to separate it from its worn-out and now discredited form. But, as Hudson has shown, when

173

the ethical is separated from the spiritual a sort of vacuum is created which must be filled, and indeed which came to be filled with a worshipful attitude towards culture, politics, science, or whatever else seemed to be a good or relevant cause.

Harvey Cox, in his 1965 *The Secular City*, gave a decidedly different perspective to this separation of the ethical from its historically spiritual origins. He quoted sociologist Max Weber on the Western belief in the sanctity of work as it originated in the monasteries of medieval Europe. With the onslaught of the Reformation, work lost its integral sanctity, '...because all ways of influencing God through traditional religious techniques had been abolished.' This situation arose naturally '...through the Calvinist doctrine of predestination in which it was taught that God had determined the elect and the damned from before the foundation of the world, and consequently nothing could be done which had the remotest chance of changing the decision' (Cox 1965:185). The upshot of this dilemma for humanity was, according to Cox, a radical shift in focus from the spiritual to the material, which happened in tandem with the rise of modern industrial society. Cox writes:

> There was no way to propitiate God. So now the energy which man had previously poured out in supplication and sacrifice had to be redirected in what Freud would call an act of massive sublimation. Religious fervor was rechanneled into energetic work in the world. Together with the invisible hand of the laissez-faire market, it provided the motor for the rise of capitalism, and the industrial revolution. Even socialism has one of its sources here, less directly. Despite so many differences, early capitalism and socialism betray marks of a common ancestor. The Marxist dialectic is the same invisible hand wearing a steel glove. The ghost of religion still prowls. Witness the exaltation of "the worker" in both Protestant ethic and in Marxism. When the history of our times is written many years from now, these two movements may be interpreted as parallel thrusts in a larger and more inclusive historical development, the wrenching redirection of man's attention and energy from heaven to earth. Town culture marks the transition phase. (Cox 1965:186.)

Certain of the intelligentsia saw in Marxist socialism Christian ethics brought to fruition on earth. Hence, already sheered of its spiritual trappings, the Christian faith took on a decidedly political and economic hue. Man's relationship to man increasingly became the most important thing, and, in this context, the coming "Russian experiment" began bearing unusual intellectual fruit in both England and the United States. Speaking in 1947, Christopher Hill, Master of Balliol College, Oxford, and staunch admirer of the Soviet system, spoke with pride concerning the model society the revolution has been able to create. 'They have acquired the prestige of demonstrated success,' he boasted. When asked: What are '...likely to be the long-run influences of the Russian Revolution?' He singled out three:

> First, soviet experience in the bringing of modern civilization to backward peoples, and especially the development of the soviet system and collective farms as a means of self-government for agrarian peoples.... Secondly, the USSR has demonstrated in practice that socialism is a system which can work even under the most unpromising conditions, and the soviet single-party system has put before all the highly industrialized countries of the world one possible solution of the conflict between economic planning and political liberty. It is becoming increasingly obvious that absolute freedom of private enterprise is incompatible with the demand of the average citizen for freedom from want and freedom from fear. The achievement of rational planning, full employment and universal economic security in the USSR has already set standards of which the rest of the world is having to take account.... Finally, reinforcing both these points, the Russian Revolution has demonstrated that the common people of the earth (and indeed of what was a very backward country) can take over power and run the state infinitely more effectively than their "betters." (Hill [1947] 1971:167-168.)

But the most noticeable feature of the Russian state can be seen in that

> ...it uplifts the poor and the downtrodden and improved their lot in the everyday things of life. This is

what most impresses in contemporary records of the revolution, and this is what is likely to be its most widespread and lasting effect. For the everyday things of life still mean most to the poor and downtrodden, and they are still the majority of the population of the world. (Hill [1947] 1971:169.)

Two men who would give hearty approval to these words were Harry F. Ward, a Methodist who taught at Union Seminary in New York from 1918-1941 (Duke:1985:85), and Norman M. Thomas; both of whom had an enormous influence on the Presbyterian Church.

As indifference to the historic tenets of the faith gave birth to both modern Liberalism and Fundamentalism, each with their attendant emotional excesses, a quiet transformation was also occurring in Presbyterianism's view of her own role in the world. Emphasis was gradually shifting away from spiritual things and the world to come to material things and the world of the here-and-now. Doctrine was yielding to a sort of a-theological ethics, that is to say, believing was being overshadowed by increasingly secular activity. All this was happening concurrent with the growth of the modern industrial society. For many in the Presbyterian Church, the embodiment of this new secular ethic was politics. Hence, to some, Marxist Socialism was seen as the most appropriate vehicle for bringing Christianity's ethical demands to fruition in the modern world. By the substitution of politics and other secular ethical constructs for the historic affirmations of the faith, Presbyterianism was slowly being given a new doctrinal content, one more appropriate for a modern society. This transformation, I suggest, was Futurist in both its theory and its practice.

5.2 Harry Ward and Norman Thomas

Born in London in 1873, Harry Frederick Ward was raised in a middle-class Methodist home. Unlike the Methodism centered on the Wesleyan liturgical order, 'the Methodism with which Ward came into contact stressed personal religious experience and human perfection' (Craig 1969:331). As the son of a tradesman, Ward had little chance of availing himself of an education in the British university system. So, when a distant uncle in Utah offered to subsidize his studies in America, Ward was on his way to the U.S. Around this time, says biographer David Duke, 'Ward experienced "conversions" ...which dramatically altered his previous understanding of Christianity: a conversion from his socially conservative, evangelical boyhood in England to a religion with a social

176

conscience, and a second related conversion to a belief that structural change was endemic to the religion of Jesus' (Duke 1985:85). This conversion was prompted by firsthand experience of man's inhumanity to man. Like many others of this period—the brothers Niebuhr for instance— Ward got his first ideological shock in and around the stockyards of Chicago. As a young cleric, Duke tells us, '...he witnessed the dehumanizing effects of corporate structures such as the meatpacking industry and Chicago's political machine' (Duke 1985:85). His sensibility to the plight of his fellow human beings was sharpened by his reading of the social manifesto of the day: Richard Ely's *The Social Aspect of Christianity*. Taking it to heart, Ward sought answers in other than the traditional avenues. To this end he traveled extensively and more than casually visited the Soviet Union on several occasions. Searching for an effective method in the modern isolated world, he studied the writings of the socialists and communists with enthusiasm.

But these experiences alone, says David Duke, '...do not completely explain Ward's intense loyalty to the Soviet Union and his persistent attempts to combine religion and Marxist philosophy. His loyalties can be adequately explained only in terms of the soteriology of the social gospel which bridged the gap between his evangelical heritage and his "evangelistic" support of the Soviet system as the first Christianized social order' (Duke 1985:86). In his Social Service Lecture for 1935, Herbert Wood, Lecturer at the University of Birmingham and a firm believer, like Ward, in the Soviet system as the end to which the Christian life tends, demonstrated how the gap between an evangelical heritage on the one hand, and an "evangelistic" support of the Soviet system on the other can be bridged.

> In its most comprehensive sense Communism simply means sharing. As an ideal, Communism claims that the best human life is the life of fellowship. Sharing should be carried to the furthest limit. Wealth should not only be owned collectively but used in common. Life itself, our interests, our emotions should be shared as far as may be. In communist society, publicity is extolled and encouraged while privacy is discouraged and suspected. In the sphere of religion the Communist will exalt occasions of public worship above acts of private devotion. He will find the essence of religion in those

experiences which break down the fences of individual life and merge the individual in some larger social whole. For the Communist the substance of religion is social. To have one's soul congregationalized is to find truth in religion. (Wood 1935:9.)

Harry Ward's social theory, however, which was the embodiment of his religion, came from the world about him; a world, as he saw it, full of need and injustice. His book, *The Gospel for a Working World* (Ward 1918), described his conclusions. His was more than just a historicist understanding of ecclesiastical teaching. Ward's faith was a political faith. His attempts to '...combine the philosophy of Marx with the "religion of Jesus"' (Duke 1985:85), as Duke describes it, was a Futurist endeavour. Ward emphatically rejected the traditional Christian concept of individual salvation (Duke 1985:89). His interest was instead in the conversion of society. This interest in society was, however, not just a practical, social out-working of orthodox teaching, because, for Ward, '...a society's conversion had taken place when it embraced socialism' (quoted by Duke 1985:91). Ward was also a prominent board member and sponsor of the People's Institute of Applied Religion (Matthews 1953:10), identified by J. B. Matthews as '...a Communist school which is run, sponsored, and subsidized by Protestant clergymen' (Matthews 1953:4), and his definition of salvation can be best found in the Institute's handbook, which he helped write: 'Salvation is the result of the collective effort of the workers and other victims of this [the capitalist] world system to save themselves from the oppressors' (quoted by Matthews 1953:4). Ward's quest took him outside the pale of Christianity to adopt a specific political stratagem as the content of his faith or, as Paul Tillich would call it, his 'ultimate concern.' In this regard also, Harry Ward was a Futurist. His political affiliations dictated the affirmations of his faith. In fact, a specific political doctrine became the content of his faith. This is a radical departure from the faith of historic Presbyterianism as embodied in the Westminster Confession of Faith. Ward's differences with historic Presbyterianism were not developments on the tenets of historic Presbyterianism; rather, I suggest that they were a distinct departure from it.

Harry Ward was first and foremost a social theorist; one with the title of minister of the Gospel. As a result, his analysis of the obstacles facing the proclamation of the Gospel is fair, but it takes up the bulk of his writing. In his *The Gospel for a Working World*, Ward's focus is almost entirely on the working world and not the gospel—although he does use a good deal of Christian terminology. Analyzing the conditions of labor and its interrelations, Ward says:

> Here are the great natural resources of the earth which God has created for the development of mankind. Out of them is made by human labor the wealth on which the world subsists. From them come food and clothes and shelter, education, inventions, comforts, luxuries. The industrial conflict centers about the question of the terms upon which men shall use these natural resources, how they shall control them, how they shall divide the wealth which comes out of them. Before a right relationship of men to each other can be completed, there must be discovered the right relationship which all men together must hold to these goods upon which the development of life depends.... That a man has little, or that he believes in cooperative ownership is no guaranty that he has discovered the spiritual meaning of property.... Unless men can discover together a different relation to property, there is no prospect of ending war. (Ward 1918:195-197.)

With these goals in mind, Ward was instrumental in the founding of The Methodist Federation for Social Service in 1907. Representing the social gospel in its maturity, the Federation expressed its purpose in its constitution as: 'To deepen within the church the sense of social obligation and opportunity, to study social problems from the Christian point of view and to promote social service in the spirit of Jesus Christ' (quoted by Hopkins 1940:289). Ward was continually busy writing and lecturing, yet rarely does he give any insight into his own motivations. In a letter from Ward to Professor Snedden, written towards the end of January, 1919, he gives us a glimpse of his objectives for the future. According to Craig, they were: '(1) To promote those social changes which he conceived to be required by the needs of humanity and the social ethics of Christianity; (2) To promote those changes on the basis of scientific knowledge and by the orderly processes of political and social evolution' (Craig 1969:339). Ward believed in the inherent immorality of capitalism with its profit motive. He also believed something of real historic importance was happening in the Soviet Union, which he visited on several occasions. Ethics, for Ward, were inextricably linked to economics, which, in turn, had been corrupted by the capitalistic system (Ward 1929:9). To find an adequate solution in the modern industrial world, he claimed his views on economics and ethics were scientific, but then so was his faith. As he himself says:

> Instead of stressing that Christianity must convert the heart of capitalism, he declared that if it did not, it would die with the failing capitalistic order. Christianity offered to industrial society the possibility of its salvation by proposing the means whereby the capitalistic system could be altered. The real aim of religion was to bring about a fully conscious society.... Both ethical religion and social science looked forward to the realization of a different economic morality and a more equitable economic process. An ethical religion would provide the direction of a new economic order based upon what science declared was possible. (Craig 1969:346-347.)

Harry Ward brought his views of religion and ethics to the Presbyterian Church when he joined the faculty of Union Theological Seminary in New York, first as lecturer from 1916 to 1918, then as professor of Christian ethics from 1918 until his retirement in 1941. Here he 'had much in common with George Coe,' Robert Handy tells us, 'for they both stressed the authority of experience and the importance of social justice' (Handy 1987:148). According to Duke, Coe, under whom Ward studied at Northwestern University, would only describe '...religion in social terms' (Duke 1985:87). Even at Union Ward was never far from a heated discussion or a controversial remark. He squared off with fellow Ethics Professor Reinhold Niebuhr in many informal discussions on the reconciliation of Christianity and communism. While Ward was an impassioned preacher, Handy says that '...as the years passed he became more and more committed to extreme radical social views...' (Handy 1987:193). Gary North says that 'Union's Harry F. Ward was the most politically radical seminary professor in America' (North 1996:924). Complaints poured in from various quarters with Elizabeth Dilling dubbing Union "The Red Seminary" (Handy 1987:193). Union, however, stood by Harry Ward as they had stood by Charles Briggs years before and even asked him to continue teaching beyond the normal age for retirement. Responding to this gesture of confidence, Ward said that Union was 'the only educational institution in the country that had shown such forbearance and freedom for teaching' (quoted by Handy 1987:193). Union Seminary, representative of the historic new school side of American Presbyterianism, evinced a much broader understanding of the nature of the church, and her historic creed, in 1941 than anyone would have countenanced in 1893. I think this is demonstrated convincingly by Nathaniel Weyl, a student at Union in the early 1940s. He wrote that

> ...when I was the leader of the radical movement on the Columbia University campus, I was invited to become an honorable member of the Atheists' Club at adjacent Union Theological Seminary. I asked rather naively how an honorable man could accept an appointment to the ministry if he didn't believe in God. The reply was that the pulpit provided a captive audience, a position of authority and a regular salary—all most useful to Socialist and Communist propagandists. I declined the invitation. (quoted by North 1996:804.)

Union's Presbyterianism by the end of Harry Ward's tenure there was, as was Ward himself, Futurist in its view of the historic affirmations of the faith, or, as North wrote, 'It (Union) was committed to the toleration of everything except orthodoxy' (North 1996:924). John Gerstner, church historian and seminary professor in the Presbyterian Church USA, wrote, in his summary of the Briggs affair: 'Thus ends the life of Calvinism in Union Theological Seminary' (Gerstner 1957:39). Paul Tillich, who taught at Union for many years, also attests to this fact. He wrote that 'when I came to America twenty years ago (1933), the theology of the Reformation was almost unknown in Union Theological Seminary [New York]...' (Tillich 1968:226). Both Harry Ward and Union Seminary trained a whole generation of Presbyterian clergy. I suggest that, because of this training, an entire generation of Presbyterian ministers was largely not committed to the historic tenets of Presbyterianism. A fact which, when combined with other developments, tended to push the entire Presbyterian Church USA in the Futurist direction.

Another Presbyterian who helped to define the Liberal/Futurist mind in the early part of the century was Norman Mattoon Thomas. His Futurism, as Ward's, was to attempt a redefinition of the historic affirmations of the faith to coincide with his vision of Christianity as manifest in the Socialist concept of society—his book *A Socialist's Faith* (Thomas 1951) was written with this goal in mind.

Born in a Presbyterian manse in Ohio to a family of credal Calvinists, Thomas seemed destined to the ministry. After a year at Bucknell College, he was provided with a stipend by a wealthy relative with the provision that he attend Princeton University. With a diploma in hand, he proceeded to New York City where he worked at the East Side Settlement for $500 a year while attending Union Theological Seminary. After graduation he was ordained and served briefly as assistant to Reverend Henry Van Dyke—who headed the confessional revision committee in 1903—at New York's Brick Presbyterian Church. Later the same year he was appointed pastor of an East Harlem Church, located in a strictly blue-collar neighborhood. About this time war was brewing in Europe, and Thomas, a pacifist, began to voice his opposition to it from the pulpit. In reaction to what they heard, the elders stopped financing the social work that he was doing in addition to his pastoral duties. Thomas promptly resigned the pastorate and joined the Socialist Party. He left the ministry of the Presbyterian Church for good on the death of his mother in 1931 (Current Biography 1944:688).

Because he did not remain within the church, Thomas's influence was more limited to the world of politics than Harry Ward's influence. He involved himself in labor disputes, spoke for socialist societal and economic planning, and ran for President of the United States on four separate occasions. All the while he saw himself as one who was furthering the church of Christ in the world. This was the case because, for Thomas, the church was the instrument of the world's salvation (Thomas 1951:121), which largely consisted of '...developing a powerful interest in worker's rights and social justice' (Thomas 1951:127). This view of salvation seems to mirror that of Harry Ward as quoted earlier from the handbook of The People's Institute of Applied Religion. For Thomas, moreover, '...there is more hope in achieving a unifying loyalty of men in the service of (this) great ideal for humanity if it is based on life's experience and not dependent on one of the many conflicting doctrines of God and creation, sin and redemption' (Thomas 1951:123).

Salvation, for Thomas, could only be spoken of in social terms because of its grounding in a historicist understanding of religious origins. Thomas was adamant that 'religion, or rather religions, emerged from the cultural patterns of the tribes' (Thomas 1951:119). Therefore, he was not the least bit enthusiastic about the type of credal faith found in the church of his fathers. In fact, he insisted that,

...if religion by definition requires a theological creed or a belief in a God who has revealed His will to us through prophets and sages, it is a serious business to claim that it is an essential answer to the confusions of our time. For one thing, religion is not singular but plural. There are many religions. Within religions like Christianity, Buddhism, and Islam are many divergent if not hostile sects. In so far as there is an ethic common to all religions, it may be questioned whether they have not derived that ethic from life rather than imposed it on life. Must we wait for a decent world until all men profess something like a common theological creed? If so, the outlook is dark indeed. (Thomas 1951:122.)

Thomas saved some of his more stinging criticisms for that branch of Christendom in which saw the faith as entirely otherworldly. In a typically Marxist criticism, Thomas considered these sects 'escapist,' and their teachings a hindrance to true religion. 'The greatest of the World's religions,' he wrote,

have professed a power to redeem the human soul. Their redemptive claims for society, short of God's apocalyptic intervention, have been less definite and more variable. Most Christian churches and sects have offered salvation out of this world. It is the church which is the City of God rather than the state which also he has ordained....Too often Christianity is loved as a way of escape from the world rather than salvation of the world. It is thus that the Protestant sects, which lately have seemed to be gaining faster than the older churches, conceive religion. Within the older churches some of the new zeal for theology is escapist, a desire for salvation out of a world irredeemably lost. (Thomas 1951:119&121.)

While Thomas's influence was neither as widespread nor as integral to the Presbyterian Church as that of Harry F. Ward, nevertheless he was still a son of the Presbyterian Church USA. Thomas was illustrative of a group of younger men that were probing the boundaries of historic Presbyterianism. They wanted a faith that was relevant; one that was consistent with their experience. Since they had few scruples about changing the historic affirmations of the faith to achieve their desired ends, I suggest that they were in the Futuristic vanguard of an entire church moving in a Futurist direction.

5.3 The Archaist Reaction

The escapism against which Thomas objected so strongly was an integral part of the emerging Fundamentalism. Sharing Liberalism's new school revival heritage (Marsden 1986), Fundamentalism tended towards an emphasis on eschatology, or last things. Dispensationalism, a system of Biblical interpretation which divided God's dealings with humanity into different epochs, was imported into the United States as early as the 1840s by John Nelson Darby and became almost immediately synonymous with Fundamentalism. Head of a controversial sect in Britain, Darby emphasized the return of Christ over all other teachings in the Bible. Darby himself traveled throughout the U.S. on several occasions between 1862 and 1877 (Sandeen 1967:70) to engage in Bible study almost exclusively among members of the clergy. Darby and his followers, the Plymouth Brethren, found their most ready acceptance among Calvinists. He wrote: '...one had to insist on the first principles of grace. No one will have it as a rule in the American churches. Old school Presbyterians, or some of them, have the most of it' (quoted by Sandeen 1967:71n). Once dispensationalism became part of the ecclesiastical landscape in America, the institution most responsible for its spread was the Bible conferences, of which, according to Sandeen, '...the most significant of these was the Niagara Conference' (Sandeen 1967:72). Growing out of the Niagara Conference were the uniquely American prophetic conferences, with their strict premillennial views regarding the future of the church and the world.

Fundamentalism was both a movement and a reaction. As a movement it was one based on conservatism in religion and politics. It was reactionary in its response to the broadening, or liberalizing, of what it perceived as America's religious heritage. Its reaction was essentially a retreat to the language of the Scriptures combined with an almost total repudiation of the world, i.e. Archaism (Rushdoony 1965:155). Ernest Gellner, after excluding the reactionary factor from his definition, sees it as a purely sociological phenomenon. His definition is helpful in putting Fundamentalism in its broader context. He believes that

When approaching fundamentalism, one should first exclude the reactiveness from the definition so as to be able to note the continuity between contemporary fundamentalism and certain earlier phenomenon—namely, what I might call the Reformation-prone religious systems, those "axial" systems which are relatively detached from social organization and which are soteriological, and *generically* soteriological. They are not, like the systems of support offered by the Fustelian-Durkheimian kind of religion, caste- or segment-specific, and they are not ailment-specific. They offer a kind of generic salvation *for all comers*, a kind of total remedy for the human condition; and it is these generic, to-whom-it-may-concern, socially disembodied religions that were historically engaged in a struggle with the persistent tendencies of the social order to return to a more Durkheimian variant of the faith. (Gellner 1995:281.)

Gellner's definition, with the reactionary element left in, would, in my opinion, be more complete. While the Fundamentalism that developed out of the prophetic conferences was conservative in its view of Christianity in general, this conservatism was primarily in reaction to Liberal historicism, which manifested itself in a critical approach to the Scriptures and a relativizing of the church's doctrinal teachings, and the Liberal stress on redemption and reconciliation as socially oriented as opposed to something intended for the individual alone. Fundamentalism's individualistic outlook was, at least in part, a reaction to the social salvation preached by the Liberals. Christ came, said Fundamentalist preachers, to seek and save the lost, individually. The communal focus of the Liberals obscured the call of Christ to the individual. Faith, without which no one can see God, was strictly individualistic in nature, not corporate. Besides, improving the working conditions of the masses does not make them Christian. Humanity is saved by faith alone.

Fundamentalism's staunch individualism was also the logical consequence of its premillennial eschatology. Most Liberals, and even a great many conservatives in the latter part of the nineteenth century, were postmillennial in their outlook for the future. They expected a future in which the world and all the institutions of society would eventually become Christian. 'This golden age of righteousness,' writes postmillennialist Lorraine Boettner, 'is, of course, not to be thought of as beginning suddenly, or on any particular date. It cannot be pinpointed on the calendar, for it comes as the result of a long, slow process' (Boettner 1957:58). To Fundamentalists, this was the greatest of heresy. Since their theology was built almost exclusively around millennial, or future, expectations of disaster and judgment, a golden age for the church of

Christ would be ushered in only by the cataclysm of the apocalypse. "Why polish the brass on a sinking ship?" quips the old Fundamentalist proverb. The mission of the church in the world, as given by Christ himself in the Great Commission (Matthew 28:19-20 AV), is to save the world individually, not collectively, and to save it out of the present world system. This Fundamentalist mind was built upon the main teachings of dispensationalism, which, curiously enough, did not seem to interfere with the denominational distinctives of any group in which it took hold. 'In brief,' writes William Cox, 'the teachings of dispensationalism are as follows:

> 1. The Jews are to be saved by repentance; they are to be left here on earth as God's earthly people.

> 2. The Gentiles are to be saved by faith; they will be taken to heaven after the Rapture. (The Rapture is God's plan for the church in the coming final cataclysm. Since, according to fundamentalist teaching, the church is not the subject of God's wrath at the end of the world, they will be taken out by secret rapture prior to the judgment of the ungodly-PB)

> 3. The church is a parenthesis in God's plan and will end in apostasy.

> 4. The kingdom of heaven and the kingdom of God are sharply differentiated, the first being the Davidic kingdom and the latter being God's universal world-wide kingdom.

> 5. God deals with men according to seven dispensations. (Cox 1963:8.)

As long as Fundamentalism was just a conservative movement within a given communion, its eschatological distinctives stood in addition to the prevailing confession. When it moved beyond denominational lines and became an inter-denominational force, eschatology became the test of orthodoxy. The main reason for this tunnel vision on the future was the Fundamentalist approach to interpreting the Bible. Dispensational hermeneutics—Biblical interpretation— popularized in America by C. I. Scofield, focused exclusively on God's dealings with His chosen people at different stages of His historical plan. Since the Old Testament was considered to be a time, or dispensation of law, and the New Testament a time of grace, both could not apply equally to the Christian in the modern world. The present time, Fundamentalism declared, was New Testament time, and the Old Testament, while illustrative of certain things, does not apply in any way to a Christian living in New Testament times (Cox 1963:13-16, Ryrie 1965). This dividing up of the Bible became an integral part of the dispensational system of interpretation. As William Cox said:

In keeping with dispensationalist views on the completely separate dispensations, the Scriptures are said to have been given dispensationally, i.e., different passages of the Bible are directed to different dispensations, Unless one interprets each passage of Scripture dispersationally, one is in a hopeless quandary and can never expect to understand the Bible. (Cox 1963:22.)

Paul Fischer, in his comparison of Fundamentalism with Modernism, argued that Modernism casts doubt on the Bible '...by the insinuation that it is entirely of human origin' (Fischer 1936:42), Fundamentalism did the same thing '...by putting question marks as to whether it is "for us" after most of the Word' (Fischer 1936:42). According to Fischer, while Fundamentalism '...insists very aggressively that every word of the Bible is inspired, ...the greater part of it cannot inspire us because it does not apply to us at all, but applies to people of different nationality and era' (Fischer 1936:22). We are now living, according to Fundamentalism, in the age or dispensation of grace; the age of the law ended with the death of Christ on the cross for all men. Fundamentalism's radical separation of the Bible into compartments, or dispensations (Cox 1963:22), had the effect of separating from Christianity much of the church's historic confession. With the dispensation of the old covenant, i.e. the Old Testament, gone, so was the moral law, taking with it any norms for the Christian life. According to Presbyterian R. J. Rushdoony, 'Most "fundamentalist" Christians are thoroughly "modernist" in their radical disregard of much of Scripture, ...and in their limitation of its authority to matters of salvation and certain limited areas of personal and social morality' (Rushdoony 1965:155).

To make up for this moral vacuum, Fundamentalism seized upon antiquated sociological norms and declared them theological distinctives. It looked back to the "good old days" and adopted sociological and cultural idiosyncrasies of a time when life seemed more pleasant and thus, more moral. Items such as dress, smoking, or drinking (temperance) now became theological distinctives, and the only marks of the true

Christian (Woolley 1957:43). This practice of Fundamentalism of substituting sociological distinctives for theological norms is historicist in both its theory and application. Sociological norms derive from, or rise out of, society's historical progression. This is not the traditional source for Christian doctrine. To substitute mores derived from society's historical progression for the traditional affirmations of the faith is a distinctly historicist venture. For Protestantism, the church of Sola Scriptura, or McGrath's tradition 1, any attempt to find the affirmations of the faith either in society's history or tradition, or anywhere other than in the Scriptures, would inevitably be classified as historicist. The outcome of this change in the source of doctrine is a change to the historical affirmations of the faith, which is decidedly Futurist. Thus, in their radical compartmentalization of the Scriptures, their historicist quest for the affirmations of the faith in society's history, and their resultant Futurism I would like to suggest, along with Paul Fischer (Fischer 1936), that the Fundamentalists were closer to their Liberal antagonists than to the Reformed faith. Confessional Calvinists maintained their insistence on the whole Bible as the only source for faith and practice. By comparison, I would suggest that both Liberalism and Fundamentalism increasingly became more identified with sociology and ethical relativity, i.e. a Futurist approach to the credal affirmations of the church.

Fundamentalism, a name derived from *The Fundamentals*—a series of conservative doctrinal essays published in 1909 that covered the whole range of Christian theology—also became a term of opprobrium applied alike to those of either an Archaist or a Centrist inclination. Fundamentalism, aside from its own Futurist inclinations, was, at this time, a reaction to the Liberal party in the church. This reaction, however, included both Archaists and Centrists who militated against the Liberals' (Futurists' also) desire to change the affirmations of the faith. As the years of the controversy progressed, the co-belligerency of Archaism and Centrism in the face of Futurism would become undone. This undoing, however, occurred over a period of years not becoming fully manifest until after the Fundamentalist/Modernist Controversy.

5.4 Conclusion

In this chapter I have tried to demonstrate the shifting climate of opinion taking place in Protestantism as a whole and in Presbyterianism in particular. Futurism was coming into clearer focus in the life and work of Harry Ward and Norman Thomas. Both men, one born a

188

Presbyterian, the other a Presbyterian by adoption, probed the fringes of Futurism. Their concern with social theory and the plight of the vanquished caused them to redefine the faith in terms of social theory. That is to say, they sought the substance of the Christian message in areas other than the historic symbols of the church. This action precluded any development of the faith since Futurism does not seek to develop the faith as it exists; it seeks to change, or to allow for the change of, the historic affirmations of the faith. This approach, also called Liberalism, was gaining significant ground within Presbyterianism. As it did so, Fundamentalism, beginning as an inter-denominational phenomenon and composed of both Archaists and Centrists, rose in opposition. In the infancy stage of this Fundamentalist opposition its constituent Archaism and Centrism were really indistinguishable. Fundamentalism as a movement, however, was not something indigenous to Presbyterianism. It was also characterized by a dispensational approach to the Scriptures, which in many ways mirrored the Modernist handling of the Bible.

Hermeneutics, however, was not the only similarity between the emerging Liberalism and the opposing Fundamentalism. In an earlier chapter I sought to demonstrate the historicism and Futurism inherent in Liberalism. In this chapter, I sought to demonstrate the historicist and Futurist inclinations of Fundamentalism also. Because of their historicism, neither Modernism/Liberalism nor the Archaist side of Fundamentalism qualifies as heir of the historic Presbyterian tradition. Tradition 1, according to McGrath, was the tradition of historic Presbyterianism, which meant simply a '...traditional way of interpreting Scripture' (McGrath 1993:136). Tradition 2: basing doctrine '...upon two quite distinct sources, Scripture and unwritten tradition' (McGrath 1993:136) has never been a part of the historic Presbyterian tradition. Hence, neither the emerging Futurism in the Presbyterian Church, nor its Archaist/Fundamentalist reaction, can be considered an heir of historic Presbyterianism.

As the Presbyterian Church moved en masse in the Futurist direction, the Fundamentalist opposition would become better defined in its constituent components. For now, the Presbyterian Church, institutionally, was guided by the Futurist vision.

Chapter 6

Centrism, Futurism, and J. Gresham Machen

It was in the midst of the shift towards Futurism in the Presbyterian Church USA that Futurism's most notable protagonist, J. Gresham Machen, was born. He eventually attended Princeton Seminary, an institution that, as I have sought to demonstrate, was representative of both the Archaist and Centrist positions within the Presbyterian Church USA. As a movement of co-belligerency, a kind of coalition, Fundamentalism was comprised of the whole spectrum from Archaism to Centrism, even harboring certain distinctly Futurist tendencies. The sides which continued to polarize in the Presbyterian Church USA were those from which the controversy took its name: Fundamentalism/Modernism. Modernism/Liberalism, in contrast to Fundamentalism, contained the Futurist element. In many ways Machen was an epitome of the Fundamentalist mind, and in others he was at variance with it. George Marsden confirmed this many sided portrait of Machen when he wrote:

> Gresham Machen (1881-1937) was not a typical fundamentalist or evangelical. He belonged to one of the sub-groups, strict Presbyterians loyal to the Old Princeton theology that looked to the Westminster Confession of Faith for its creed. He did not like being called a fundamentalist, he was an intellectual, he was ill-at-ease with the emotionalism and over-simplifications of revival meetings.... Yet he was willing to make common cause with popular fundamentalism. In his view modernist theology threatened to undermine Christianity by proclaiming another gospel. His volume *Christianity and Liberalism* (1923) cast him as the foremost spokesperson for the fundamentalist coalition. (Marsden 1991:182.)

In this chapter I would like to delve in to the trials and tribulations of J. Gresham Machen in the latter half of the Fundamentalist/Modernist Controversy. While many people, some of great importance in ecclesiastical circles, were involved in the controversy, I believe that

Machen was the central figure. With this in mind, I would like first to survey Machen's life and then turn to his role in the controversy which, in its latter stages, swept through the halls of Princeton Theological Seminary, culminating in his dismissal from the Presbyterian Church after a protracted dispute over the newly formed Independent Board for Foreign Missions—a Machen creation. Interspersed throughout, I will endeavor to tie up any loose ends our narrative has generated thus far, the most notable of which being the long term effect of the Cumberland Presbyterian merger.

6.1 J. Gresham Machen

John Gresham Machen was born in Baltimore on 28 July 1881, just prior to the decade that Henry Steel Commager has dubbed '...the watershed of American history' (Commager 1950:41). In a sense he was born at the crossroads of the modern world: the Industrial Revolution, waves of immigration from Europe flooding into American cities, and the social gospel were well under way (Hudson 1953:110-156, Ashton 1948). His childhood was a happy one in almost every respect; never having to taste the grinding poverty which was so much a part of city life (Stonehouse [1954]1987:40-57). In all respects his family life seemed to be a model of decorum, not inconsistent with that of a typical Calvinistic household. His father, Arthur Machen, was a successful attorney and an elder in the Franklin Street Presbyterian Church. 'One can see the image of the son in the father,' writes William Masselink, '...Machen's father was a profoundly Christian man. He was a man of wide reading and earnest meditation upon the sacred things of holy faith. He was not of an emotional type but his Christian experience was rather "a quiet stream whose waters ran deep." He was not a superficial ascetic but rather an earnest consecrated Christian.' (Masselink [S.a.]:3-4). Machen's mother, Mary, or Minnie as she was affectionately known, was the real inspiration for her son's firm grounding in the faith as set forth in both the Scriptures and the Westminster Confession and Catechisms. Already in his early youth he was compelled to memorize the kings of Israel and Judah, as well as the Westminster Shorter Catechism. On his death, the faculty of Westminster Seminary issued a statement which read in part: 'the home in which he was reared was a home of culture and refinement, but first of all a home of childlike faith. In that faith of his childhood Dr. Machen continued to live and in the joy of the sufficiency of that faith he died' (quoted by Masselink [S.a.]:5).

Machen attended private but secular primary and secondary schools and graduated at the tender age of seventeen. Thereupon he immediately set his sights on the Johns Hopkins University and graduated with the Bachelor of Arts in 1901. Throughout his college career, Machen excelled in the classics. Even after graduation, he decided to stay on for an additional year's tutelage under the renowned classicist Professor Basil L. Gildersleeve. In 1902, at the urging of Francis Landey Patton, Princeton Seminary's newly elected president, Machen entered Princeton Seminary and a course that would extend for the next twenty seven years. Machen biographers abound in speculation regarding his emotional and psychological state during this period (Hart 1994:17, Coray 1981:17, Stonehouse [1954]1987:58-60). That he was hesitant to enter the ministry is an understatement. But was Machen rootless, given to a sort of wanderlust of the mind, and unable to commit himself to a specific course for life? Darryl Hart leaves this impression by his portrayal of Machen in his student days as self-absorbed, exuding a decidedly cavalier attitude to all his responsibilities (Hart 1994:10-34). Machen's problems might well have been, however, more in the way of mental reservations. William Masselink, however, speaks almost exclusively of the influence that Benjamin Warfield had on the young man (Masselink [S.a.]:6-10). Machen seems to have been severely perturbed by the apparent intellectual difficulties of the faith (Hart 1994:23); not difficulties in the sense of insurmountable problems inherent within the very nature of the faith, but rather, because Christianity as it was generally taught and preached, lacked, for him, intellectual cohesion. Doctrine was being submerged in favor of the more amorphous concept "life." 'These were the signs' relates Darryl Hart, 'of "the extremely low intellectual standard among the future ministers of the Presbyterian Church." For them, "true piety, high motives," but also "deep ignorance" was the rule' (Hart 1994:27). Machen saw the climate of American Protestantism as "sentimental" and "anti-intellectual" (Hart 1994:24), and distinctly not to his liking.

During the years 1905 and 1906 Machen studied at the Universities of Marburg and Göttingen, initially concentrating his efforts in the field of New Testament under the able tutelage of Adolf Jülicher. Gradually his attention shifted to systematic theology and the towering personality of Wilhelm Herrmann, a disciple of the Rischlian School. Herrmann's teaching was not bound by the strictures of history in its views of Christianity. Christianity for Hermann was rather a-historical in nature but valid with respect to its sublime ethical content. Hermann's chief interest was God's kingdom, and that kingdom as it was found within. 'The chief end of every religion,' writes Herrmann,

> is to secure God's communion with the individual soul.... In the soul of the man who stands amid such revelation religion is established; and that participation in the divine life, towards which our religious longing yearns, consists in a man's becoming conscious that he means something to God, and that God is entering into communion with him. He who does not admit these propositions to be true does not know what religion is. We feel that we have a common understanding with all who show that they understand religion thus, whether they are Christians or not.... (But) we see that we have no inner life at all until we recognise the good and let it rule in our hearts; and the clearer this becomes the more painfully are we sensible that all the forces of our existence are in conflict with the good. (Herrmann1909:199 & 99-100.)

Machen admitted on many occasions during this period in his life that Herrmann was the most dynamic speaker he had ever heard. According to Hart, 'Herrmann represented a model for reconciling the seemingly divergent worlds of religion and academic rigor' (Hart 1994:22). In a letter to his mother, Machen describes Herrmann thus: 'Such an overpowering personality I think I almost never before encountered—overpowering in the sincerity of religious devotion. Herrmann may be illogical and one-sided, but I tell you he is alive' (quoted by Stonehouse [1954] 1987:106). He admitted four days later in a letter to his father that 'He (Herrmann) speaks right to the heart; and I have been thrown all into confusion by what he says—so much deeper is his devotion to Christ than anything I have known in myself during the last few years. I don't know at all what to say as yet, for Herrmann's views are so revolutionary' (quoted by Stonehouse [1954] 1987:106). Gradually it dawned on Machen that Herrmann was not correct in his views of the Christian faith. As Stonehouse relates:

> Later Machen was to see that the "Christ" to whom Herrmann was fervently devoted never really existed and that religious experience is not as such self-validating. Evidently to a significant extent he became aware even

while he heard and read Herrmann of basic weaknesses and inadequacies. He certainly never came to the point of substituting Herrmann's views for those of orthodox Christianity. Nevertheless, he was profoundly unsettled and even overwhelmed by his encounter with this man whose fervor and moral earnestness put many Christians to shame. And even when he came to reject this theology without qualification he remained affected by the experience at least to the extent of being concerned to deal in dead earnest with the views of his opponents and of being tenderly sympathetic with those who might be passing through similar struggles of doubt. (Stonehouse [1954] 1987:108.)

The time spent studying at the great theological faculties of Marburg and Göttingen were to be of inestimable value in the theological war brewing at home, a war in which Machen would command an important position. In his thesis, William Masselink gives a valuable assessment of Machen's years in Germany. 'In which way did this liberal theology of Marburg and Göttingen influence Machen?' he ponders.

Several facts must here be stated. In the first place his stay in Germany gave him direct and firsthand information in regard to this liberal movement which he later combated. Machen also states that his studies in Germany gave him a new respect for the Princeton theology. When he came back to Princeton, he appreciated more than ever before the thoroughly scientific methods of the Princeton Seminary. He saw with convincing clearness that great scholars like Armstrong and Warfield had not dodged the real questions at issue, but had presented the liberal views with a conscientious honesty which one must admire and respect. Machen also learned from his stay in Germany the scientific methods which the various critics used against their opponents. He made use of these himself. One of Machen's keenest weapons against his liberal opponents is to answer them out of the mouth of other liberals. In this way he makes one liberal annihilate the hypothesis of another. But the stay in Germany also influenced his Religion. He tells us that it was here that he faced the greatest spiritual struggle of his life. Not that these doubts had never perplexed his mind before, but now they certainly came to their consummation. In the agony of his soul he faced the question, Is Christianity true or is it false? Is it based upon facts or only upon subjective experience? The outcome of this spiritual battle was glorious. His difficulties were solved one by one. Especially Machen's mother must be credited for giving genuine spiritual guidance to her doubting son in the midst of these dark clouds. When faith was restored to its equilibrium he was better prepared than ever before to face the great task of his life in defending the old faith against the liberal criticism. (Masselink [S.a.]:12.)

A new clarity of mind became evident in the months that followed Machen's return to Princeton. He approached his work with a renewed vigor. Could it be that his doubts about the ministry and its distinct lack of interest in the intellectual side of the faith had finally been assuaged? None of the letters written to members of his family during this time period can settle this question conclusively. Although, during this period, Machen's main concern does seem to have been his own personal reconciliation of the intellectual and the spiritual side of the Christian Faith (Hart 1994:26-27), the one event that points to a resolution of these earlier antagonisms was his decision finally to seek ordination; he was subsequently licensed to preach in 1914.

The resolution of his inner conflict helped to focus Machen's attention and his formidable powers of analysis upon more pressing matters. Throughout his writings he always seems to be grappling, in one way or another, with problems posed by the conflict between time and eternity. That is to say, we live in a world of the senses, a creation which is fallen but, at the same time, it is all that humanity knows. Because of the Christian faith, humanity seeks a world unlike anything presently accessible and one not comprehended by any means presently available. How do the two relate? This same question put another way is the apparent paradox that the Reformed Theology posits between saint and sinner. The two, existing in the same space, in the very same body, are juxtaposed in the same thinking subject. The antagonism between the fallen creation and the realm of the spirit is seen in the person of every one for whom Christ died. And this ongoing struggle of the flesh with the spirit, between the old and the new is carried on in every detail of this present earthly life. The questions to which Machen lent his pen were the same problems that were also foremost in the minds of others (Hart 1994:30). Charles Briggs, not so many years before, was looking at the same dilemma under the heading of Christ and culture. Machen did the same and simultaneously defended his position as the true or orthodox one. Machen saw collaboration and compromise as evils, not as new forms of efficiency (Hart 1994:27-34). The world was not a helper to the church but her nemesis. Criticizing the church for abandoning her calling in favor of a more enlightened cooperation, Machen chides:

> In a day of increased specialization, of renewed interest in philology and in history, of more rigorous scientific method, let the Church go on abandoning her Bible to her enemies. They will study it scientifically, rest assured, if the Church does not. Let her substitute sociology altogether for Hebrew, practical expertness for the proof of her gospel. Let her shorten the preparation of her ministry, let her permit it to be interrupted yet more and more by premature practical activity. By doing so she will win a straggler here and there. But her winnings will be temporary. The great current of modern culture will sooner or later engulf her puny eddy. God will save her somehow—out of the depths. But the labor of centuries will have been swept away. God grant that the Church may not resign herself to that. God grant she may face her problem squarely and bravely. That problem is not easy. It involves the very basis of her faith. Christianity is the proclamation of an historical fact—that Jesus Christ rose from the dead. Modern thought has no place for that proclamation. It prevents men even from listening to the message. (Machen 1913:12.)

To Machen, the church was doing more than just accommodating herself to certain facets of modern culture, and by implication to the world. She was acquiescing in her very nature to the things of the world. She was bringing the world into her sphere of activity and baptizing its philosophy and activities so as to make them acceptable. She was blurring the distinction between herself and the world. She was breaking down the wall of antithesis. And, subtly, this same mind, one bent on accommodation, was being detected within the walls of Princeton Seminary (Hart 1978:30, 50-54 & Rian [1940] 1992:37-56). Trying to give his colleagues the benefit of the doubt, Machen wrote:

> The Church is puzzled by the world's indifference. She is trying to overcome it by adapting her message to the fashions of the day. But if, instead, before the conflict, she would descend into the secret place of meditation, if by the clear light of the gospel she would seek an answer not merely to the questions of the hour but, first of all, to the eternal problems of the spiritual world, then perhaps, by God's grace, through His Holy Spirit, in His good time, she might issue forth once more with power, and an age of doubt might be followed by the dawn of an era of faith. (Machen 1913:15.)

Machen's defensive posture was interpreted by others as intolerance and even vindictiveness. There were those on the Princeton Seminary faculty, not necessarily theological Liberals, who could not, or would not, understand Machen's militant position. Ronald Clutter, in his 1982 doctoral thesis on the re-organization of Princeton Seminary, maintains that the rift that developed in the Princeton faculty during this time period set the teachers of the theoretical subjects against those more disposed to the practical disciplines. Clutter is quick to point out that Princeton '...entered the twentieth century with an educational philosophy established for the seminary in 1811' (Clutter 1982:226). This was considered a drawback given the changes happening in the modern world to which Christianity must make a relevant contribution. Princeton Seminary, by its adherence to the strict Calvinism prescribed in its charter, was loosing students to the other seminaries in the denomination, which were taking a more hands-on, practical approach to the ministry. In response to calls for a more practical emphasis to be given to the curriculum, the faculty reiterated its expectation that a student apply himself to the studies at hand and not to side issues. The faculty minutes for the meeting of 29 April 1903 indicate a decision taken in this matter as:

> One. That the students without exception will gain more profit by devoting their attention solely to seminary duties during the session than by surrendering a portion of their time each week to church work in neighboring cities. It has been the theory of this seminary from the

beginning that the seminary session is for study and the long vacation for such purposes as obtaining practical experience in ministerial work. Two. That there is no immediate necessity for the seminary to depart from its traditional policy. (quoted by Clutter 1982:227.)

The debate over the practical, however, would not go away by simple faculty pronouncement; in fact, it intensified. This intensification took the form of the person of J. Ross Stevenson, who was elected to the presidency of Princeton Seminary in 1914—Stevenson, as was pointed out earlier, was one of the initial supporters of the plan of union between the Presbyterian Church USA and the Cumberland Presbyterian Church that was ratified in 1906. His predecessor, Francis Landey Patton, had approached his position as president of the faculty as *primus inter pares*, the first among a gathering of equals. Stevenson did not follow suit. As Edwin Rian relates: 'He (Stevenson) came to Princeton not appreciating fully its theological position and emphasis, and at the same time accepting the office of president on the terms set forth in the plan of the seminary which he interpreted in the plain sense, but which interpretation had never been enforced at the institution.' Additionally, Rian reminisces,

> From the stand point of administration, Dr. Stevenson conceived of his position as that of the real head of the institution who was to have a leading part in forming its policies, choosing its professors, inviting men to address the students and representing the seminary before the church. One who did not know the history of Princeton and its administrative policy would be likely to accept that interpretation of the president's position from a reading of the plan of the seminary. On the other hand, the faculty had always believed that the president was little more than a presiding officer who, together with his colleagues, decided on the entire educational program for the institution. (Rian [1940] 1992:40-41.)

It is impossible to tell if the board that sought out his services for the seminary expected Stevenson to recreate the office to which he was appointed. The probability was that such changes were indeed expected of the new president. His qualifications differed significantly from the rest of the faculty over which he was expected to preside effectively. The Princeton faculty at the time of Stevenson's hire was a select group of highly trained and specialized scholars. Most had published widely and were internationally known. Stevenson, by contrast, was not a scholar but a pastor. Clutter (1982) has argued that in selecting Stevenson the seminary board was attempting to secure a man who could bridge what was perceived as a widening gap between the seminary and the church. Stevenson was a churchman, and an acknowledged master in the pastoral arts, and it was because of his pastoral expertise that his services were sought by the seminary. But, as Paul Woolley, late Professor of Church History at Westminster Theological Seminary, argues, the pastoral and experiential were all Stevenson knew.

> It was an evil day for the seminary for, pious and believing though he was, he had no understanding of, or love for, the great tradition which the theologians of Princeton had been building for ninety years. Elected in 1914 to the presidency of the institution, he made it his goal to end the distinctive contribution of Princeton and to make it instead a seminary which should be representative of all the streams of theology, widely variegated though they were, to be found in the Presbyterian Church in the U. S. A. Stevenson was impressive in the pulpit. In his later years he frequently recited from memory in very moving fashion long catenae of biblical passages which might feed the soul. It was hard to realize that such a pious person was bending every effort to disrupt the legacy of the earlier Princeton theologians which a majority of the faculty and directors were defending. (Woolley 1977:11.)

Stevenson, in his inaugural address to the office of president, seemed to deny that any such inclusive view of the church, including the seminary and its work, was to be part of his administrative tenure. Nevertheless, his speech was sufficiently vague to warrant suspicion on the part of his colleagues. Stevenson declared that:

> This institution bears as her official title "The Theological Seminary of the Presbyterian Church in the U. S. A." While her gates are open to all students of all Christian churches, and as a matter of fact her service has been of the widest interdenominational character as our alumni catalogue records, nevertheless by foundation

anchorage, by legal ties, and by covenanted obligation this seminary is bound to heed the demands of the age as interpreted and emphasized by the Presbyterian Church. (quoted by Clutter 1982:93.)

On another occasion Stevenson further clarified his intentions to the Princeton Seminary faculty by stating: 'We (Princeton Seminary) are the agency of the combined Old School and New School and my ambition as President of the Seminary is to have it represent the whole Presbyterian Church and not any particular faction of it' (quoted by Rian [1940] 1992:42). From the outset the faculty clashed with the ideas and policies of the new president. Machen did not believe in President Stevenson's sincerity. To the contrary, he believed that Stevenson's inauguration was the beginning of the end of the institution he had come to love dearly. In retrospect, Machen stated for the record that,

> Never has Dr. Stevenson given any clear indication by the policy that he has followed as President of the Seminary, that he recognizes the profound line of cleavage that separates the two opposite tendences (sic) within the Presbyterian Church, and the necessity that if Princeton Seminary is to be true to the moral obligations involved in the distinctive basis upon which it has always appealed for support, it must, in this great contention, definitely and unequivocally take sides. Such recognition, which we seek in vain in President Stevenson, would not necessarily prejudge the question whether both tendencies should be tolerated within the Presbyterian Church: but it would certainly mean at least that Princeton has the right and indeed the very solemn obligation of maintaining a *distinctive* position within the larger unity of the Church. It is true, then, that Dr. Stevenson's policy is in a very important sense an inclusive policy, and that such an inclusive policy is contrary to the obligations which, on account of its entire history, Princeton Seminary has very solemnly assumed. (Machen 1927:9-10.)

Machen went on to plead for the historic position of Princeton as opposed to the broader, more inclusive position which was gaining adherents in high places. He saw the inclusiveness that was being promoted as unnatural for the church, any church. For it meant nothing less than including the unbelieving world in the church. The church was, however, according to the Confession, the Scriptures, and her historic stance exclusive of the unrepentant world. For Machen, the world was fallen and an object of the church's evangelistic efforts; not, as Stevenson would have it, just another 'tendency' in Christendom. Maybe, in this instance, Machen was also a prophet, since, it seems, he accurately predicted the end from the beginning with regard to Stevenson's policies. He foresaw that:

> If that policy (Stevenson's inclusive vision for the church) becomes dominant in Princeton Seminary, then the Princeton position has very definitely been given up. And if the change is wrought by ecclesiastical action, then all the high-sounding words which have recently been uttered about peace and tolerance will be mocked. In that case, there will be liberty in the Presbyterian Church for Modernists, but none for conservatives; and those who hold the conservative view will have to go elsewhere for the maintenance of those convictions that are dearer to them than life itself. (Machen 1927:10-11.)

Machen foresaw the anarchy that would characterize the Presbyterian Church if these "tendencies" were allowed to develop. He foresaw the transformation that eventually would take place in Presbyterianism, but, as the prophets of old, he was not accepted in his own house. His own rejected his vision as fantastic. All of this, however, served to strengthen Machen in his resolve that what he was doing was right

6.2 The Controversy

There is scholarly disagreement as to exactly who fired the opening salvo that erupted in all-out war between the two 'tendencies' in the Presbyterian Church. That this war eventually became known as the Fundamentalist/Modernist Controversy is agreed upon by all. That it had been simmering just beneath the surface of civility for some time is only beginning to receive recognition (Weston 1997).

Those who called themselves Liberals were dissatisfied with the lack of toleration accorded their views by their more conservative brothers (Weston 1997:104-112). They wanted much more latitude in what they would continue to maintain was their 'interpretation' of the confession and related documents. James Everitt Clarke, a Cumberland Liberal, had answered Benjamin Warfield as early as 1904, questioning '...whether Dr. Warfield's interpretation is the only interpretation permissible and orthodox within the Presbyterian Church' (quoted by Ames 1971:79). The question was a rhetorical one, the obvious answer being a resounding, 'No!' Underlying Clarke's words was a minor document popularly known as the *Brief Statement*—see appendix II for the text in its entirety— referred to by the more conservative element as a "constitutional technicality." This document, it seems, held much more importance for the Cumberland brethren than for the Presbyterian Church at large in the merger of 1906. Clarke, editor of *The Cumberland Presbyterian* and later *The Presbyterian Advance* and a vocal proponent of the Cumberland cause, was generally in favor of the union of 1906. His understanding of the significance and mechanics of it, however, differed greatly from that of the Princeton professors.

Clarke was a native New Yorker who became dissatisfied with some of the more Calvinistic distinctives he encountered in the north. Not wishing to commit himself to an interpretation of the Westminster Confession that he found objectionable, he emigrated south. It was in the state of Tennessee that he finally found a theological home. Clarke was to find himself in a unique situation when talks of a merger began after the confessional revision of 1903. Regarding the revision and the prospects of returning to the church of his birth, Clarke was positive. He observed that:

> ...the recent revision of the Westminster Confession has removed or explained away all of the expressions to which he (Clarke) had always taken exception. The revised confession plainly says that all infants are saved; that if any man is not saved it is wholly his own fault and not because God foreordained that some should be condemned; that Christ's redemptive work is for the whole human race; that the Holy Spirit operates on the whole world in such a manner as to leave all men inexcusable. (quoted by Ames 1971:64.)

In response to a question from one of his readers, Clarke clarified his views on the revision and its position in the context of the reunion of the two churches. Clarke responded that Cumberland Presbyterians were not required or expected to disavow or renounce their old doctrines. There is no intention... expressed, implied, or intimated in the Plan of Union that they should do so. Unquestionably there will be the amplest freedom... in matters of doctrine. In the recently adopted 'Declaratory Statement' emphasis is placed upon the fact that, in their ordination vow, ministers and elders and deacons subscribe, not to particular doctrines, but to the Confession of Faith as containing only the SYSTEM of doctrine taught in the Scriptures. And this liberty of belief is specifically secured by the Declaratory Statement, as to chapters III and X which contained the doctrines that were particularly objectionable to our (Cumberland) fathers. (quoted by Ames 1971:64.)

Not to be misunderstood, Clarke recognized that there were indeed differences between the revised Confession of 1903 and the Cumberland Confessions, and many of these were of significance. Yet the *Concurrent Declaration*, adopted by both the Cumberland Presbyterian and the Presbyterian Church USA at their General Assemblies in 1904, said there was agreement between the two churches on two counts. The first was that the systems of theology contained in the Cumberland Confession and the revision of 1903 were, except for minor differences, identical. The second reason, as John Ames indicates, was that there was '...agreement in the practical, actual, teachings of the churches' (Ames 1971:69). The *Concurrent Declaration* reads in part:

In adopting the Confession of Faith of the Presbyterian Church in the United States of America, as revised in 1903, as a Basis of Union it is mutually recognized that such agreement now exists between the systems of doctrine contained in the Confessions of Faith of the two Churches as to warrant this union—a union alike honoring to both. Mutual acknowledgment is also made of the teaching and defense of essential evangelical doctrines held in common by these Churches, and of the divine favor and blessing that have made this common faith and service effectual. It is also recognized that liberty of belief exists by virtue of the provisions of the Declaratory Statement, which is part of the Confession of Faith..., and which states that 'the ordination vow of ministers, ruling elders and deacons, as set forth in the Form of Government, requires the reception and adopting of the Confession of Faith, only as containing the system of doctrine taught in the Holy Scriptures.' This liberty is specifically secured by the Declaratory Statement, as to Chapter III, and Chapter X, Section 3 of the Confession of Faith. It is recognized also that the doctrinal deliverance contained in the 'Brief Statement of the Reformed Faith,' adopted in 1902 by the General Assembly of the Presbyterian Church... 'for better understanding of our doctrinal beliefs,' reveals a doctrinal agreement favorable to reunion. (quoted by Ames 1971:60-61.)

The document in which the Cumberland Church placed so much hope for the merger was the *"Brief Statement."* This document, drawn up by the same revision committee that was responsible for the revision of 1903 in the Presbyterian Church USA, was adopted by the General Assembly to express '...so far as possible, in untechnical terms for the purpose "of giving information and a better understanding of our beliefs and not with a view to its becoming a substitute or an alternative of our Confession of Faith"' (Schaff [1931]1985:920). Nevertheless, the importance of this *"Brief Statement"* for Clarke and others concerned about the terms of reunion cannot be overestimated. In this connection, Ames adds:

The very existence of this statement, approved by the General Assembly, indicated to Clarke that the actual theology of the Presbyterian Church, except in a few cases, was not contained in the Westminster Confession and its catechisms, but in the "Brief Statement." Clarke knew that it was not part of the doctrinal standards of the Presbyterian Church, through what he called a "constitutional technicality" in that it had not been submitted to the presbyteries for adoption. But he felt that "really, and in the popular mind" it was clothed with as much authority as the Confession; and, quoting "an eminent Presbyterian minister," Clarke said that the authority of the "Brief Statement" would "grow and grow." The action of the General Assembly in ordering it printed in the hymnbook was, according to "the eminent minister," a "practical adopting act of the widest and most far-reaching influence. It will become, it has become, the real confession of our faith as a church." Earlier Clarke had argued that "had the 'Brief Statement' not been made, covering as it does the whole Confession," it is doubtful there would have been an overture from the Cumberland Presbyterians towards union. He admitted that the revision itself was incomplete, but insisted that the "Brief Statement" made statements "as clear as any Cumberland Presbyterian could ask." (Ames 1971:69-70.)

Not all on the Cumberland side were happy with the merger either. Some felt that it was engineered by certain Cumberland ministers desirous of the kinds of well-paying ministerial positions the northern ministers were believed to have. Others such as Elder Ben Eli Guthrie of Missouri saw the Liberals of the northern church luring the Cumberland Presbyterians into union in order to strengthen their own Liberal ranks. At the Cumberland General Assembly of 1904 he made himself perfectly clear.

> The liberal party in the Northern Church is waiting like Wellington at Waterloo for reinforcements. The Cumberland Presbyterian Church is its Blucher. The Southern Presbyterian Church is the Grouchy for whose aid the conservatives are looking. The question for us is this: shall Blucher or Grouchy get there first? (quoted by Ames 1971:82.)

The years following the merger were a time of silent consolidation, in which each side was trying to figure exactly where it stood. There were times when the controversy, bubbling beneath the surface, came into full view. After several years of "experiencing" the united church, conservatives used their influence in the General Assembly to publish an abbreviated statement of faith to which they demanded that all subscribe. Known as the *Doctrinal Deliverance of 1910*, this document, as I indicated in the previous chapter, stipulated five doctrines which it claimed were "essential and necessary" (Armstrong, Loetscher, and Anderson 1956:280), namely: the inspiration and inerrancy of Scripture, the virgin birth, the atonement, the resurrection of Christ, and the validity of Miracles (Armstrong, Loetscher, and Anderson 1956:281). Because of the intervention of World War I, the response to this *1910 Deliverance* was not quick in coming. When it did come, however, James Everitt Clarke was in the forefront, and the response was known as the *Auburn Affirmation*.

The stir caused by the publication of the *Auburn Affirmation* in 1924, about which more will be said later, was enormous. Still, its impact would have been even greater had it not been for a famous sermon, delivered two years earlier by a Baptist minister named Harry Emerson Fosdick, serving a Presbyterian charge in New York, that exploded on the scene first. The Reverend Fosdick set out to compose a conciliatory address, or so he said. To underscore its irenic content in the minds of his audience, he entitled his sermon: "Shall the Fundamentalists Win?" Although it was meant to be a 'plea' for 'good will,' the sermon fell wide of its mark. Indeed, it seemed to bring the Fundamentalist/Modernist Controversy to an even higher level of hostility. The climate in general, however, was ripe for discord. William Jennings Bryan's articles in the *New York Times* condemning evolution, plus his book *In His Image* (Bryan 1922) set the stage for some form of retaliation from the growing Liberal caucus (North 1996:453-456). An inflammatory article in the *New York Times Book Review and Magazine*, dated just three months before Fosdick's sermon, was a Liberal response to Bryan's book and editorials, as well as another straw on the conservative camel's back. The author, Austin Hay, seems to have said what was on the minds of many Liberals at the time. His assessment that:

> It is not generally recognized that, parallel with the great march of science during the last sixty years, religion, so far from retrogressing, has also advanced; and that never before in the history of the world has the interest in the spiritual side of life been keener, nor the quality of religious thought finer and nobler. Religion, indeed, has also been undergoing an evolutionary process and adapting itself to modern ideas, modern conditions and modern needs. Many dogmas have been discarded and the essential truths of religion and morality separated from the obsolete husks which formerly surrounded them. Not the least part of this progressive movement has been carried on by theologians and professional teachers of religion. Naturally, from the standpoint of crude and outmoded beliefs the new faith looks like a

collection of heresies. The primitive religionist still imagines that to accept the truths of science is to become an "infidel"; and, since there still survive those who hold this restricted view, an occasional recrudescence of Pre-Darwinian superstition is to be expected. (quoted by North 1996:456.)

While these volleys may have served to set the stage, it was Fosdick who threw down the gauntlet with his truly memorable sermon. Fosdick began by exhorting his audience '...to think of the Fundamentalist controversy which threatens to divide the American churches, as though already they were not sufficiently split and riven' (Fosdick [1922] 1968)170). He characterized the Fundamentalist as one whose basic quality was intolerance (Fosdick [1922]1968:172), intolerance for those who did not hold the same opinions regarding the doctrines of Christianity. It became evident, in the hearing, that Fosdick's opinions "regarding" Christian doctrine should be rephrased as the opinions "of" Christian doctrine, because, to Fosdick, the two were inseparable. He admitted that the Fundamentalists saw clearly the theological shift that had been taking place, and accurately assessed it as resulting from new knowledge. In speaking of this new knowledge, which he properly defined as the recent findings of both science and philosophy, Fosdick defined the role of both Liberals and Fundamentalists in the current crisis. He concluded that:

A great mass of new knowledge has come into man's possession: new knowledge about the physical universe, its origin, its forces, its laws; new knowledge about human history and in particular about the ways in which the ancient peoples used to think in matters of religion and the methods by which they phrased and explained their spiritual experiences; and new knowledge, also, about other religions and the strangely similar ways in which men's faiths and religious practices have developed everywhere. Now, there are multitudes of reverent Christians who have been unable to keep this new knowledge in one compartment of their minds and the Christian faith in the other. ...the new knowledge and the old faith had to be blended in a new combination. Now, the people in this generation who are trying to do this are the liberals, and the Fundamentalists are out on a campaign to shut against them the doors of the Christian fellowship. Shall they be allowed to succeed? ... If they (Fundamentalists) had their way, within the Church, they would set up in Protestantism a doctrinal tribunal more rigid than the Pope's. (Fosdick [1922]1968:173,172.)

In order to save the Presbyterian Church, Fosdick suggested an accommodation between the credal statements of historic Presbyterianism and the new knowledge. This course of action was, however, the very course taken by Arius in the fourth century and it eventually led to his being anathemized by the Centrist party (Murray 1964:54). In the developing crisis within Presbyterianism, Fosdick was of the Futurist mind. He proposed to change the historic affirmations of the faith to accommodate the ever-changing pronouncements of science and philosophy. This inclination was, moreover, not limited to Fosdick. It was a hallmark of theological Liberalism as a whole within the Presbyterian Church.

This new knowledge, for Fosdick, also embraced an intimate knowledge of the historical process itself and the indelible stamp that it leaves on the Christian religion with each new discovery (Fosdick [1922]1968:172). I believe that Kenneth Cauthen puts Fosdick's position, and all Futurists for that matter, into the larger context of doctrinal development when he comments on the 'evolutionary notions taken up by (Liberal) scholars' (Cauthen 1962:23). He writes:

> Historical research ...indicated that the religious ideas of the Hebrews had undergone a long period of development from primitive polytheism to the lofty heights of the ethical monotheism of II Isaiah and had come to its climax after many centuries more in the religion of Jesus. Thus, it became evident that there was not one complete, perfect, and static body of religious truth contained within the Bible. Rather, the Bible was seen to contain a developing religion which embraced many stages from its primitive beginnings to its maturity in the New Testament. There were many theologies and points of view in the Bible. Different levels of truth and value were seen to exist side by side. The Bible came to be thought of as a record of the progressive discovery of God in human experience, not as a static body of

209

theological dogmas all equally inspired and all of equal religious value. (Cauthen 1962:23.)

With this perspective in mind, it is easier to understand Fosdick's reservations on the traditional definition of the virgin birth of Christ. Fosdick complained that it is phrased '... in terms of a biological miracle that our modern minds cannot use' (Fosdick [1922] 1968:175). The same charge, however, with slight modification, could be laid against any of the doctrines that make up the credal system of historic Presbyterianism. 'As I plead thus for an intellectually hospitable, tolerant, liberty loving Church,' Fosdick warned, 'I am, of course, thinking primarily about this new generation. We have boys and girls growing up in our homes and schools, and because we love them we may well wonder about the Church which will be waiting to receive them' (Fosdick [1922] 1968:180).

Fosdick attacked the prevailing definition of Presbyterianism as it had been historically and traditionally defined in the Westminster Confession of Faith. Even though his own concept of Presbyterianism, it seems, was influenced by an evolutionary view of development, he still criticized the opposition for basing their views on tenuous grounds. To Fosdick, this extremely conservative view, characterized by Reformed Theology, was based not on the Westminster Confession but on the more abridged *Doctrinal Deliverance of 1910*. A document which, according to Fosdick, focused almost exclusively on the doctrine of inerrancy in each of its five points (Kim 1983:169). It is Kim's belief that both 'the Fosdick case and the Auburn Affirmation were protests against the binding ecclesiological policy, which attempted to maintain a doctrinally pure church. As the opponent power rose, the militant spirit was added to the extreme conservative ecclesiology, and this fact even more stimulated the conflict' (Kim 1983:170).

Fosdicks's preaching, especially his most famous sermon: "Shall the Fundamentalists Win," caused both an uproar in conservative circles and a protest demanding his reprimand to be lodged with the presbytery of New York. The New York presbytery, however, took the matter "under advisement." Finally, two years later, much to the chagrin of the conservatives, the presbytery of New York exonerated him of all charges. Fosdick went on to be pastor at the Riverside Church in upper Manhattan, clearly a promotion for his pulpit abilities, his theological affinities notwithstanding.

It was a combination of the Fosdick affair and the perceived ascendance of Liberalism in the Presbyterian Church USA that caused Machen to take up his pen in defense of what he believed was the church's historic stance. 'As Machen witnessed modernism making inroads into the Presbyterian Church,' argues Clutter, 'he realized the need to engage the enemy before the infiltration could reach irreversible proportions' (Clutter 1982:105). Thus, a New Testament professor by profession, Machen became the apologist for credal Presbyterianism. He began his new, popular literary career with *Christianity and Liberalism*, a book that turned out to be the bombshell of the decade. Against what he saw as a spurious and dangerous new theology, one that recast the historic affirmations of the faith in accommodation with the "new knowledge," as Fosdick called it, emanating from the Liberal/Futurist contingent in the church, Machen spoke and wrote in a singularly uncompromising manner. Machen called this new 'accommodation' of the Liberals a new religion entirely (Machen [1923]1946:2). As he put it: '...what the liberal theologian has retained after abandoning to the enemy one Christian doctrine after another is not Christianity at all, but a religion which is so entirely different from Christianity as to belong in a distinct category' (Machen [1923]1946:6-7). The alternative that Machen presented, the historic credal stance of the Presbyterian Church, can be seen in virtually every page that he wrote. As early as 1925 Robert Hastings Nichols defined the difference between the rival parties in the Presbyterian Church as hinging on an understanding of just what makes one a Presbyterian, a creed or something else. In an article on the subject he said,

> It has been said ...that scriptural literalism is at the root of it (Fundamentalism). This is true, yet something else lies even deeper. It is also often said, and truly, that the real theological interest of the movement is the maintenance of the supernatural, as the fundamentalists construe this. It is a powerful recrudescence of the ancient feeling that God is manifested only in what is outside normal experience, and that if abnormal things are taken away, God is lost. The five points (the Doctrinal Deliverance of 1910), or any other list of fundamentals, reveal this emphasis. But deeper than either literalism or crude supernaturalism is a certain conception of the church. (quoted by Kim 1983:117-118.)

Machen's ecclesiology was credal, in concert with the historic Presbyterian position. If one was in agreement with the creed, one was free to bind oneself to that creed or not (Machen [1923]1946:164-165). This was the extent of the freedom accorded in the idea of "voluntary association" in Machen's thought (Machen [1923]1946:168-170), about which the Liberals said so much (Loetscher 1954:117). Machen's reason for stressing the notion of voluntary association was in the hope of convincing the Liberals to leave and form a church in accord with their own principles, thus ending their efforts to remake the historic Presbyterian Church in their own image, something it never was (Machen [1923]1946:160, 164-168). He had already seen, with a clarity that few of his contemporaries possessed, that if the Liberals gained the ascendancy, regardless of their present pleas for tolerance, there would be no place found for the adherents of historic Presbyterianism. 'At this point a question may arise,' Machen wrote in *Christianity and Liberalism*,

> If there ought to be a separation between the liberals and the conservatives in the Church, why should not the conservatives be the ones to withdraw? Certainly it may come to that. If the liberal party really obtains full control of the councils of the Church, then no evangelical Christian can continue to support the Church's work. If a man believes that salvation from sin comes only through the atoning death of Jesus, then he cannot honestly support by his gifts and by his presence a propaganda which is intended to produce an exactly opposite impression. To do so would mean the most terrible bloodguiltiness which it is impossible to conceive. If the liberal party, therefore, really obtains control of the Church, evangelical Christians must be prepared to withdraw no matter what it costs. (Machen [1923] 1946:166.)

Speaking specifically of the historic credal faith of the church, Machen treated together all the doctrines that have traditionally made up the Reformed and Presbyterian tradition in order to show the unbridgeable gulf that separates the two sides in the then current debate. To Machen, the struggle for ascendancy in the church was between two different religions, one of which was anti-Christian in character.

At any rate, the situation cannot be helped by ignoring facts. The plain fact is that liberalism, whether it be true or false, is no mere "heresy"—no mere divergence at isolated points from Christian teaching. On the contrary it proceeds from a totally different root, and it constitutes, in essentials, a unitary system of its own. That does not mean that all liberals hold all parts of the system, or that Christians who have been affected by liberal teaching at one point have been affected at all points. There is sometimes a salutary lack of logic which prevents the whole of a man's faith being destroyed when he has given up a part. But the true way in which to examine a spiritual movement is in its logical relations; logic is the great dynamic, and the logical implications of any way of thinking are sooner or later certain to be worked out. And taken as a whole, even as it actually exists to-day, naturalistic liberalism is a fairly unitary phenomenon; it is tending more and more to eliminate from itself illogical remnants of Christian belief. It differs from Christianity in its view of God, of man, of the seat of authority and of the way of salvation. And it differs from Christianity not only in theology but in the whole of life. It is indeed sometimes said that there can be communion in feeling where communion in thinking is gone, a communion of the heart as distinguished from a communion of the head. But with respect to the present controversy, such a distinction certainly does not apply. On the contrary, in reading the books and listening to the sermons of recent liberal teachers—so untroubled by the problem of sin, so devoid of all sympathy for guilty humanity, so prone to abuse and ridicule the things dearest to the heart of every Christian man—one can only confess that if liberalism is to return into the Christian communion there must be a change of heart fully as much as a change of mind. God grant that such a change may come! But meanwhile the present situation must not be ignored but faced. Christianity is being attacked from within by a movement which is anti-Christian to the core. (Machen [1923] 1946:172-173.)

Well-known Washington publicist, Walter Lippmann, believed Machen had written a marvelous book. In his *A Preface to Morals* (1929), he referred in a particularly gracious manner to *Christianity and Liberalism* and its author. Lippmann stated emphatically that 'It is an admirable book. For its acumen, for its saliency, and for its wit this cool and stringent defense of orthodox Protestantism is, I think, the best popular argument produced by either side in the current controversy. We shall do well to listen to Dr. Machen' (Lippmann 1929:32). Lippmann's book, *A Preface to Morals*, written in 1929 and thus viewing the events about which he commented in retrospect, still prompted him to declare that 'the liberals have yet to answer Dr. Machen when he says that "the Christian movement at its inception was not just a way of life in the modern sense, but a way of life founded upon a message."' He hastened to add, however, that: 'Complete as was Dr. Machen's victory over the Protestant liberals, he did not long remain in possession of the field' (Lippmann 1929:33&34). Even as Machen was writing and editing the proofs for *Christianity and Liberalism*, the Liberals were preparing yet another volley. This broadside, which was first issued in January of 1924, struck with full force only months after the publication of Machen's thoroughgoing analysis of their position. It became known as the *Auburn Affirmation*, after the town in New York state where it was drafted, and its declared purpose was '...to safeguard the unity and liberty of the Presbyterian Church in the United States of America' (quoted by Rian [1940] 1992:205). Consistent with its stated purpose, the twofold contention of the document is, in Rian's estimation, 'First, that the general assembly has no constitutional right to elevate the five doctrines mentioned (*1910 Doctrinal Deliverance*) as special tests for ordination to the ministry, unless the constitution be changed by a vote of presbyteries; and secondly, that the five doctrines enumerated in the assembly's action are non-essential to the system of doctrine taught in the holy Scriptures and are merely theories of those facts and doctrines' (Rian [1940] 1992:25-26).

At the meeting of the next General Assembly in Grand Rapids, Michigan, in May of 1924, an overture was presented from the presbytery of Cincinnati advising the Assembly of the controversial contents of the *Auburn Affirmation*. A debate ensued which lasted the course of the next five days, during which time, to quote Charles Quirk's account,

J. Gresham Machen, a commissioner from New Brunswick Presbytery, released one of his typical attacks on the <u>Affirmation</u>, characterizing it as "... anti-theological and anti-Christian to the core." Machen allowed for the possibility that Christian men were among the signers, many of whom, according to Machen, may have been deceived by the Christian terminology of the document. (Quirk 1967:251.)

The result of the prolonged, heated debate over this document was absolutely nothing. The Committee on Bills and Overtures to which the *Auburn Affirmation* was presented for further endorsement recommended that no action be taken (Rian [1940] 1992:33). Kim's interpretation of these events is contra the interests of those he terms the "extreme conservatives."

> The Special Commission of the Assembly ignored extreme conservatives' interpretation of Church history, their desire to maintain a doctrinally conservative church, and their understanding of constitutional issues. The majority wanted to have a peaceful church instead of a noisy one. They attempted to maintain the church's unity rather than its purity. Therefore the Presbyterian Church became far more inclusive by moving towards pluralism and broadened itself theologically. The fundamentalist campaign failed. Fundamentalism now needed to change its method to preserve the last stamp of orthodoxy. (Kim 1983:170.)

Kim's analysis is telling. While he is in no way supportive of what he calls the Fundamentalist position, yet, he understands the issues under consideration by the Presbyterian Church in Machen's day to be theological in nature. Additionally, he fully acknowledges the desirability on the part of the majority present at the 1924 General Assembly for unity versus purity of doctrine and peace instead of noise. In so doing, Kim also attests to the fact that the issues under consideration by the 1924 General Assembly went largely unresolved.

In the wake of the merger between the Presbyterian Church USA and the Cumberland Presbyterian Church in 1906, all seemed relatively quiet for the reunited church. Yet, just beneath the surface, rumblings of discord were becoming more noticeable. In response to the merger of 1906, a more conservative element in the united church passed the *Doctrinal Deliverance of 1910* in order to safeguard the church's doctrinal integrity from perceived threats. The response from the Liberal camp took fourteen years to formulate, and it was still a bombshell when it was unveiled. Part of the publicity accorded this Liberal response, known as the *Auburn Affirmation*, was a controversial sermon by Harry Emerson Fosdick. Fosdick's sermon and the publication of the *Auburn Affirmation* became the necessary impetus for Princeton's J. Gresham Machen to take up his pen in defense of what he saw as threats to the affirmations of historic Presbyterianism. The battle lines were fast taking shape, and Machen was the center of the foray

6.3 Cumberland Influence

The long-term results of the Cumberland reunion of 1906 had become evident by the 1920s in the *Auburn Affirmation*, and James Everitt Clarke was one Cumberland Presbyterian who had taken an active role in its publication. A Cumberland Presbyterian minister, Clarke returned with the reunion only to see that, as time passed, all that was promised as a condition of union was not being honored. An activist by nature and a liberal by conviction, Clarke set about to remedy the situation. His standard throughout his life remained theological liberty for all. While Clarke might not have countenanced everything the Northern Liberals stood for, motifs such as '... the centrality of Christ, the immanence of God and the universality of his love, the basic goodness of man, and the social dimensions of Christianity' (Ames 1971:117) continually characterized his work. As John Ames puts it:

> Clarke was an active church man, and when he became convinced that the freedom of theological belief, which had been guaranteed to the Cumberland Presbyterians in the merger of 1906, was being denied through the efforts of what he called the "belligerent conservatives," who sought to make all officers of the church accept their interpretation of Presbyterian theology, he responded to this challenge and became one of the principal liberal leaders during the "fundamentalist controversy." A member of the committee that prepared and issued the "Auburn Affirmation," Clarke was instrumental in securing support for the liberal cause

216

from among former Cumberland Presbyterians, and from among Presbyterians in the South and Midwest. He was one of the architects of the strategy that secured for the liberals the support of the moderates, mostly conservative theologically though unwilling to allow the fundamentalists to dominate the church to the exclusion of all other views. (Ames 1971:iv-v.)

Neither the Liberals nor the Fundamentalists, at this juncture, had the votes needed to dominate the Presbyterian Church (Ames 1971:114). Hence, the field of endeavor was accorded to the more moderate Liberal contingent, referred to throughout by Weston as "institutional loyalists" (Weston 1997). Clarke was so successful in his campaign for the *Auburn Affirmation* that more than fifteen percent of the final 1200 signatures were from former Cumberland Presbyterians—made up essentially of this moderate/loyalist contingent (Weston 1997). This percentage, it should be noted, does not reflect the actual number of Cumberland Presbyterians in the Presbyterian Church; at that time they comprised about five percent of the total number. In its plea for liberty in the interpretation of the standards of the Church, the *Auburn Affirmation* appealed to the *Adopting Act of 1729* as guaranteeing the minister the right to 'scruple' concerning the non-essential articles of the Christian faith. The *Auburn Affirmation* roundly condemned the actions of the General Assembly in approving the *Doctrinal Deliverance of 1910* and ratifying it several more times in the interim. The claim for liberty of interpretation alone, as espoused by the document, was rendered suspect by the words of section IV:

> Furthermore, this opinion of the General Assembly attempts to commit our church to certain theories concerning the inspiration of the Bible, and the Incarnation, the Atonement, the Resurrection, and the Continuing Life and Supernatural Power of our Lord Jesus Christ....Some of us regard the particular theories contained in the deliverance of the General Assembly of 1923 as satisfactory explanations of these facts and doctrines. But we are united in believing that these are not the only theories allowed by the Scriptures and our standards as explanations of these facts and doctrines of our religion, and that all who hold to these facts and

doctrines, whatever theories they may employ to explain them, are worthy of all confidence and fellowship. (quoted by Rian [1940] 1992:208.)

For Machen, however, all this was absurd. How could one separate the historical event in the Scriptures from the interpretation of that event, or its theological significance, also given by the Scriptures. Doctrine was God's own explanation of the mighty acts that He did, both of which were contained in the same pages.

> From the beginning, the Christian gospel, as indeed the name "gospel" or "good news" implies, consists in an account of something that had happened. And from the beginning, the meaning of the happening was set forth; and when the meaning of the happening was set forth then there was Christian doctrine. "Christ died"—that is history; "Christ died for our sins"—that is doctrine. Without these two elements, joined in their indissoluble union, there is no Christianity.... The world was to be redeemed through the proclamation of an event. And with the event went the meaning of the event; and the setting forth of the event with the meaning of the event was doctrine. These two elements are always combined in the Christian message. The narration of the facts is history: the narration of the facts with the meaning of the facts is doctrine. "Suffered under Pontius Pilate, was crucified, dead and buried"—that is history. "He loved me and gave Himself for me"—that is doctrine. (Machen [1923]1946:27 & 29.)

To take a part of salvation history and say that the interpretation given to it by God in the pages of His Word was a theory was, for Machen, both a denial of the truthfulness of the Scriptures and of the laws of logic. It was essentially gibberish; but, nevertheless, as Machen contended, an artful vehicle for discarding those portions of the Bible that were offensive to those of a more 'enlightened' mind.

The reunion of the Cumberland Church with the Presbyterian Church USA strengthened the Liberal segment in the new united church considerably. James Everitt Clarke, who was instrumental in the publication of the *Auburn Affirmation*, and the many other Cumberland ministers, who, along with Clarke participated in signing of the *Auburn Affirmation*, contributed greatly to this new-found strength and influence.

218

The Cumberland presence, moreover, was felt in the united church in great disproportion to their actual numbers. The Liberal camp now had the numbers, in good measure because of the Cumberland reunion, and their overall influence was growing steadily.

6.4 The Re-organization of Princeton Seminary

The waters stirred up by the *Auburn Affirmation* and the gradual shift of the more "moderate" contingent in the church in the direction of the Liberals was eventually to cause Machen problems in the very halls of Princeton. J. Ross Stevenson was not the only member of the seminary faculty to be classified as a moderate; Charles R. Erdman also fell into this category (Longfield 1991). These men wanted peace in the church above all else, and they firmly believed that the proper authorities, the church courts, would ensure the desired orthodoxy of belief without resorting to the flamboyant methods of Dr. Machen (Clutter 1982:230). These men also entertained a pastoral outlook on the events taking place in the church and concentrated on the training of pastors irrespective of which theological winds were blowing.

Machen could not convince them that anything was amiss, let alone motivate them to take any positive action on behalf of the Reformed faith. This was primarily because, according to George Marsden, Machen '...stood for a narrow Old School confessionalism and exclusivism that many people today find appalling' (Marsden 1991:200-201). Many in Machen's day also found his stance hard to take. Most of those of the Stevenson and Erdman variety of moderates would and did fall into this category. For this reason, Machen viewed theological moderates as '...even more dangerous than theological liberals because they could reassure conservatives while cutting deals with modernists' (Hart 1994:150). Further, Machen firmly believed '...that the enemies of the gospel are not only those who overtly deny the resurrection but also those who refuse to stand up for it. Theories may differ from each other only in degree, but whether or not the great gospel events have happened is the difference between something else' (Davis 1986:253). Since Machen believed that the church is defined by the content of her belief as it is best set forth in the Westminster Confession of Faith, he incurred the wrath of those who wanted change and also of those who just wanted peace.

In addition to the winds of discord in the denomination in general, personal animosity helped to fuel the growing ill-will and discord inside Princeton Seminary, in turn, prompting calls from within the denomination for something to be done. Part of the reason for this was that 'The Seminary at Princeton represented in microcosm the Presbyterian Church at large' (Selden 1992:91). Another part was what appeared to be an ongoing feud between Machen and Practical Theology Professor, Charles R. Erdman. According to Presbyterian elder and church historian, William K. Selden, the feud between Machen and Erdman went back to the General Assembly of 1924, in which Machen supported conservative Clarence Edward Macartney over the more moderate Erdman for the position of Moderator of the General Assembly, even though Erdman was Machen's colleague at Princeton. In retaliation, Erdman, together with Princeton's Seminary's President J. Ross Stevenson, opposed Machen's promotion to the chair of Apologetics, recently vacated by William B. Greene, citing character deficiencies as their reason. As Selden relates, events just seemed to be spiraling out of control.

> (Clarence Edward) Macartney was a Princeton Seminary classmate of Machen, director of the Seminary, an accomplished preacher, who was elected Moderator of the General Assembly in 1924 with the active support of the majority of members of the faculty of the Seminary in a contest with Charles R. Erdman, their fellow faculty member. Some months later the directors of the seminary offered Macartney the professorship of apologetics and Christian ethics that was being vacated by Professor William B. Greene, Jr. After a period of deliberation Macartney declined the offer, following which the Board of Directors then approved the promotion of Machen to this position and reported its action to the General Assembly in 1926. At this session of the Assembly strong opposition was presented by Stevenson and Erdman, the latter having been elected moderator succeeding Macartney. Consequently, action was deferred by the Assembly with respect to Machen's promotion, and this fact only added to the various festering sores that were afflicting the Seminary and the church during this turbulent decade. Charles Erdman was a seminary graduate in the class of 1891 following which he held

pastorates in the Philadelphia Presbytery and was a director of the Seminary before his election to the faculty in 1906 as Professor of Practical Theology. His appointment gave recognition to the need to broaden the curriculum and include instruction in Christian education, evangelism, homiletics, pastoral care, polity, and especially English Bible for which the students had been petitioning. ...The strains between Machen and Erdman were accentuated by their association with the First Presbyterian Church of Princeton. Machen's appointment as supply minister in 1923 received notoriety when Henry Van Dyke, former director of the Seminary, moderator of the General Assembly in 1902 and subsequent United States Ambassador to the Netherlands (also an associate and defender of Charles Briggs, chairman of the committee to revise the Westminster Confession in 1903, and "avowed modernist" (Hart 1978)), publicly announced that he was wasting no more time "in listening to such dismal, bilious travesty of the Gospel. Until he [Machen] is done, count me out, and give up my pew in the church. We want to worship Christ our Savior." He did not return until Erdman was appointed the pastor in 1924, a pastorate which Erdman served until 1934 concurrently with his professorship at the Seminary. (Seldon 1992:92-93.)

After Erdman replaced Machen in the pulpit of First Church, Henry Van Dyke quietly returned to his pew. When this happened, the editor of *The Presbyterian*, a publication on which Machen held an editorship, the only member of Princeton Seminary's faculty to do so, commented,

Does the return of such a profound and avowed Modernist as Dr. Van Dyke to the old church, under the new pastor, mean that he is anticipating more liberal preaching under the new regime? But Dr. Machen and Dr. Erdman are both professors in the same seminary and [share] the Standards of the Presbyterian Church to which it belongs. Does this action of Dr. Van Dyke signify that two parties are developing in the faculty of

Princeton Seminary, or does it simply show a confusion outside? (Longfield 1991:131.)

Erdman's response was '...a blistering repudiation of the implication ...that his ministry was strengthening the forces of rationalism' (Stonehouse [1954]1987:375) in either the church or the Seminary. This response was also a personal attack on Machen as the only faculty member who was also an editor on the publication. Machen tried subsequently, in a letter to *The Presbyterian*, to redirect attention away from personal animosity and to doctrinal concerns. Machen wrote that:

> I regret the personal tone in which the letter is couched. If I have ever said anything in controversy either with Dr. Erdman or with others, to justify such a characterization of me, it has not yet been brought to my attention. I differ from Dr. Erdman profoundly, but I have tried never to allow our differences to prevent me from holding him in high personal esteem.... Dr. Erdman does not indeed reject the doctrinal system of our church, but he is perfectly willing to make common cause with those who reject it, and he is perfectly willing on many occasions to keep it in the background. I, on the other hand, can never consent to keep it in the background. Christian doctrine, I hold is not merely connected with the gospel, but it is identical with the gospel... It is, I hold, only as He is offered to us in the gospel—that is in the "Doctrine" which the world despises—that Christ saves sinful men; and never will I create the impression that there can be Christian prayer or Christian service except on the basis of those redeeming facts which are now called in question by a large party in our church.... (Stonehouse [1954]1987:376.)

Machen's attempt to redirect the focus of the editorials from one of personal attacks to doctrinal concerns was unsuccessful. While Erdman suffered no permanent effects from the exchange, Machen was not able to clear his name. Subsequently, '...this incident likewise was used to support charges being given widespread circulation in the church and before the general public that Machen was engaging in a personal campaign against Erdman' (Stonehouse [1954]1987:377).

The presidency of J. Ross Stevenson became the focal point as the problems in Princeton Seminary continued to deepen. John Hart lends some insight into the motivation of the president.

> From his early days at Princeton Seminary, Stevenson indicated his desire to broaden the influence of the Seminary. Although he proudly referred to Princeton as "the West Point of the Church," Stevenson wanted the Seminary to be more than merely the voice of Old School-Princeton Theology-Calvinism. Stevenson regretted that many Presbyterians viewed Princeton as a representative of only one wing of the Church; he feared that the Seminary was heading towards theological isolation and imbalance. Stevenson constantly expressed his desire that Princeton would become an inclusive seminary which would represent the whole spectrum of Presbyterian Calvinism. (Hart 1978:51.)

A large portion of the faculty did not support Stevenson in his vision for a new, inclusive institution. He consistently took positions which appeared at variance with the traditional stance of the school. As such, he was viewed by Machen and others on the faculty with distrust, even suspicion. Machen believed Stevenson's inclusive policies would spell the death of the institution which he both loved and served. As Darryl Hart observes, all this just added to the growing tide of animosity in the seminary.

> The Faculty at the Seminary, in the tradition of Hodge and Warfield, believed that the Princeton Theology should be maintained and continued at that institution. They realized that it was a distinctive position within the Church; yet, since this view was represented nowhere else, and since many other views were taught at other Presbyterian seminaries, Princeton's testimony "for the traditional faith should be clear and unequivocal." The majority of the Faculty felt that it was impossible for the Seminary to represent the whole church and remain true to its Charter and history. Thus, although the Church had merged with the New School in 1869, revised its creed in 1903, and merged with the Cumberland Church

in 1906, Princeton Seminary had the responsibility to propagate and defend the Old School theology (the Westminster Confession of Faith). Inclusivism was not an abstract issue, as members of the Seminary community clearly voiced their opinions on it in the religious press. As a result, on November 16, 1923, Stevenson called a special Faculty meeting to discuss the tensions at Princeton over this issue. At the meeting, he asked if any member of the Faculty doubted his loyalty to the Reformed Faith and to the historic attitude of the Seminary. All professors expressed confidence in his position except one—Machen. The tension between the President and the Faculty increased as the issue of inclusivism came before the Church at large with the Fosdick affair and the Auburn Affirmation. Stevenson took a moderate stand on these issues, while several of the Faculty members were leaders in the conservative party. Consequently, the conservative majority of the Faculty thought Stevenson was doctrinally indifferent; if he was tolerant towards these liberals in the Church he must be open to a wide range of views in the Seminary itself. These ecclesiastical differences among the Faculty were hard to conceal in a Seminary such as Princeton; professors and directors were recognized leaders in the Church.... J. Ross Stevenson was not favored by the majority of Faculty at Princeton during the search for a new President because he was neither a "Princeton man" nor an eminent scholar. But as he actively supported a policy of inclusivism in the Church at large and in the Seminary in particular, Stevenson soon found that he was actually being opposed by the Faculty at the Seminary. (Hart 1978:52-54.)

At a meeting of the Board of Directors in May of 1925, Stevenson was asked for his opinion on the problems that continued to develop at the Seminary. Stevenson responded by reminding the Board of what he believed his commission at Princeton to be, namely, '...to bring Princeton back in touch with the Church' (Hart 1978:64). Furthermore, he '...claimed that the breach in the Seminary was due to a disagreement over Church policy, not doctrine, and that the issues had become incarnated in the Erdman-Machen quarrel' (Hart 1978:64). At the

224

meeting, Stevenson also requested a committee of Directors to investigate the dissension which was currently dividing the school (Hart 1978:64). This request was answered by the 1926 General Assembly who appointed a five-man committee '...to investigate the "welfare of Princeton Seminary" and to attempt to "harmonize differences."' (North 1996:604). The five-man committee, after intense investigation and interviews with faculty members concluded that:

> "The minority (Stevenson's supporters) believe in peace and work, the majority believe in controversy in defense of the truth and work." The real problem was not theological; it was administrative, the report concluded: "The root and source of the serious difficulties at Princeton, and the greatest obstacle to the removal of these difficulties, seem to be in the plan of government by two boards." (North 1996:604.)

Actually, the division so prominent in the faculty eventually spilled over into both the Board of Directors and the Board of Trustees (Hart 1978:63 & 70). (Princeton, as stipulated in its charter, was to be governed by two separate and distinct Boards: a Board of Directors and a Board of Trustees (Clutter 1982:15-18 & 21-22 & Hart 1978:49).) Once the divisions in the faculty became mirrored in the two Boards, even the day-to-day operations of the seminary were increasingly hampered. Machen saw the problem as theological; Stevenson, however, maintained that the problem was solely administrative. Overlooking some of Gary North's theological verve and provocative description, I think he adds some interesting insights into the matter of the two Boards.

> From the point of view of the moderate and liberal wings, the conservative Board of Directors had to be thwarted, since the Board was in charge of all appointments to the faculty, the school's curriculum, and all other matters except financial, which was the responsibility of the Trustees. Therefore, any attempt to put Princeton under one Board of Control was a direct thrust at the conservative orthodoxy of Princeton Seminary. The legal implication of the committee's report was that the Board of Trustees was really an organization equal in responsibility to the Board of Directors in the management of Princeton's affairs, a view which Machen

225

would later challenge. But the legal implication was only one aspect of the report. The other was far more revealing. The committee stated that the root of the problem was the division of control into two boards. In other words, *the problem was institutional and governmental, not theological.* This had been the standard argument of the liberals from the beginning: divisions were never admitted to be theological, but only institutional and personal ("unloving attitudes," "extremism"). The liberals had by this time gained an enormous advantage over their opponents. They had framed the terms of the debate. (North 1996:604-605.)

In his book on the proposed re-organization of Princeton Seminary, Machen concluded that the real question in the matter of the two boards was which theological orientation was to govern the seminary, conservative or liberal.

> The real question at Princeton, as has already been pointed out, is the question whether the conservative majority now in control of the institution is to be ejected and the present minority represented by Dr. Stevenson is to be placed in charge. The particular means by which this result is to be attained is the establishment, to replace the present Boards of Directors and Trustees, of a single board of control. The question whether we are to have one board or two boards has, indeed, sometimes been represented as though it were a mere administrative question; but in reality it is a question upon which the whole character of the institution depends. Maintain the authority, in spiritual affairs, of the Board of Directors, which alone has kept the institution (so far as its theological position is concerned) what it is, and Princeton will continue to maintain its historic stand in the defence and propagation of the faith that is taught in the Word of God; substitute for that authority the authority of a single board of control, and the fine old institution, with all its noble traditions, will be dead. (Machen 1927:22.)

The cause which Machen championed went from one crushing defeat to another, each time at the hands of moderates who claimed to have the interests of the church foremost in their sights. Machen opposed the administrative re-organization of Princeton Seminary, knowing full well that it meant her demise. He pleaded his case cogently, but it fell on deaf ears. He finally took his arguments to the rank and file saying:

> Princeton could be saved still, if the evangelical people in our Church had any understanding of what was going on. Indeed, even among those who disagree with our position regarding the great religious issue of the day there are some, we think, who will hardly be willing to stoop to methods so unfair as those which were employed by Dr. Thompson's committee last year (the five-man committee); and if there are any persons in our church in whom evangelical convictions are really clear and strong, they will engage earnestly in prayer that the continuity of Princeton Seminary may be preserved and that thus we may have at least one institution in the Presbyterian Church that shall proclaim clearly and without compromise the gospel of our Lord Jesus Christ as it is found in God's Word.... But our chief appeal is to the rank and file of our Church. We have a just cause; and the heart of the Church, we hope, is still true. If the whole body of the Church could only be acquainted with the facts, we think that Princeton might be saved next May. (Machen 1927:39.)

During the course of deliberations in the General Assembly, Machen was given the opportunity to voice his opinion on the subject of re-organization. With candor and poise he began:

> I cannot show you how that is true; for I have but a few minutes to speak; but there are many throughout the world who will know that it is true. I cannot show you how unjust it is; but there are many of Christ's little ones whom the injustice of it grieves to the very heart. With these grieved and burdened souls, who are perplexed by the uncertainty of the age, and who are looking to Princeton Seminary for something to be said against

modern unbelief and in favor of the full truthfulness of God's Word—with these we are united today in a blessed fellowship of sympathy and prayer. To that fellowship I believe that most of you would belong if you only knew the facts. It is hard for me to look into your faces and see many of you ready to do the ruthless thing which, if you only knew its meaning, you would be the first to deplore. I cannot reach your minds, for the times (sic) does not suffice for that; and God has granted me no gift of eloquence that I might reach your hearts. I can only hope that a greater and more mysterious persuasion may prevent you from doing unwittingly that which is so irrevocable and so wrong. One thing at least is clear— there are many Christians in many lands who will feel that if the old Princeton goes, a light will have gone out of their lives. Many are praying today that you may be kept from putting out that light. If you destroy the old Princeton today, by destroying the board of directors which has made it what it is, there are many, I admit, who will rejoice; for there are many who think that the old gospel and the old Book are out of date. But if there are many who will rejoice, there are also those, Mr. Moderator, who will grieve. (quoted by Clutter 1982:219-220.)

After Machen spoke, there was a long silence. Shortly thereafter a vote was taken, and the re-organization of Princeton Seminary was a reality. J. Ross Stevenson, and others, expressed their gratitude to the General Assembly and its members for their vote of confidence. They painted a picture of a bright future in which cooperation would permeate the atmosphere, and where all that made Princeton what it was as a defender of the historic faith would remain. Nothing changed that day, or the next day, or the next week, but slowly, gradually the old Princeton was replaced by the new. Change did come. As Gary North says:

He (Machen) predicted that if the reorganization went through, Princeton would soon go modernist. In one way, he was correct; in another, he was not. Princeton by 1933 had moved publicly towards neo-orthodoxy: Adolph Keller's Stone Foundation lectures. (In 1933, the prestigious Stone Foundation Lectures of Princeton Seminary featured German theologian, Adolph

Keller, who introduced the theology of Karl Barth to the students (North 1996:639).) In 1939, Emil Brunner was a guest faculty member. Princeton adopted what Van Til in 1947 would call the new modernism. (North 1996:626.)

According to Ronald Clutter, in his thesis specifically on Princeton Seminary's re-organization, Machen was proved correct in the end (Clutter 1982:224), but Machen, Wilson, Allis, Van Til, and Murray chose, rather than remain at an institution which they now regarded as lost, to found a new seminary to carry on the traditions of the Princeton that they all had loved so much. Thus, Westminster Theological Seminary was born in 1929.

6.5 The Independent Board for Presbyterian Foreign Missions

Three years later in 1932, a book-length inquiry into the theory and method of modern missions, known as *Rethinking Missions*, was published by a multi-denominational lay committee with representatives from the Presbyterian Church USA. Edited by William Ernest Hocking of Harvard, the inquiry promoted an eclectic approach to foreign missions:

> It is no longer, which prophet? Or which book? It is whether any prophet, book, revelation, rite, church is to be trusted. All the old oracles are seeing a new sign: the scorn on the faces of students who know the experiments in anti-religion in Russia and non-religion in Turkey, and the actual religionlessness of much western life.... The case that must now be stated is the case for any religion at all.... Thus it is that Christianity finds itself in point of fact aligned in this world-wide issue with the non-Christian faiths of Asia.... There are thus several factors conspiring to one end: namely, the necessity that the modern mission make a positive effort, first of all to know and understand the religion around it, then to recognize and associate with whatever kindred elements there are in them. (Hocking 1932:32-33.)

Noted author, Pearl Buck, was, at the time of its publication, a missionary of the Presbyterian Church USA to China. She was favorably impressed with *Rethinking Missions*, and related this impression in an interview with the Liberal church paper *The Christian Century*. Bubbling with enthusiasm, Mrs. Buck stated:

> I have not read merely a report. I have read a unique book, a great book. The book presents a masterly statement of religion and its place in life, and of Christianity and its place in religion. The first three chapters are the finest exposition of religion I have ever read.... I think this is the only book I have ever read which seems to me to be literally true in it's every observation and right in its every conclusion. I want every American Christian to read this book. I hope it will be translated into every language. (quoted by Machen 1933:13.)

In a lengthy article written for *Harpers Magazine*, Pearl Buck gave greater insight into her own views of the gospel message, a message which she was actively promulgating under the auspices of the Presbyterian Church USA. She candidly admitted that:

> Some of us (Christians) believe in Christ as our fathers did. To some of us he is still the divine son of God, born of the Virgin Mary, conceived by the Holy Spirit. But to many of us He has ceased to be that.... Let us face the fact that the old reasons for foreign missions are gone from the minds and hearts of many of us, certainly from those of us who are young.... Even though it is proved in some future time that there never lived an actual Christ and what we think of as Christ should some day be found as the essence of men's dreams of the simplest and most beautiful goodness, would I be willing to have that personification of dreams pass out of men's minds....? In the old days it was plain enough. Our forefathers believed sincerely in a magic religion. They believed simply and plainly that all who did not hear the gospel, as they called it, were damned, and every soul to whom they preached received in that moment the chance for salvation from hell. Though heard but for a single moment, the preacher gave that soul the opportunity of a choice for eternity. If the soul paid no heed or did not believe, the preacher could not take the responsibility. He was absolved. There are those who still believe this, and if

they sincerely believe, I honor that sincerity, though I cannot share the belief. I agree with the Chinese who feel their people should be protected from such superstition. (quoted by Machen 1933:13-15.)

Machen believed he could sit by no longer. Here was a woman, a missionary of the very church in which he was a minister of the Gospel, saying that the objects of the church's missionary endeavors needed to be shielded from the very Gospel that was intended to be their salvation (quoted by Machen 1933:15). To remedy the situation, Machen introduced an overture to the Presbytery of New Brunswick on 24 January 1933 (Machen 1933:4). He argued for the removal of Mrs. Buck from the rolls as missionary and for the establishment of guidelines to ensure the orthodoxy of future missionaries (Machen 1933:1). By making these demands, Machen was taking on the entire Board of Foreign Missions and its revered secretary Robert E. Speer. Speer steadfastly defended his turf, and, ironically, Machen was put on the defensive. Before anything could be done about Pearl Buck, she resigned her commission as missionary in the Presbyterian Church (Hart 1994:203), a resignation, moreover, that was received with profound regret by the Board of Foreign Mission and Dr. Speer (Stonehouse [1954]1987:478). Not seeing his way clear to reform the church's Foreign Mission board, Machen, together with others of like mind formed their own (Stonehouse [1954]1987:482-484). Known as the Independent Board for Presbyterian Foreign Missions, this board was launched to take the place of the one currently in 'enemy' hands.

The Presbyterian Church USA was not amused by Machen's actions, regardless of how sincere he appeared to be. Consequently, at the 1934 General Assembly the following action was taken with the Independent Board in mind:

A church member or an individual church that will not give to promote the officially authorized missionary program of the Presbyterian Church is in exactly the same position with reference to the Constitution of the Church as a church member or an individual church that would refuse to take part in the celebration of the Lord's Supper or any other of the prescribed ordinances of the denomination as set forth in Chapter VII of the Form of Government. (McIntire 1935:92.)

231

In his defense, Machen wrote a one hundred page pamphlet outlining what he believed the issues to be and orchestrating his own defense (Machen 1934). Machen's associate Carl McIntire had this to say with respect to the 1934 decision:

> One wonders if this could be "the law of the Church" to which Dr. Speer refers and which men violate when they criticize the Board for its Modernism. There is nothing in our Constitution which prohibits a man from directing attention to evidence of Modernism in an agency of the Church. In fact, every minister and elder is under oath to study the *purity* of the Church. So far as the Constitution of the United States is concerned, it guarantees "freedom of speech," and freedom of public assembly, and this is more than the policy of the Board will tolerate. Criticisms must be silenced by force. If we are to remain Presbyterian, if our inestimable heritage is to remain as a channel of blessing, the time has come when every truth-honoring and liberty-loving Presbyterian must oppose with all his might the usurpation of authority in the Church and demand that the agencies of the Church be the servants of the Church and of the Church's only Head, Jesus Christ. (McIntire 1935:92.)

Reverend A. L. Latham, D.D., pastor of the Third Presbyterian Church in Chester, Pennsylvania, who was neither a member of the controversial Board for Foreign Missions nor an ally of Machen, wrote:

> I have no connection with the Independent Board, and never have had any. Nevertheless, I believe there is abundant ground for the formation of the same. The pity is this, that the church council and the General Assembly have done nothing to remove these grounds... the Assembly has not sought to remove the disturbing cause; but rather, to coerce. (quoted by Rian [1940]1992:115-116.)

Machen and those involved with the Independent Board were warned to quit the new Board or action would be taken. Machen, choosing to obey his conscience, did not sever his association with the Board. No one, not even Machen, believed that the Presbyterian Church would take action on a decision as controversial as that agreed upon by the 1934 General Assembly. All, including Machen, were proved wrong. On the night of 20 December 1934, at the meeting of the Presbytery of New Brunswick, Machen was formally charged.

> That Presbytery prefer charges against the Rev. J. Gresham Machen, D.D., for offenses which are as follows: with the violation of his ordination vows; with his disapproval of the government and discipline of the Presbyterian Church in the USA; with renouncing and disobeying the rules and lawful authority of the Church; with refusal to sever his connection with the Independent Board for Presbyterian Foreign Missions as directed by the General Assembly, with not being zealous and faithful in maintaining the peace of the church; with contempt of and rebellion against his superiors in the church in their lawful counsels, commands and corrections; with breach of his lawful promises; and with refusing subjection to his brethren in the Lord. (quoted by Rian [1940]1992;120.)

Edwin Rian, friend and contemporary of J. Gresham Machen, believed the trial that ensued was a complete sham. The prosecution, it seems, did not want to engage any doctrinal questions which would explain Machen's actions, as it might also hold up the actions of the church court to scrutiny. Thus, the prosecution obtained an injunction barring the introduction of '...anything that goes back to Princeton Seminary, or the doctrinal phase of the case' (Rian [1940]1992:121). There was, however, no "non-doctrinal" phase of the case, and the issuance of the injunction by the court all but eviscerated Machen's defense. Rian wrote that 'On March 7, 1935, at the third session the dramatic and tragic point of the trial was reached' (Rian [1940]1992:123). To quote Rian at some length on this matter: after Machen pleaded "not guilty" to the six charges against him,

> ...the farcical and disgusting aspect of the entire proceedings followed immediately. The Book of Discipline states, "Questions as to order or evidence, arising in the course of the trial, shall, *after* the parties have had the opportunity to be heard, be decided by the moderator, subject to an appeal to the judicial commission, to be determined without debate."

Disregarding this rule and making the trial even more ridiculous, the commission issued the following ruling: "1. This court rules that it cannot accept and hear any further arguments or inferences based on the Auburn Affirmation, or on its signing by certain members of the Presbyterian Church USA. 2. This court rules that it cannot accept and hear any further arguments or inferences against the Board of Foreign Missions of the Presbyterian Church in the USA. It is not within the province of this Commission to hear either defence or attack of the Board of Foreign Missions in our Church, since both the General Assembly and the Presbytery of New Brunswick, from which this Commission derives its power, have given the Board of Foreign Missions their vote of approval. 3. This court rules that it cannot accept and hear any further arguments or inferences based on the Princeton-Westminster Seminary controversy. We cannot entertain any arguments directed against any individuals, Boards, Agencies, Institutions, or Judicatories, against which no charges have been presented in the Presbytery of New Brunswick, and which are not on trial before this Judicial Commission. 4. This court rules that it cannot accept or regard any arguments questioning the legality or validity of the Mandate of the General Assembly in reference to the 'Independent Board for Presbyterian Foreign Missions.' It is one of the well established and fundamental principles of the Presbyterian system that a subordinate judicatory cannot sit in judgment upon the acts or deliverances of a superior judicatory, whether or not we think those acts or deliverances have been wise, equitable, and for the edification of the Church. So long as such acts and deliverances stand this Commission has no power but to obey." (Rian [1940] 1992:123-124.)

Machen, on the basis of this judgment, was essentially not allowed to defend himself. The whole case was one with significant doctrinal overtures, none of which were ever allowed a hearing. The results of this decision by the Judicial Commission were simply to deny Machen any defense at all. As Rian concludes:

...As a result of this unexpected and unfair move by the commission, the rest of the proceedings became more or less meaningless. The opening speech by the prosecution was given by the Rev. D. Wilson Hollinger, in which he reiterated that the case was not doctrinal but administrative and that the Presbytery of New Brunswick and the church were perfectly orthodox. After this the prosecution offered various documents, mostly pamphlets issued by the Independent Board, as evidence to prove their case against Dr. Machen. The whole procedure was little short of ridiculous, especially since the defendant was not allowed to prove that his charges against the Board of Foreign Missions were true. As a formality, the defense moved for a verdict for the defense which was overruled by the commission. The defense then expressed the willingness to prove that Dr. Machen's charges against the Board of Foreign Missions were true. When the court refused to hear this evidence, the counsel for the defense stated: "Mr. Moderator, the rulings of this court relating to argument and evidence have deprived this defendant of the right to introduce facts and arguments essential to his defense against these charges, and to be heard concerning the same. Since this defendant is thus precluded from offering a defense to which he is entitled by the constitution of the Church, the exercise of which right has been denied by this commission, he does not find himself able to present a so-called 'case' which would not include these essential facts and arguments, for such a 'case' would not be the case which, by the law of the Church, he is entitled to present. Therefore, Mr. Moderator, under these circumstances the defense has nothing further to say." (Rian [1040]1992:125-126.)

Unable to explain his actions or motivations because of the decision taken by the Judicial Commission disallowing anything of a doctrinal nature in his defense, Machen had no defense. He was unable to explain himself and thus clear himself of the charges pending against him. Thus at the final session of the trial on 29 March 1935, Machen was found guilty and suspended from the ministry of the Presbyterian Church USA.

This decision was finalized by appeal to the Permanent Judicial Commission of the General Assembly in 1936. Edwin Rian commented that 'The shift of the church from the conservative to the liberal doctrinal position and also a drift towards tyranny can be seen quite clearly from this procedure. Such action would have been incredible twenty-five years earlier' (Rian [1940]1992:132). Ten days after confirmation of his suspension from the ministry by the higher judicatory, a new Presbyterian denomination was formed with its center in Philadelphia and Machen as moderator (Hart & Muether 1995:37).

Troubles were not yet over, however, and in one sense they were just getting started. Those who left the Presbyterian Church USA with Machen to found a new church were a curious amalgam of what I have called Centrists and Archaists. While this coalition held together as long as there was a common enemy, once the reason for co-belligerency was removed, the coalition proceeded to disintegrate. Edward John Carnell, late President of Fuller Seminary, has described Machen as '...a friend of the fundamentalist mentality (Archaism)' (Carnell 1959:115). He also added, however, that '...Machen was a foe of the fundamentalist... (and) an outspoken critic of the fundamentalist movement' (Carnell 1959:114,115). The reason given by Carnell for Machen's opposition to the Fundamentalist movement was that 'He (Machen) argued with great force that Christianity is a system, and not a list of fundamentals' (Carnell 1959:114). Machen argued for a complete system of divinity, much of which is not expressly set down in the Scriptures, but which must be arrived at by reasoning and deduction (Leith 1982:195). For the Archaist (Fundamentalist) who would only admit what is expressly found in the sacred text, the sacred words so to speak, Machen's Centrist approach was abhorrent. According to Darryl Hart and John Muether, both formerly of Westminster Seminary, the main ingredient around which the troubles in the new denomination began to brew was "dispensational premillennialism" (Hart & Muether 1995:43); a feature of Fundamentalism which Machen, as a confessionalist and a Centrist who held tenaciously to the historic affirmations of the faith as set forth in the Westminster Confession of Faith, could not possibly accept. Which is why according to Hart and Muether, 'he began to see more clearly the serious ways in which dispensationalism undermined the Reformed faith, in fact, that theological differences separated fundamentalism and Presbyterians which could not be harmonized' (Hart & Muether 1995:45). George Marsden has described the trouble in Machen's new church as arising directly from the inability of Carl McIntire, one time

236

Machen associate and co-founder of the new denomination, to persuade the General Assembly of the new church to adopt a policy of total abstinence from alcoholic beverages (Marsden 1970:246-247). If true, it would be another example of Fundamentalism taking a point of social order and making it a theological distinctive, thereby demonstrating the open-ended nature of Archaist theology and, thus, the stark similarity of Archaism to Futurism.

The Archaist/Centrist coalition which made up the bulk of Machen's support was not strong enough to stand the test of time. Shortly after Machen's death in 1937, the coalition began to come apart. Long time associates of Machen, Clarence Edward Macartney and Edwin Rian, went back to the Presbyterian Church USA (Longfield 1991:111-112), not willing to follow Machen further in building a new church. Macartney retired in 1953 from the First Presbyterian Church in Pittsburgh and Rian went on to become assistent to the President of Princeton Seminary. The largest schism to hit Machen's fledgling church was the exit of the Fundamentalists (those whom I have called Archaists) in 1938 to form the Bible Presbyterian Church along more Dispensational lines under the leadership of Carl McIntire (Hart & Meuther 1995:50). According to Darryl Hart and John Meuther, the reasons for these divisions was that 'The church (Machen's church) was established not on the basis of fundamentalism but out of a deep commitment to and love for Calvinist theology, Presbyterian church government, and Reformed piety' (Hart & Meuther 1995:54). Machen's church continued the heritage of historic confessional Presbyterianism, what I have chosen to call Centrism.

If we view the events that transpired at Princeton as indicative of Presbyterianism as a whole, as William Seldon bids us to do (Seldon 1992:91), I believe it is unmistakable that a significant shift in the theological orientation of the Presbyterian Church USA had indeed taken place. Just how significant a shift this was is shown in a document submitted for consideration to the General Assembly of the Presbyterian Church USA in 1991, which reads:

> Young people, regardless of their sexual orientation, need to understand the institutional power of heterosexism and the injustice that it perpetuates. As the church is called to speak a truthful word about sexuality, it does so in the name of God's call to justice—a call that

invites gay and lesbian adolescents to explore the goodness of their sexuality within the community of God's people. (North 1996:dustjacket.)

This is essentially the direction—that of a progressive rejection of biblical, confessional theology and morality—that Machen predicted would be taken if the problems of his day were not remedied. The Liberal/Futurist design was to change the historic affirmations of the faith, and they eventually succeeded. Machen, however, was in staunch opposition to the Liberal/Futurist plans for the future of the Presbyterian Church. Machen's colleagues at Princeton, especially Erdman and Stevenson, were not thoroughgoing Modernists—which is why I have labeled them "moderates." Moderates were essentially for the toleration of Modernism in the church in the name of peace and unity. To Machen, this was ecclesiastical suicide. He accused the moderates of being doctrinally indifferent. 'It concerns the question not of this doctrine or that,' wrote Machen, 'but of the importance which is to be attributed to doctrine as such' (quoted by Hart 1978:58). The program of the moderates won out. In doing so, however, it furthered the agenda of the Futurist contingent. When Futurism finally won the day, it is significant that the majority of these moderates did not feel uncomfortable in their new environment. Centrism and Archaism were co-belligerents throughout the latter stages of the Fundamentalist/Modernist Controversy. Only after the split from the Presbyterian Church USA and the formation of a new Presbyterian Church did the true differences between Centrism and Archaism become manifest, which resulted in yet another split, this time from each other.

Machen was a Centrist. Unlike Futurism, he did not believe that the faith of the church was based on "the Christian consciousness" or "Christian experience" (Machen [1923]1946:78). For Machen, this source for doctrinal content would result in constantly changing affirmations of the faith. This is not to say that he repudiated doctrinal development. Machen believed that 'Such doctrinal advance is certainly conceivable' (Machen 1973:156), but, rightly or wrongly, he thought that '...such doctrinal advance to be just now extremely unlikely. We are living in a time of widespread intellectual as well as moral decadence, and the visible church has unfortunately not kept herself free from this decadence' (Machen 1973:156). This decadence would include any who, in the way of historicism, sought to build the edifice of Christianity on the collective experience of believers, ie Futurism. Contrariwise, as a Centrist, Machen saw development as greater precision and clarity for existing doctrines, not in their abandonment for new doctrines.

6.6 Conclusion

It was, in my opinion, the Presbyterian Church USA that left the intellectual and spiritual traditions of historic Presbyterianism, not Machen. He sought to develop the faith as outlined in the historic symbols of Presbyterianism, by comparing and contrasting them to the growing results of Futurism. Futurism, however, wanted to change the affirmations of the faith, and, eventually, it did. A decision which led directly to Machen, and others of like mind, leaving the denomination to form a new church to carry on the intellectual and spiritual heritage that they now felt was lost.

The process which led to the Futurist ascendancy in the Presbyterian Church USA was essentially a slow process. Beginning with the reunion with the Cumberland Presbyterian Church, which itself was based on the confessional revision of 1903, the Liberal contingent began to gain in both numbers and influence. William Weston has argued that as long as the Liberal faction tried to press their theological agenda on the Presbyterian Church they were rebuffed by the institutional loyalists. But as soon as they began to plead for tolerance, they were accorded both room for their theological agenda as well as the support of the institutional loyalists. With respect to William Weston, I am not so sure that his categories are so clearly distinguishable. Additionally, I have tried to demonstrate that the whole church was moving slowly in the Liberal/Futurist direction.

Machen opposed this trend from the very beginning. In the wake of the Cumberland reunion, the distinctly conservative general Assembly of 1910 passed the *Doctrinal Deliverance of 1910* in an effort to safeguard certain tenets of the faith which they believed were under attack. The Liberal response came in the *Auburn Affirmation* of 1924, calling these same tenets, outlined in the *Doctrinal Deliverance of 1910*, "theories." These "theories," as the Liberals called them, were open to restructuring, reinterpretation, and even abandonment in the event of more favorable discoveries from other branches of knowledge.

In response to the growing Liberal/Futurist consensus, Machen wrote *Christianity and Liberalism*, which was both a popular critique and a devastating assessment. This work, however, put Machen in the vanguard of the growing controversy, effectively making him the spokesman for a militant and growing Fundamentalist faction in the Presbyterian Church USA. It was in direct response to the Liberal threat that Fundamentalism, a coalition of confessional Centrists, like Machen, and dispensational Archaists, such as Carl McIntire, became a significant voice in the Presbyterian Church.

The Liberal/Futurist wing of the church, however, had both the numbers and the influence, neither of which were on Machen's side. This state of affairs led to Machen's ouster from the Presbyterian Church in a manner which even denied him a reasonable defense. The Presbyterian Church USA did not change overnight. It was rather a gradual drift in a distinctly Futurist direction, one whose trajectory was set from the days of the Cumberland reunion and even before. The coalition of Archaists and Centrists which left the Presbyterian Church USA in the wake of Machen's trial held together for less than a year. Those of an Archaist/Fundamentalist mind, such as Carl McIntire, left with a sizable portion of Machen's new church to form the distinctly Fundamentalist Bible Presbyterian Church in 1938.

Machen was a Centrist, however, in contrast to the Archaists, with whom he made common cause and the Futurists with whom he had little in common. He defended the historic affirmations of the faith from the Liberal rejection of them in much the same way as Athanasius had defended the faith in the course of the Arian Controversy. In a sense, Machen developed the faith in the same way that Athanasius before him, by giving better definition and clearer exposition to the existing tenets of the faith in the face of conflict. In *Christianity and Liberalism*, which has often been ignored, Machen gave both a precise definition of and a devastating critique of the Liberalism of his day. He proceeded to compare and contrast this Liberalism with the historic stance of the Presbyterian Church in order to demonstrate the degree to which this Liberalism had departed from the historic affirmations of the faith. This was, in effect, doctrinal development on Machen's part, as he further defined and clarified the faith in contrast to what he perceived as error. This is Centrism, and this was Machen's legacy.

Conclusion

Taking a paradigm from John Courtney Murray, which he applied with such success to the Arian Controversy in the Fourth century, I have sought to shed some new light on the Fundamentalist/Modernist controversy in the Presbyterian Church in our own century. According to Murray, there were three factions in the Arian struggle: The Futurists, the Centrists, and the Archaists. The Futurists, including Arius himself, sought to accommodate the faith to the times by subordinating it to the then current philosophical ideas. Simply put, Futurists endeavored to change the historic affirmations of the faith to accommodate outside, temporal, influences. Archaists, represented by Eusebius of Caesarea, would have none of this. They believed that if the very wording of the affirmations of the faith were not themselves contained in the Holy Writ, then regardless of what doctrinal formulation one arrived at, it was still invalid. In the end, doctrine proved to be open-ended for both the Futurists and Archaists. Open-ended for the Futurists, because the very affirmations of the faith themselves were mutable, and indeed must be, in order to stay current, and thus relevant, with the very latest results from other branches of knowledge. Open-ended for Archaists, because of their insistence that unless the very words, "sacred words," of Scripture are strictly adhered to, doctrinal truth will not coincide with God's revelation and will tend to fly off in every direction, even changing the very sense of the Scriptural affirmations. The Centrists, while believing in doctrinal development, never lost sight of the historic affirmations of the faith and developed doctrine accordingly.

It is into these categories that I have endeavored to transpose the Fundamentalist/Modernist Controversy. My reason for doing so is the tremendous insight that these categories give into the Presbyterian tradition. The first thing that I tried to show was the extent of the controversy. Previous studies on the subject usually limit the time-frame for the Fundamentalist/Modernist Controversy to the 1920s and 1930s. I have followed William Weston's groundbreaking lead and extended the time frame to cover the trial of Charles Briggs in the 1890s, as well as the confessional revision of 1903 and the Cumberland reunion of 1906. These events, to my mind, were integral parts of the Fundamentalist/Modernist Controversy in the Presbyterian Church.

In relating and analyzing these events, I have tried to demonstrate that a profound theological change occurred within the Presbyterian Church USA. The course of this theological change was the result of a battle that was taking place between the Archaists, the Centrists, and the Futurists. Ideas from the Enlightenment, current philosophical speculation, and historical criticism of the Scriptures, each contributed to making the traditional confessional stance of the Presbyterian Church seem untenable in the eyes of certain prominent leaders. Futurists, known more commonly as Liberals or Modernists, endeavored to change the historic affirmations of the faith in order to accommodate them to this new and growing body of knowledge. They came to believe that experience was the final authority and source for Christian truth and not the historic symbols of the church. Their position was essentially historicist in character inasmuch as they tended to see the historic symbols as relative expressions of the experience of believers at given points in time, rather than as permanent points of departure for all subsequent theological reflection.

During the Briggs affair, Futurism tried to adjust the historic affirmations of the faith to the new found historical-criticism. This move was countered by a coalition of Archaism and Centrism that emanated from Princeton Seminary. The faculty at Princeton, the primary critics of Professor Briggs, endeavored to maintain the historic creeds over against any encroachments by this new critical thought. Briggs believed himself to be developing the historic faith by making it relevant to the modern Christians. Warfield and others at Princeton disagreed strenuously, stating that development consisted in better definition and further clarification of existing doctrines, not something new. Warfield himself, however, joined the Archaist camp when, in order to counter Briggs and his critical theories, he sought to redefine those portions of the Westminster Confession that spoke to the inspiration of the Scriptures; seeking to ensure that these confessional statements referred only to the now lost original autographs as opposed to those copies which are extant. Warfield's doctrine of inerrancy was novel and was itself a change in the historic affirmation of faith with regard to the Bible.

The years which followed the Briggs affair saw the Westminster Confession of Faith revised in 1903 and the reunion with a large portion of the Cumberland Presbyterian Church both become realities. While the confessional revision was essentially just a clarification of the existing doctrines contained in the Confession, and as such was a Centrist endeavor, such was not the case with the Cumberland reunion of 1906.

The Cumberland reunion was the merging of two doctrinally unequal churches, the Presbyterian Church USA and the Cumberland Presbyterian Church. Having broken away from the Presbyterian Church more than a hundred years earlier in 1814 because of doctrinal differences, the Cumberland Presbyterian Church sought reunion with the Presbyterian Church USA in the wake of the confessional revision of 1903, citing essential doctrinal agreement as their reason. I have tried to show that the Cumberland confession from 1814, adopted at that church's inception, was already far removed from even the changes adopted by the Presbyterian Church USA in 1903. However, this was not the end of it. In 1883, the Cumberland Church ratified yet another revision, if it can indeed be called a revision, which made the subsequent church unrecognizable from a confessionally Reformed perspective. The Cumberland Presbyterian Church, by their successive confessional revisions, had significantly changed the historic affirmations of the faith as found in the Westminster Confession, the traditional symbol of historic Presbyterianism. The Cumberland Presbyterian Church was, therefore, characterized by Liberalism/Futurism in its approach to the historic affirmations of the faith. Liberals/Futurists in the Presbyterian Church USA were instrumental in uniting these two doctrinally dissimilar churches in 1906. Those opposed to the union in both churches seemed to have diagnosed correctly the reason for the union. The Liberal/Futurist contingent in the Presbyterian Church USA seems to have perceived that they could greatly enhance both their numbers and their influence by the reunion, since most on the Cumberland side were sympathetic to their cause. This is, in fact, what happened. The reunion gave the Liberal/Futurist camp in the reunited church the power and the influence to carry out their agenda. In the now reunited church, Futurism became the controlling ideology, which, in turn, set the theological tone for the whole church.

The reunion pushed the Presbyterian Church USA further away from its historic confessional stance, and Centrism was ineffective in its defense of the historic position of the church. As Futurism was gaining ground everywhere throughout Protestantism, so Archaism was fast transforming itself into an inter-denominational movement called Fundamentalism. The concept of a system of theology, such as was accepted in the Presbyterian and Reformed tradition, was alien to Fundamentalism. On the one hand, Fundamentalism wanted an abbreviated statement of faith encompassing only those statements which could be found directly in the Bible, i.e., sacred words. Theological deductions from the sacred text were regarded, therefore, as inadmissible. On the other hand, Fundamentalism by its dispensational hermeneutics divided the Scriptures up in such as manner as to call into question exactly for whom certain portions were written, the Jews or the Church. In this, and in their drive to make social tenets from a bygone age theological imperatives, Fundamentalism (Archaism) mirrored Futurism, effectively demonstrating the open-ended, changeable, and non-permanent, nature of the historic affirmations of the faith, which was characteristic of both groups.

With Harry Ward and Norman Thomas, Futurism was on a rise within the Presbyterian Church. Those of a more moderate theological persuasion at Princeton Seminary, by not resisting this rise of Futurism helped, perhaps unconsciously, to solidify its position and to enable it eventually to gain its objectives. Archaism and Centrism again were co-belligerents in the struggle against Futurism, this time being labeled collectively as Fundamentalism. Futurism, however, won the battle. And while nothing of immediate significance took place, the historic affirmations of the faith were gradually changed. Machen and many of both the Centrist and Archaist stripe left the Church to found a new Presbyterian Church to replace the one they believed was permanently lost. Shortly after the founding of this new church, this amalgam of Archaism and Centrism split over the affirmations which should characterize the new church.

The Fundamentalist/Modernist Controversy was essentially a struggle between Futurism on the one hand and Archaism allied with Centrism on the other. The Presbyterian Church changed in the direction of Futurism, with Archaism and Centrism exiting to found a replacement. Futurism, consistent with its nature, broke with the historic tradition of Presbyterianism; not all at once but gradually. In answer, then, to the question as to whether there was doctrinal development during the time of the Fundamentalist/Modernist Controversy, in my estimation, largely there was not. I say, largely, because the answer is both "yes" and "no."

As I have tried to demonstrate, the only doctrinal development seems to have occurred with the confessional revision of 1903 and with J. Gresham Machen in the wake of the *Auburn Affirmation*. In 1903, the Presbyterian Church USA was in the midst of a grass roots movement to revise the Westminster Confession, in order to clarify certain more obscure points of doctrine and to rephrase some it's of the more objectionable language. I suggest that the revision accomplished this objective; hence, it was both Centrist in thrust and true doctrinal development. My reasons for adopting this position are really provided by the opposition to the revision from both the Archaist and Futurist sides. The Futurists, represented by Charles Briggs and others, centered in Union theological Seminary in New York City, wanted an entirely new confession; one of their own making that would not be at variance with the findings of research in other fields. This they did not get. Their response to the revision as it was adopted was scorn. They saw the revision as no revision at all, and were thus greatly upset with what they deemed token changes. The Archaists, represented by Warfield et al, with their center at Princeton theological Seminary, also complained bitterly about the revision. They also, however, had really nothing specific to say about the revision outside of some rather loud generalities. Warfield, as quoted earlier, was forced to admit, grudgingly, in the wake of the revision that '...it may possibly be true that some elements of truth not always recognized as provided for in our doctrinal system are emphasized in it' (Warfield 1904b:298). This is an admission on Warfield's part that the revision of 1903 was indeed doctrinal development. The revision did just what doctrinal development usually does; it further defined and clarified the existing affirmations of the faith while, at the same time, not seeing the need to be bound to a prescribed list of sacred words. Thus, I suggest that the confessional revision of 1903 was indeed doctrinal development and work of Centrism in the church.

The other instance of doctrinal development during the course of the Fundamentalist/Modernist Controversy was, as I tried to show, in the work of J. Gresham Machen. Machen's scholarly output was significant, ranging in scope from his extremely popular *Christianity and Liberalism* to articles on "Christianity and Culture" and "the Creeds and Doctrinal Advance." In all of these, especially *Christianity and Liberalism*, Machen contended for the credal faith of historic Presbyterianism. In many ways I picture him as Athanasius, carefully defining the truth while in the midst of conflict. Machen's work is characterized by precise definition and careful exposition of the truths that make up the corpus of historic Presbyterianism. I have tried to show that he developed the faith by means of precise definition and careful exposition of the historic faith in sharp distinction from what he saw as the prevailing Liberal/Futurist errors. Just as Athanasius developed the faith by carefully distinguishing it from the errors of Arius, so Machen developed the faith by his careful and meticulous distinction of it from the errors of Modernism. The Liberal faction did not want to answer Machen, as Walter Lippmann said (Lippmann 192932-34), because they could not do so effectively. So, instead, their strategy was to ignore him and then, eventually, to be rid of him. They succeeded on both counts. After Machen's dismissal, the Presbyterian Church USA became decidedly Futurist in orientation. There was no longer any effective opposition.

There are other events that I have dealt with as part of the Fundamentalist/ Modernist Controversy which I feel were definitely not doctrinal development. In fact, I suggested that they were Futurist endeavors, brought about by theological Futurists, and I tried to portray them as such. These people and events include the work of Charles Briggs, the Cumberland reunion and its effects, Harry Ward, Norman Thomas, the *Auburn Affirmation*, Harry Emerson Fosdick, the reorganization of Princeton, and ultimately, the defrocking of J. Gresham Machen. In each case, Futurism held center stage. Charles Briggs did not just want a new confession; he saw the very idea of confessional subscription as being no longer relevant or desirable. He wanted a faith that was fully in tune with the findings of modern scientific research and, as such, he had no place for the historic tenets of the faith. The Cumberland reunion served only to strengthen the numbers and influence of the Liberal/Futurist element in the Presbyterian Church USA. After the reunion, Futurism held sway in the newly reunited church, and, thereafter, it did not relinquish its position of dominance. Harry Ward and Norman Thomas were men who probed the frontiers, the outer limits of Futurism. Norman Thomas eventually left the Church altogether. Both men substituted a political ideology for the historic affirmations of the faith. They did this because they felt that a particular ideology, Marxist Socialism, was the best possible manifestation of the Christian Faith in action. Each became progressively radical as their careers progressed, so much so, it seems, that each came to hold a political ideology in place of the historic Christian Faith. Harry Emerson Fosdick, the *Auburn Affirmation*, the reorganization of Princeton Seminary, and the defrocking of J. Gresham Machen were each part of the later Futurism in the Presbyterian Church USA as the church turned progressively in the Futurist direction. I see no doctrinal development in any of these latter events.

Futurism sought to replace the historic tenets of the faith with a new faith drawn from the collective experience of Christians in history. I

246

suggest that this is historicism. I do not deny that history has a certain effect on doctrine as it is handed down from one generation to the next. I draw the line, however, at the point where the historical process yields up doctrine. For this, I believe, is historicism, and, as I have tried to show throughout, this is the source of Futurism's faith. This is not doctrinal development. This is, instead, supplanting the historic affirmations of the faith with a faith taken from an ever-changing history. These are not the same. I suggest that they are diametrically opposed to one another. Was there doctrinal development during the Fundamentalist/Modernist Controversy? The answer, as I have tried to show is both "yes" and "no," but with "no" predominating.

Appendix I

Brief Statement of the Reformed Faith

Adopted May 22, 1902, by the General Assembly of the

Presbyterian Church in the United States of America.

Article I. Of God

We believe in the ever-living God, who is a Spirit and the Father of our spirits; infinite, eternal, and unchangeable in His being and perfections; the Lord Almighty, most just in all His ways, most glorious in holiness, unsearchable in wisdom and plenteous in mercy, full of love and compassion, and abundant in goodness and truth. We worship Him, Father, Son, and Holy Spirit, three persons in one Godhead, one in substance and equal in power and glory.

Article II. Of Revelation

We believe that God is revealed in nature, in history, and in the heart of man; that He has made gracious and clearer revelations of Himself to men of God who spoke as they were moved by the Holy Spirit; and that Jesus Christ, the Word made flesh, is the brightness of the Father's glory and the express image of His person. We gratefully receive the Holy Scriptures, given by inspiration, to be the faithful record of God's gracious revelations and the sure witness to Christ, as the Word of God, the only infallible rule of faith and life.

Article III. Of the Eternal Purpose

We believe that the eternal, wise, holy, and loving purpose of God embraces all events, so that while the freedom of man is not taken away nor is God the author of sin, yet in His providence He makes all things work together in the fulfillment of His sovereign design and the manifestation of His glory; wherefore, humbly acknowledging the mystery of this truth, we trust in His protecting care and set our hearts to do His will.

Article IV. OF the Creation

We believe that God is the creator, upholder, and governor of all things; that He is above all His works and in them all; and that He made man in His own image, meet for fellowship with Him, free and able to choose between good and evil, and forever responsible to his Maker and Lord.

Article V. Of the Sin of Man

We believe that our first parents, being tempted, chose evil, and so fell away from God and came under the power of sin, the penalty of which is eternal death; and we confess that, by reason of this disobedience, we and all men are born with a sinful nature, that we have broken God's law, and that no man can be saved but by His grace.

Article VI. OF the Grace of God

We believe that God, out of His great love for the world, has given His only begotten Son to be the Savior of sinners and in the Gospel freely offers His all-sufficient salvation to all men. And we praise Him for the unspeakable grace wherein He has provided a way of eternal life for all mankind.

Article VII. OF Election

We believe that God, from the beginning, in His own good pleasure, gave to His Son a people, and innumerable multitude, chosen in Christ unto holiness, service, and salvation; we believe that all who come to years of discretion can receive this salvation only through faith and repentance; and we believe that all who die in infancy, and all others given by the Father to the Son who are beyond the reach of the outward means of grace, are regenerated and saved by Christ through the Spirit, who works when and where and how He pleases.

Article VIII. Of Our Lord Jesus Christ

We believe in and confess the Lord Jesus Christ, the only Mediator between God and man, who, being the Eternal Son of God, for us men and for our salvation became truly man, being conceived by the Holy Ghost and born of the Virgin Mary, without sin; unto us He had revealed the Father, by His Word and Spirit making known the perfect will of God; for us He fulfilled all righteousness and satisfied eternal justice, offering Himself a perfect sacrifice upon the cross to take away the sin of the world; for us He rose from the dead and ascended into heaven, where He ever intercedes for us; in our hearts, joined to Him by faith, He abides forever as the indwelling Christ; over us, and over all for us, He rules: wherefore, unto Him we render love, obedience, and adoration as our Prophet, Priest, and King forever.

Article IX Of Faith and Repentance

We believe that God pardons our sins and accepts us as righteous solely on the ground of the perfect obedience and sacrifice of Christ received by faith alone; and that this saving faith is always accompanied by repentance, wherein we confess and forsake our sins with full purpose of, and endeavor after, a new obedience to God.

Article X. Of the Holy Spirit

We believe in the Holy Spirit, the Lord and Giver of Life, who moves everywhere upon the hearts of men, to restrain them from evil and to incite them unto good, and whom the father is ever willing to give unto all who ask Him. We believe that He has spoken by holy men of God in making known His truth to men for their salvation; that, through our exalted Savior, He was sent forth in power to convict the world of sin, to enlighten men's minds in the knowledge of Christ, and to persuade and enable them to obey the call of the Gospel; and that He abides with the Church, dwelling in every believer as the spirit of truth, of holiness, and of comfort.

Article XI. Of the New Birth and the New Life

We believe that the Holy Spirit only is the author and source of the new birth; we rejoice in the new life, wherein He is given unto us as the seal of sonship in Christ, and keeps loving fellowship with us, helps us in our infirmities, purges us from our faults, and ever continues His transforming work in us until we are perfected in the likeness of Christ, in the glory of the life to come.

Article XII. Of the Resurrection and the Life to Come

We believe that the law of God, revealed in the Ten Commandments, and more clearly disclosed in the words of Christ, is forever established in truth and equity, so that no human work shall abide except it be built on this foundation. We believe that God requires of every man to do justly, to love mercy, and to walk humbly with his God; and that only through this harmony with the will of God shall be fulfilled that brotherhood of man wherein the kingdom of God is to be made manifest.

Article XIII. Of the Law of God

We believe that the law of God, revealed in the Ten Commandments, and more clearly disclosed in the words of Christ, is forever established in truth and equity, so that no human work shall abide except it be built on this foundation. We believe that God requires of every man to do justly, to love mercy, and to walk humbly with his God; and that only through this harmony with the will of God shall be fulfilled that brotherhood of man wherein the kingdom of God is to be made manifest.

Article XIV. Of the Church and the Sacraments

We believe in the Holy Catholic Church of which Christ is the only Head. We believe that the Church Invisible consists of all the redeemed, and that the Church Visible embraces all who profess the true religion together with their children. We receive to our communion all who confess and obey Christ as their divine Lord and Savior, and we hold fellowship with all believers in Him. We receive the sacraments of Baptism and the Lord's Supper, alone divinely established and committed

252

to the Church, together with the Word, as means of grace; made effectual only by the Holy Spirit, and always to be used by Christians with prayer and praise to God.

Article XV. Of the Last Judgment

We believe that the Lord Jesus Christ will come again in glorious majesty to judge the world and to make a final separation between the righteous and the wicked. The wicked shall receive the eternal award of their sins, and the Lord will manifest the glory of His mercy in the salvation of His people and their entrance upon the full enjoyment of eternal life.

Article XVI. Of Christian Service and the Final Triumph

We believe that it is our duty, as servants and friends of Christ, to do good unto all men, to maintain the public and private worship of God, to hallow the Lord's Day, to preserve the sanctity of the family, to uphold the just authority of the State, and so to live in all honesty, purity, and chastity, that our lives shall testify of Christ. We joyfully receive the word of Christ, bidding His people go into all the world and make disciples of all nations, and declare unto them that God was in Christ reconciling the world unto Himself, and that He will have all men to be saved and to come to the knowledge of the truth. We confidently trust that by His power and grace, all His enemies and ours shall be finally overcome, and the kingdoms of this world shall be made the kingdom of our God and of His Christ. In this faith we abide; in this service we labor; and in this hope we pray, Even so, come, Lord Jesus.

(This Statement was usually found inside the front cover of the Presbyterian Hymnal. It made its appearance in the hymnal in 1906 and remained there until the early 1960s.)

Appendix II

The Revision of the Westminster Confession, 1903

which includes a Declaratory Statement bearing on the subjects of God's decrees and the salvation of infants, changes in three chapters and two new chapters.

as found in:

Schaff, p (ed.) [1931] 1985. The Creeds of Christendom with a History and Critical Notes, Volume 3: The Evangelical Protestant Creeds with Translations. Sixth edition. Grand Rapids, Michigan: Baker: 920-922.

Declaratory Statement.

While the ordination vow of ministers, ruling elders, and deacons, as set forth in the Form of Government, requires the reception and adoption of the Confession of Faith only as containing the System of Doctrine taught in the Holy Scriptures, nevertheless, seeing that the desire has been formally expressed for a disavowal by the Church of certain inferences drawn from statements in the Confession of Faith, and also for a declaration of certain aspects of revealed truth which appear at the present time to call for more explicit statements, therefore the Presbyterian Church in the United States of America does authoritatively declare as follows:

First, With reference to Chapter III. Of the Confession of Faith: that concerning those who are saved in Christ, the doctrine of God's eternal decree is held in harmony with the doctrine of His love to all mankind, His gift of His Son to be the propitiation for the sins of the whole world, and His readiness to bestow His saving grace on all who seek it. That concerning those who perish, the doctrine of God's eternal decree is held in harmony with the doctrine that God desires not the death of any sinner, but has provided in Christ a salvation sufficient for all, adopted to all, and freely offered in the Gospel to all; that men are fully responsible for their treatment of God's gracious offer; that His decree hinders no man from accepting that offer; and that no man is condemned except on the ground of his sin.

Second, With reference to Chapter X., Section 3, of the Confession of Faith, that it is not to be regarded as teaching that any who die in infancy are lost. We believe that all dying in infancy are included in the election of grace, and are regenerated and saved by Christ through the Spirit, who works when and where and how He pleases.

Changes in Chapters.

XVI., 7. Works done by unregenerate men, although for the matter of them they may be things which God commands, and in themselves praiseworthy and useful, and although the neglect of such things is sinful and displeasing unto God; yet, because they proceed not from a heart purified by faith; nor are done in a right manner, according to His Word; nor to a right end, the glory of God; they come short of what God requires and do not make any man meet to receive the grace of God.

XXII., 3. Whosoever taketh an oath ought duly to consider the weightiness of so solemn an act, and therein to avouch nothing but what he is fully persuaded is the truth. Neither may any man bind himself by oath to anything but what is good and just, and what he believeth so to be, and what he is able and resolved to perform.

XXV., 6. The Lord Jesus Christ is the only head of the Church, and the claim of any man to be the vicar of Christ and the head of the Church, is unscriptural, without warrant in fact, and is a usurpation dishonoring to the Lord Jesus Christ.

The Added Chapters.

XXXIV. Of the Holy Spirit.—I. The Holy Spirit, the third person in the Trinity, proceeding from the Father and the Son, of the same substance and equal in power and glory, is, together with the Father and the Son, to be believed in, loved, obeyed, and worshiped throughout all ages.

II. He is the Lord and Giver of life, everywhere present in nature, and is the source of all good thoughts, pure desires, and holy counsels in men. By Him the Prophets were moved to speak the Word of God, and all writers of the Holy Scriptures inspired to record infallibly the mind and will of God. The dispensation of the Gospel is especially committed to Him. He prepares the way for it, accompanies it with His persuasive power, and urges its message upon the reason and conscience of men, so that they who reject its merciful offer are not only without excuse, but are also guilty of resisting the Holy Spirit.

III. The Holy Spirit, whom the Father is ever willing to give to all who ask Him, is the only efficient agent in the application of redemption. He convicts men of sin, moves them to repentance, regenerates them by His grace, and persuades and enables them to embrace Jesus Christ by faith. He unites all believers to Christ, dwells in them as their Comforter and Sanctifier, gives to them the spirit of Adoption and Prayer, and performs all those gracious offices by which they are sanctified and sealed unto the day of redemption.

IV. By the indwelling of the Holy Spirit all believers being vitally united to Christ, who is the Head, are thus united one to another in the Church, which is His body. He calls and anoints ministers for their holy office, qualifies all other officers in the Church for their special work, and imparts various gifts and graces to its members. He gives efficacy to the Word, and to the ordinances of the Gospel. By Him the Church will be preserved, increased until it shall cover the earth, purified, and at last made perfectly holy in the presence of God.

XXXV. Of the Love of God and Missions.—I. God, in infinite and perfect love, having provided in the covenant of grace, through the mediation and sacrifice of the Lord Jesus Christ, a way of life and salvation, sufficient for and adapted to the whole lost race of man, doth freely offer this salvation to all men in the Gospel.

II. In the Gospel God declared His love for the world and His desire that all men should be saved, reveals fully and clearly the only way of salvation; promises eternal life to all who truly repent and believe in Christ; invites and commands all to embrace the offered mercy; and by His Spirit accompanying the Word pleads with men to accept His gracious invitation.

III. It is the duty and privilege of everyone who hears the Gospel immediately to accept its merciful provisions: and they who continue in impenitence and unbelief incur aggravated guilt and perish by their own fault.

IV. Since there is no other way of salvation than that revealed in the Gospel, and since in the divinely established and ordinary method of grace faith cometh by hearing the Word of God, Christ hath commissioned His Church to go into all the world and to make disciples of all nations. All believers are, therefore, under obligation to sustain the ordinances of religion where they are already established, and to contribute by their prayers, gifts, and personal efforts, to the extension of the kingdom of Christ throughout the whole earth.

Bibliography

Abzug, RH 1994. *Cosmos Crumbling: American Reform and the Religious Imagination*. New York & Oxford: Oxford University Press.

Ahlstrom, SE 1955. The Scottish Philosophy and American Theology, in *Church History* 24 (1955): 257-272.

Ames, J T. 1971. James Everitt Clarke: A Cumberland Liberal and the Social and Theological Development of American Presbyterianism. Ph.D. Thesis. Durham: Duke University.

--- 1974. Cumberland Liberals and the Union of 1906, in *Journal of Presbyterian History* 52 (Spring 1974): 3-18.

Armington, RQ & Ellis, WD 1984. *More: The Rediscovering of American Common   Sense*. Chicago: Regnery Gateway.

Armstrong, MW, Loetscher, LA, & Anderson, CA 1956. *The Presbyterian Enterprise: Sources of American Presbyterian History*. Philadelphia: Westminster Press.

Ashton, TS 1948. *The Industrial Revolution 1760-1830*. London: Oxford University Press.

Atwell, RL 1981. The Heritage of the Orthodox Presbyterian Church, in *New Horizons*   Vol. 2, no. 5, May-June 1981:1.

Bahnsen, GL 1988. Forward. In Gary DeMar, *The Debate over Christian Reconstruction*. Fort Worth, Texas: Dominion Press.

Balmer, RH 1982. The Princetonians and Scripture: A Reconsideration, in *Westminster Theological Journal* 44 (1982): 352-365.

Bangs, C 1971. *Arminius: A Study in the Dutch Reformation.* Nashville & New York: Abington.

Bannerman, J [1869] 1991. *The Church of Christ: A Treatise on the Nature, Powers, Ordinances, Discipline and Government of the Christian Church.* Volume 1. Edmonton, Alberta: Still Waters Revival Books.

Barth, K c1956. *Church Dogmatics,* Volume 1: *The Doctrine of the Word of God,* Part 2. Edinburgh: T. & T. Clark.

--- c1975. *Church Dogmatics,* Volume 1: *The Doctrine of the Word of God,* Part 1. Edinburgh: T. & T. Clark.

Beidelman, TO 1974. *W. Robertson Smith and the Sociological Study of Religion.* Chicago & London: University of Chicago Press.

Berkouwer, GC 1976. *Studies in Dogmatics: The Church.* Grand Rapids: Eerdmans.

Bible. Authorized King James Version. 1983. *The Holy Bible: Containing the Old and New Testaments.* (s.l.): National Publishing Co.

Biemer, G 1967. *Newman and Tradition.* New York: Herder & Herder.

Blenkinsopp, J 1968. *A Sketchbook of Biblical Theology.* New York: Herder & Herder.

Bloch, R 1985. *Visionary Republic: Millennial Themes in American Thought, 1756-1800*. Cambridge: Cambridge University Press.

Boettner, L 1957. *The Millennium*. Philadelphia: Presbyterian & Reformed.

Bolich, GG 1980. *Karl Barth and Evangelicalism*. Downers Grove: Inter Varsity Press.

Boseman, TD 1977. *Protestants in an Age of Science: The Baconian Ideal and Antebellum American Religious Thought*. Chapel Hill: University of North Carolina Press.

Briggs, CA 1870. Biblical Theology, with Especial Reference to the New Testament, in *The American Presbyterian Review*. New Series, Volume 2. (January): 105-133, (April): 293-306.

--- 1880a. The Documentary History of the Westminster Assembly, in *The Presbyterian Review* 1 (January 1880): 127-163.

--- 1880b. The Robertson Smith Case, in *The Presbyterian Review*, 1 (1880): 737-745.

--- 1883a. *Biblical Study: Its Principles, Methods, and History*. New York: Scribners.

--- 1883b. A Critical Study of the History of Higher Criticism with Special Reference to the Pentateuch, in *The Presbyterian Review* 4 (1883): 69-130.

--- [1891] 1972. *Inaugural Address and Defense*. New York: Arno Press.

--- 1885. *American Presbyterianism: Its Origin and Early History*. New York: Scribners.

--- 1889. *Whither? A Theological Question for the Times*. New York: Scribners.

--- 1890a. *How Shall We Revise the Westminster Confession of Faith: A Bundle of Papers*. New York: Scribners.

--- 1890b. Revision of the Westminster Confession, in *Andover Review* 13 (January 1890): 45-68.

--- 1893a. *The Bible, The Church and The Reason: The Three Great Fountains of Divine Authority*. Second Edition. New York: Scribners.

--- 1893b. *The Higher Criticism of the Hexateuch*. New York: Scribners.

--- [1900] 1970. *General Introduction to the Study of Holy Scripture*. Revised Edition. Grand Rapids: Baker.

--- 1909. *Church Unity: Studies of its Most Important Problems*. New York: Scribners.

Brown, RE 1985. *Biblical Exegesis and Church Doctrine*. New York & Mahwah: Paulist Press.

Bryan, WJ 1922. *In His Image*. New York: Revell.

Calvin, J 1960. *Institutes of the Christian Religion*, Vol. II: *Books III.XX to IV.XX*. The Library of Christian Classics, Volume XXI. Edited by John T. McNeill. Philadelphia: Westminster Press.

Carnell, EJ 1959. *The Case for Orthodox Theology*. Philadelphia: Westminster Press.

Cauthen, K 1962. *The Impact of American Religious Liberalism*. New York & Evanston: Harper & Row.

Chadwick, O 1957. *From Bossuet to Newman: The Idea of Doctrinal Development*. Cambridge: Cambridge University Press.

Chalmers, TW 1891. The Inaugural Address of Professor Briggs, in *Presbyterian and Reformed Review* 2 (1891): 482-494.

Clark, GH 1963. *Karl Barth's Theological Method*. Philadelphia: Presbyterian and Reformed.

--- 1986. *Logical Criticisms of Textual Criticism*. Jefferson, Maryland: The Trinity Foundation.

Clarke, WN 1899. *The Christian Doctrine of God*. International Theological Library. C. A. Briggs & S. D. F. Salmond eds. New York: Scribners.

--- 1909. *An Outline of Christian Theology*. New York: Scribners.

Clutter, RT 1982. The Reorientation of Princeton Theological Seminary 1900-1929. Th.D. Thesis. Dallas: Dallas Theological Seminary.

Commager, HS 1950. *The American Mind: An Interpretation of American Thought and Character since the 1880s*. New Haven: Yale University Press.

--- 1978. *The Empire of Reason: How Europe Imagined and America Realized the Enlightenment.* Garden City, NY: Anchor Press/Doubleday.

Coray, HW 1981. *J. Gresham Machen: A Silhouette.* Grand Rapids: Kregel Publications.

Cox H 1965. *The Secular City: Secularization and Urbanization in Theological Perspective.* New York: Macmillan.

Cox, WE 1963. *An Examination of Dispensationalism.* Phillipsburg, New Jersey: Presbyterian & Reformed.

Craig, RH 1969. An Introduction to the Life and Thought of Harry F. Ward, in *Union Seminary Quarterly Review* 24/4 (Summer 1969): 331-356.

Croce, B 1955. *History as the Story of Liberty.* New York: Meridian.

Cumberland Presbyterian Church 1815. *The Constitution of the Cumberland Presbyterian Church, in the United States of America: Containing the Confession of Faith, A Catechism, The Government and Discipline, and the Directory for the Worship of God; Ratified and Adopted by the Synod of Cumberland, held at Sugg's Creek, in Tennessee State, April the 5ᵗʰ, 1814, and Continued by Adjournments, until the 9ᵗʰ of the Same Month.* Nashville: M. & J. Norvell.

--- [1884] 1985. *Confession of Faith and Government of the Cumberland Presbyterian Church, Adopted 1883.* Memphis: Frontier Press.

Cunliffe-Jones, H (ed.) 1978. *A History of Christian Doctrine.* Philadelphia: Fortress.

Cunningham, W [1863] 1991. *Discussions on Church Principles: Popish, Erastian, and Presbyterian.* Edmonton, Alberta: Still Waters Revival Books.

Current Biography 1944. Thomas, Norman (Mattoon), in *Current Biography, Who's News and Why 1944*. Edited by Anna Rothe. New York: H. W. Wilson: 688-691.

--- 1962. Thomas, Norman (Mattoon), in *Current Biography Yearbook 1962*. Edited by Charles Moritz. New York: H. W. Wilson: 416-419.

Davis, DC 1986. Machen and Liberalism, in Dennison & Gamble 1986:247-258.

Deist, F 1990. *A Concise Dictionary of Theological and Related Terms*. Second revised and enlarged edition. Pretoria: van Schaik.

DeMar, G 1994. *Last Days Madness: Obsession of the Modern Church*. Atlanta, American Vision.

Dennison, CG & Gamble, RC (eds.) 1986. *Pressing Towards the Mark. Essays Commemorating Fifty Years of the Orthodox Presbyterian Church*. Philadelphia: The Committee for the Historian of the Orthodox Presbyterian Church.

Dennison, CG 1992. *The History of the Orthodox Presbyterian Church: An Annotated Bibliography*. Philadelphia: The Committee for the Historian of the Orthodox Presbyterian Church.

Dorner, IA 1872. *History of the Development of the Doctrine of the Person of Christ*, Volume 1: *First Four Centuries*. Clark's Foreign Theological Library. Edinburgh: T. & T. Clark.

Douglas, JD (ed.) 1978. *The New International Dictionary of the Christian Church*. Grand Rapids: Zondervan.

--- 1992. William Robertson Smith, in *Who's Who in Christian History*, edited by J. D. Douglas & Philip W. Comfort. Wheaton, Illinois: Tyndale House.

Duke, DN 1985. Harry F. Ward: From Conservative Evangelical to Social Radical, in *Union Seminary Quarterly Review* 40: 85-96.

Dykstra, RJ 1998. Abraham Kuyper and the Union of 1892, in *The Standard Bearer*. Vol. 75, no. 2 (October 15, 1998): 36-38.

Eliot, TS 1940. *The Idea of a Christian Society*. New York: Harcourt, Brace.

Epp, EJ 1976. The Eclectic Method in New Testament Textual Criticism: Solution or Symposium? in *Harvard Theological Review* 69: 3 & 4 (July - October 1976): 211-257.

Ewing, F [1814] 1826. Presbyterians, Cumberland, in *A Theological Dictionary Containing Definitions of All Religious Terms*. Edited by the late Rev. Charles Buck. Philadelphia: Joseph J. Woodward: 485-489.

Fenn, WW 1913. Modern Liberalism, in *The American Journal of Theology* 17/4 (October 1913): 509-519.

Fischer, PB 1936. *Ultra-Dispensationalism is Modernism: Exposing a Heresy among Fundamentalists*. Chicago: Weir Brothers.

Fosdick, HE [1922] 1968. Shall the Fundamentalists Win? in *American Protestant Thought in the Liberal Era*. Edited by William R. Hutchison. Lanham, Maryland: University of Press of America.

Gaybba, BP 1988. *Aspects of the Mediaeval History of Theology*. Pretoria: University of South Africa.

Gellner, E 1995. Fundamentalism as a Comprehensive System: Soviet Marxism and Islamic Fundamentalism Compared, in *Fundamentalisms Comprehended*. Edited by Martin E. Marty & R. Scott Appleby. Chicago & London: University of Chicago Press: 277-287.

Gerstner, JT 1957. American Calvinism until the Twentieth Century especially in New England, in Hoogstra 1957:13-39.

Green, WH 1893. Dr. Briggs' Higher Criticism of the Hexateuch Examined, in *The Presbyterian and Reformed Review*, 4 (1893): 529-561.

Greene, WB 1906. Broad Churchism and the Christian Life, in *Princeton Theological Review* 4 (July 1906): 306-316.

Guelzo, AC 1986. Jonathan Edwards and the New Divinity, 1758-1858, in Dennison & Gamble 1986: 147-167.

--- 1989. *Edwards on the Will: A Century of American Theological Debate*. Middletown: Wesleyn University Press.

Gusfield, JR 1963. *Symbolic Crusade: Status Politics and the American Temperance Movement*. Urbana, Illinois: University of Illinois Press.

Handy, RT 1984. *A Christian America: Protestant Hopes and Historical Realities*. Second edition, revised and enlarged. New York & Oxford: Oxford University Press.

--- 1987. *A History of Union Theological Seminary in New York*. New York: Columbia University Press.

Hanson, RPC 1988. *The Search for the Christian Doctrine of God: The Arian Controversy 318-181*. Edinburgh: T. & T. Clark.

Harris, H 1975. *The Tubingen School: A Historical Investigation of the School of F. C. Baur*. Oxford & New York: Oxford University Press.

Hart, DG 1988. "Doctor Fundamentalis:" An Intellectual Biography of J. Gresham Machen, 1881-1937. Ph.D. Thesis. Baltimore: Johns Hopkins University.

--- 1994. *Defending the Faith: J Gresham Machen and the Crisis of Conservative Protestantism in Modern America*. Baltimore & London: Johns Hopkins University Press.

Hart DG, & Muether, J 1995. *Fighting the Good Fight: A Brief History of the Orthodox Presbyterian Church*. Philadelphia: Committee on Christian Education and the Committee for the Historian of the Orthodox Presbyterian Church.

Hart, JW 1978. The Controversy within the Presbyterian Church, USA in the 1920s with Special Emphasis on the Reorganization of Princeton Theological Seminary. A Senior Thesis Submitted to the History Department of Princeton University in Partial Fulfillment of the Requirements for the Degree of Bachelor of Arts. Princeton: Princeton University.

Hatch, CE 1969. *The Charles A. Briggs Heresy Trial: Prologue to Twentieth-Century Liberal Protestantism*. New York: Exposition.

Hatch, NO 1989. *The Democratization of American Christianity*. New Haven & London: Yale University Press.

Herrmann, W 1909. *The Communion of the Christian with God*. Third English Edition. London: Williams & Norgate.

Hill C [1947] 1971. *Lenin and the Russian Revolution*. Harmondsworth: Penguin.

Hocking, WE (ed.) 1932. *Re-thinking Missions: A Layman's Inquiry after One Hundred Years*. New York & London: Harper & Brothers.

Hodge, AA [1869] 1983. *The Confession of Faith: A Handbook of Christian Doctrine, Expounding the Westminster Confession*. Edinburgh: Banner of Truth.

--- 1881. *The Life of Charles Hodge. DD, LL.D., Professor in the Theological Seminary, Princeton*. London: T. Nelson & Sons.

Hodge, AA & Warfield, BB 1881. Inspiration, in *The Presbyterian Review* 2 (1881): 225-260.

Hodge, C 1839. Transcendentalism, in *The Biblical Repertory and Princeton Review*. Vol. IX, no.1. Philadelphia: James A. Peabody: 37-101.

--- 1979. *Systematic Theology*. Volume 1. Grand Rapids: Eerdmans.

Hodge, EB 1904. The Story of the Cumberland Presbyterian Church, in *Princeton Theological Review* 2 (April 1904): 283-294.

Hoeksema, H 1966. *Reformed Dogmatics*. Grand Rapids: Reformed Free Publishing Association.

Hoogstra, JT (ed.) 1957. *American Calvinism: A Survey*. Grand Rapids: Baker.

Hopkins, CH 1940. *The Rise of the Social Gospel in American Protestantism, 1865-1915*. New Haven: Yale University Press.

Hudson, WS [1953] 1963. *The Great Tradition of the American Churches*. Torchbook Edition. New York & Evanston: Harper & Row.

Jeschke, CR 1966. The Briggs Case: The Focus of a Study in Nineteenth Century Presbyterian History. Ph.D. Thesis. Chicago: University of Chicago.

Johnson, DF 1968. The Attitudes of the Princeton Theologians towards Darwinism and Evolution from 1859-1929. Ph.D. Thesis. Iowa City: University of Iowa.

Johnson, GLW 1987. Briggs vs. Warfield: Rogers/McKim Revisited. MTh. Dissertation. Philadelphia: Westminster Theological Seminary.

Kendall, RT 1979. *Calvin and English Calvinism to 1649*. Oxford: Oxford University Press.

Kerr, HT 1988. The Story of the Other Wise Man by Henry Van Dyke, in *American Presbyterians* 66 (Winter 1988): 294-298.

Kim, Ki-Hong 1983. Presbyterian Conflict in the Early Twentieth Century: Ecclesiology in the Presbyterian Tradition and the Emergence of Presbyterian Fundamentalism. Ph.D. Thesis. Madison: Drew University.

Kuyper, A [1871] 1998. Modernism: A Fata Morgana in the Christian Domain, in *Abraham Kuyper: A Centennial Reader*. Edited by James D. Bratt. Grand Rapids: Eerdmans: 87-124.

Leith, JH (ed.) 1982. *Creeds of the Churches: A Reader in Christian Doctrine from the Bible to the Present*. Third Edition. Atlanta: John Knox.

Letis, TP 1984. Edward Freer Hills's Contribution to the Revival of the Ecclesiastical Text. MTS. Thesis. Atlanta: Candler School of Theology, Emory University.

--- 1990. The Protestant Dogmaticians and the Late Princeton on the Status of the Sacred Apographa, in *The Scottish Bulletin of Evangelical Theology* 8 (1990): 16-42.

--- 1991. B. B. Warfield, Common-Sense Philosophy and Biblical Criticism, in *American Presbyterians* 69:3 (Fall 1991): 1-16 (Galley Proof).

Lindsell, H 1976. *The Battle for the Bible*. Grand Rapids: Zondervan.

Lippman, W 1929. *A Preface to Morals*. New York: Macmillan.

Loetscher, LA 1954. *The Broadening Church: A Study of Theological Issues in the Presbyterian Church since 1869*. Philadelphia: University of Pennsylvania Press.

--- 1978. *A Brief History of Presbyterians*. Fourth Edition. Philadelphia: Westminster Press.

--- 1983. *Facing the Enlightenment and Pietism: Archibald Alexander and the Founding of Princeton Theological Seminary.* Westport & London: Greenwood Press.

Longfield, BJ 1991. *The Presbyterian Controversy: Fundamentalists, Modernists, and Moderates.* New York & Oxford: Oxford University Press.

Lundén, R 1988. *Business and Religion in the American 1920s.* Contributions in American Studies #91. Westport & London: Greenwood Press.

Machen, JG 1913. Christianity and Culture, reprinted from *The Princeton Theological Review* 11 (January 1913):1-15.

--- 1915. History and Faith, reprinted from *The Princeton Theological Review* 13 (July 1915): 1-15.

--- [1923] 1946. *Christianity and Liberalism.* Grand Rapids: Eerdmans.

--- 1925. *What is Faith.* New York: Macmillan.

--- 1927. *The Attack upon Princeton Seminary: A Plea for Fair Play.* Philadelphia: Johnson & Prince.

--- 1933. *Modernism and the Board of Foreign Missions of the Presbyterian Church in the USA.* (S.l.): J. Gresham Machen.

--- 1934. *Statement to the Special Committee of the Presbytery of New Brunswick in the Presbyterian Church in the USA which was Appointed by the Presbytery at its Meeting on Tuesday, September 25, 1934, to "Confer Further with Dr. Machen with Respect to his Relationship with the Independent Board for Presbyterian Foreign Missions, and to Make Recommendations to Presbytery for the Disposition of the Matter Involving the Mandate of the General Assembly to the Presbytery and the*

Relation of Dr. Machen to the Independent Board for Presbyterian Foreign Missions". Philadelphia: J. Gresham Machen.

--- 1973. The Creeds and Doctrinal Advance, in *Scripture and Confession: A Book about Confessions Old and New*. Edited by John H. Skilton. Nutley, New Jersey: Presbyterian and Reformed.

--- 1976. *The New Testament: An Introduction to Its Literature and History*. Edinburgh: Banner of Truth.

--- 1991. Karl Barth and "The Theology of Crisis", in *Westminster Theological Journal* 53 (1991): 197-207.

Marsden, GM 1970. *The Evangelical Mind and the New School Presbyterian Experience: A Case Study of Thought and Theology in Nineteenth-Century America*. New Haven & London Yale University Press.

--- 1986. The New School Heritage and Presbyterian Fundamentalism, in Dennison & Gamble 1986: 169-182.

--- 1991. *Understanding Fundamentalism and Evangelicalism*. Grand Rapids: Eerdmans.

Massa, MS 1990. *Charles Augustus Briggs and the Crisis of Historical Criticism*. Harvard Dissertations in Religion # 25. Minneapolis: Fortress.

Masselink, W [s.a.]. *J. Gresham Machen: His Life and Defense of the Bible*. Grand Rapids: Zondervan.

Mathews, S 1924. *The Faith of Modernism*. New York: Macmillan.

Matthews, JB 1953. Reds and Our Churches, in *The American Mercury*. July 1953: 3-13.

May, H 1975. *The Enlightenment in America*. New York: Oxford University Press.

McGrath, AE 1993. *Reformation Thought: An Introduction*. Second Edition. Grand Rapids: Baker.

McIntire, C 1935. *Dr. Robert E. Speer, The Board of Foreign Missions of the Presbyterian Church in the USA and Modernism*. (S. l.): Rev. Carl McIntire.

Meyer, D [1960] 1988a. *The Positive Thinkers: Popular Religious Psychology from Mary Baker Eddy to Norman Vincent Peale and Ronald Regan*. Revised Edition. Middletown: Wesleyan University Press.

--- [1965] 1988b. *The Protestant Search for Political Realism. 1919-1941*. Second Edition. Middletown: Wesleyan University Press.

Miller, S 1839. *The Utility and Importance of Creeds and Confessions: Addressed Particularly to Candidates for the Ministry*. Philadelphia: Presbyterian Board of Publication.

Morrow, HW 1965. The Background and Development of Cumberland Presbyterian Theology. Ph.D. Thesis. Nashville: Vanderbilt University.

--- 1994. *Covenant Theology and the Cumberland Presbyterian Church*. Russelville, Arkansas: HW Morrow.

Morrow, TWJ 1983. Infallibility as a Theological Concept: A Study in the Use of the Concept 'Infallible' in the Writings of B. B. Warfield and C. A. Briggs. Ph.D. Thesis. Edinburgh: University of Edinburgh.

Muller, RA 1991. *God, Creation, and Providence in the Thought of Jacob Arminius: Sources and Directions of Scholastic Protestantism in the Era of Early Orthodoxy*. Grand Rapids: Baker.

--- 1994. The Covenant of Works and the Stability of Divine Law in Seventeenth-Century Reformed Orthodoxy: A Study in the Theology of Herman Witsius and Wilhelmus A'Brakel, in *Calvin Theological Journal* Vol. 29, no. 1 (April 1994): 75-100.

Murray, JC 1964. *The Problem of God: Yesterday and Today*. New Haven & London: Yale University Press.

Newman, JH [1878] 1949. *The Development of Christian Doctrine*. Edited by Charles Frederick Harrold. London: Longmans, Green.

--- 1908. *The Arians of the Fourth Century*. London: Longmans, Green.

Nigg, W 1962. *The Heretics*. New York: Alfred A. Knopf.

Noll, MA 1985. Common Sense Traditions and American Evangelical Thought, in *American Quarterly* 37 (Summer 1985): 216-238.

--- 1991. *Between Faith and Criticism: Evangelicals, Scholarship, and the Bible in America*. Second Edition. Grand Rapids: Baker.

North, G 1996. *Crossed Fingers; How the Liberals Captured the Presbyterian Church*. Tyler, Texas: Institute for Christian Economics.

Pauck, W 1950. *The Heritage of the Reformation*. Revised and enlarged edition. Oxford: Oxford University Press.

Pelikan, J 1962. Forward, in Kenneth Cauthen, *The Impact of American Religious Liberalism*. New York & Evanston: Harper & Row.

--- 1969. *Development of Christian Doctrine: Some Historical Prolegomena*. New Haven & London: Yale University Press.

--- 1984. *The Vindication of Tradition*. New Haven & London: Yale University Press.

Pope Pius X 1907. Encyclical Letter: Pascendi Gregis, appended to Paul Sabatier, *Modernism*. New York: Scribners.

Prentiss, GL 1899. *The Union Theological Seminary in the City of New York: Another Decade of its History*. Asbury Park, New Jersey: M., W. & C. Pennypacker.

Quirk, CE 1967. The "Auburn" Affirmation: A Critical Narrative of the Document Designed to Safeguard the Unity and Liberty of the Presbyterian Church in the United States of America in 1924. Ph.D. Thesis. Iowa City: University of Iowa.

Rian, EH [1940] 1992. *The Presbyterian Conflict*. Philadelphia: The Committee for the Historian of the Orthodox Presbyterian Church.

Robbins, J 1998. Karl Barth, in *The Trinity Review*. # 156 (February 1998).

Rogers, MG 1964. Charles Augustus Briggs: Conservative Heretic. Ph.D. Thesis. New York: Columbia University.

--- 1966. Charles Augustus Briggs: Heresy at Union, in *American Religious Heretics, Formal and Informal Trials*. Edited by George H. Shriver. Nashville & New York: Abington Press.

Runia, K 1962. *Karl Barth's Doctrine of Holy Scripture*. Grand Rapids: Eerdmans.

Rushdoony, RJ 1965. *The Nature of the American System*. Fairfax, Virginia: Thoburn Press.

Ryrie, CC 1965. *Dispensationalism Today*. Chicago: Moody Press.

Sabatier, P 1908. *Modernism*. New York: Scribners.

Sandeen, ER 1962. The Princeton Theology: One Source of Biblical Literalism in American Protestantism, in *Church History* 31 (September 1962): 307-321.

--- 1967. Towards a Historical Interpretation of the Origins of Fundamentalism, in *Church History* 36 (1967): 66-83.

--- 1970. *The Roots of Fundamentalism: English and American Millenarianism 1800-1930*. Chicago & London: University of Chicago Press.

Sawyer, MJ 1994. *Charles Augustus Briggs and Tensions in Late Nineteenth-Century American Theology*. Lewiston, New York: Mellen University Press.

Schaff, P 1890. *Creed Revision in the Presbyterian Churches*. New York: Scribners.

Schaff, P (ed.) [1931] 1985. *The Creeds of Christendom, With a History and Critical Notes*, Vol II: *The Greek and Latin Creeds with Translations*. Sixth Edition. Grand Rapids: Baker.

--- [1931] 1985. *The Creeds of Christendom, With a History and Critical Notes*, Vol III: *The Evangelical Protestant Creeds with Translations*. Sixth Edition. Grand Rapids: Baker.

Selden, WK 1992. *Princeton Theological Seminary: A Narrative History, 1812-1992*. Princeton: Princeton University Press.

Shedd, WGT 1893. *Calvinism: Pure and Mixed, A Defense of the Westminster Standards*. New York: Scribners.

Smith, HP 1913. Charles Augustus Briggs, in *The American Journal of Theology*, Vol. XVII, no. 4 (October 1913): 497-508.

Smith, TL [1957] 1976. *Revivalism and Social Reform: American Protestantism on the Eve of the Civil War*. Gloucester: Peter Smith.

Smith, WR 1912. *Lectures and Essays of William Robertson Smith*. Edited by John Sutherland Black & George Chrystal. London: Adam & Charles Black.

Sorokin, PA 1941. *The Crisis of Our Age*. New York: E. P. Dutton.

Stonehouse, NB [1954] 1987. *J. Gresham Machen: A Biographical Memoir*. Third Edition. Edinburgh: Banner of Truth.

Sweet, WW [1944] 1976. *Revivalism in America: Its Origin, Growth and Decline*. Gloucester: Peter Smith.

Thayer, F 1998. The Role and Status of Women in Hitler's Germany, in *The Barnes Review*. Vol. 4, no. 3, (May/June 1998): 45-48.

Thomas, N 1951. *A Socialist's Faith*. New York: W. W. Norton.

Tillard, JMR 1996. Dogmatic Development and Koinonia, in *New Perspectives on Historical Theology. Essays in Memory of John Meyendorff*. Edited by Bradley Nassif. Grand Rapids: Eerdmans: 172-185.

Tillich, P 1968. *A History of Christian Thought*. New York: Harper & Row.

Van Til, C 1947. *The New Modernism: An Appraisal of the Theology of Barth and Brunner*. Philadelphia: Presbyterian and Reformed.

Vidler, A 1934. *The Modernist Movement in the Roman Catholic Church, Its Origins and Outcome*. Cambridge: Cambridge University Press.

von Balthasar, HU 1971. *The Theology of Karl Barth*. New York: Holt, Rinehart & Winston.

Vos, G 1894. *Inauguration of the Rev. Geehardus Vos, Ph.D., DD., as Professor of Biblical Theology*. New York: Anson D. F. Randolph.

Ward, HF. 1918. *The Gospel for a Working World*. New York: Missionary Education Movement of the United States and Canada.

--- 1929. *Our Economic Morality and the Ethic of Jesus*. New York: Macmillan.

Warfield, BB 1887. *An Introduction to the Textual Criticism of the New Testament*. New York: Thomas Whittaker.

--- [1893] 1983. The Inerrancy of the Original Autographs, in *The Princeton Theology 1812-1921*. Edited by Mark Noll. Phillipsburg, New Jersey: Presbyterian & Reformed: 268-274.

--- 1904a. The Confession of Faith as Revised in 1903, in *The Union Seminary Magazine* 16/1 (October-November 1904): 1-37.

--- 1904b. The Proposed Union with the Cumberland Presbyterians, in *Princeton Theological Review* 2 (April 1904):295-316.

--- [1932] 1981. *The Works of Benjamin B. Warfield*, Vol. 10: *Critical Reviews*. Grand Rapids: Baker.

Watson, R 1832. *Theological Institutes: or, A View of the Evidences, Doctrines, Morals and Institutions of Christianity*, Vol. III. Third Edition. London: James Mason.

Watts, R 1882. *The Newer Criticism and the Analogy of Faith. A Reply to Lectures by William Robertson Smith, MA on the Old Testament in the Jewish Church*. Third Edition. Edinburgh: T. & T. Clark.

Weber, O 1953. *Karl Barth's Church Dogmatics*. London: Lutterworth Press.

--- 1981. *Foundations of Dogmatics*. Volume 1. Translated and annotated by Darrell Gruder. Grand Rapids: Eerdmans.

--- 1983. *Foundations of Dogmatics*. Volume 2. Translated and annotated by Darrell Gruder. Grand Rapids: Eerdmans.

Welch, C 1972. *Protestant Thought in the Nineteenth Century*, Vol I: *1799-1870*. New Haven & London: Yale University Press.

--- 1985. *Protestant Thought in the Nineteenth Century*, Vol II: *1870-1914*. New Haven & London: Yale University Press.

Westminster Assembly [1647] 1983. *The Confession of Faith; The Larger and Shorter Catechisms, with the Scripture Proofs at Large: Together with the Sum of Saving Knowledge*. Inverness, Scotland: Free Presbyterian Publications.

Weston, WJ 1997. *Presbyterian Pluralism: Competition in a Protestant House.* Knoxville: University of Tennessee Press.

Wood, HG 1935. *Communism, Christian and Marxist. The Social Service Lecture, 1935*. London: Epworth Press.

Woolley, P 1957. American Calvinism in the Twentieth Century, in Hoogstra 1957:40-63.

Woolley, P 1977. *The Significance of J. Gresham Machen Today.* Nutley, New Jersey: Presbyterian & Reformed.

www.ingramcontent.com/pod-product-compliance
Lightning Source LLC
Chambersburg PA
CBHW031946090426
42739CB00006B/98